Thumbing Through the '70s

Maggie O'Brien

To order additional copies of this book, contact:
Xlibris
800-056-3182
www.Xlibrispublishing.co.uk
Orders@Xlibrispublishing.co.uk
517055

Dedication

For my gran Daisy Morgan who used to sing to me

"Around the world I searched for you.
I travelled on when hope was gone
to keep a rendezvous."

Harry Hillis.1903

For(e)ward

Well, what do you know? I'm told I've become a living historical document.

I never saw that coming.

Over the past few years I've been badgered by a lot of younger people to write down my experience of the 1970s. The freedom the world offered us to just get up and go back then has apparently become legendary. Who knew?

The final clincher came in Argentina in 2016. Backstage at a huge musical festival I fell to talking with some fabulous youngsters. As best I could, I answered their questions about that infamous decade. They practically begged me to write a first- hand account of what it was like to travel overland from Britain to India and to be there at the beginnings of their idols, those iconic rock bands still around today.

As a result I made promises. This book is the result.

It's not intended to be an autobiography but I felt I should begin with some pages to set the context.

Memory is a remarkable thing. I have to thank my grandad for teaching me to value it. He taught me to pay attention.

"Keep an eye on history as you live through it my girl. When you get older you won't recognise it in any history book."

'Talking 'bout my Generation....'

The Who

In 1969 I flew the coop. The home world I grew up in (loving and nurturing as it was) felt too small for me. I had no money to speak of but that wasn't going to stop me. To this day I don't understand anyone who says 'I want to travel but I don't have the money.' I was 17 and had flown to Berlin for eight weeks of Voluntary Service Overseas. Everything was funded by that organisation.

On the first full day of my newly-found independence we were given a welcoming tour of the city. We had just come from Checkpoint Charlie on the Berlin Wall and stood where J.F.K. gave his famous 1963 speech announcing he was a jelly-filled doughnut.

It was July 20th 1969 and crowds were gathering in front of a shop window. I joined them to see what was going on. We were soon watching a bank of televisions showing grainy black-and-white footage of the first moon landing.

Considering this was my own maiden flight, the slogan from the moon that day should always have been "'That's one small step for mankind, one giant leap for a Maggie." I'd gone off-world too. But they weren't to know. It was auspicious though, don't you think?

It was also the summer leading up to my leaving home for university 200 miles north of Southmead in Bristol where I grew up. I was on the move. My wings were working fine. To mix metaphors I had caught the travel bug. From that year onward I would never again be embedded in conformity or popular culture.

The 1970s rocked! The decade was an amazing time for the young to be alive in and, if not? You were on a different planet than me.

Sure, Britain was in a mess but wasn't it always? More important things were going on. Roger Daltrey had found his voice, Simon and Garfunkel were in their heyday; Cassius Clay was floating like a butterfly and stinging like a bee; Cat Stevens was drop dead gorgeous; the Moody Blues were carrying us all away with great concept albums and the Beatles were splitting up. It's a place in time that some now call the 'Me Decade.' After all the recent war and upheaval there was a general and genuine sense that the political had failed to improve the world and maybe individualism was the way to go. Whatever it was I was more than happy to be part of it; to break rules if need be and dress as crazy as I wanted.

In the '60s the Hippies had blown a lot of old thinking sky high (to coin a phrase) and in the '70s we reaped the rewards. Individuals as well as cultures have a tendency to glorify a past epoch as some Golden Age. In my case the very late '60s and the '70s were unquestionably a golden time for young people to travel. The whole world was wide open; only one decision and one step away for those of us who had 'travellin' shoes' and the itchy feet to match.

We were the generation who witnessed the arrival of baby bands that went on to be mega. We were there at their beginning. As university students we had a hand in making them. As Pete Townshend so famously said, "If the pirate radio stations drove the first wave of rock, then universities drove the second."

We were counted among the top 2% in the country. We knew it. We made the most of it. I sometimes think our generation gave students a bad name but maybe we just worsened it.

In 1970 Leeds University was the place for bands to play. The Who played at Leeds for my birthday in February of 1970. I would be a full-time student there by the September. Seems strange now but a hall that could take over 2,000 was a big venue back then. We were spoiled rotten. The Who, Led Zeppelin, Pink Floyd, The Stones, Rod Stewart and the Faces, the Free, Cream, Derek and the Dominoes (Clapton) the list goes on and on. They trucked along to play for us every Saturday night and we let them know exactly what we felt. Did we know they would go on to be stellar? Nah, of course not. Neither did they. We were all young. The young don't think that far ahead.

Yes, they all turned up every Saturday and we paid our £1. Sometimes we'd go as high as £1.50 but that was pushing it. That was cause for debate. Back then a pound could get you 15 pints in the student bar. I clearly remember a heated discussion about whether or not to pay 10 shillings (50p) to go and see a new guy called Elton John. For all we knew he was a whining piano player who had a single "Your Song" in the charts. That fact did not endear him to us. We didn't much fancy it.

I don't know what made us go along after all but we did. Oh boy! Back then could young Elton rock! But then he was just 23 years old. As for Rod Stewart? Thanks Rod. You made damn sure that every time I walked into any student bar or the main union, a crowd would bellow "Maggie I wish I'd …never… seen your face."

My state education was completely free. Yep! From the age of 4½ - 22 the government picked up the tab for everything. Odd now to think that '70s Britain was supposed to be poor but education, healthcare, dentistry, eye treatment and prescriptions were all free. Now? Britain is allegedly wealthy but none of those services are free. How did that happen? I digress.

The University year had three terms. Each term was eight weeks long. You do the sums. You got it! We had 28 weeks of the year off. In those long holidays we grabbed a job in a bar, a Bingo Hall, a department store, an office or factory. After a month of that we took off down through Europe or wherever we wanted. We lived on beaches, in forests or wherever took our fancy.

My mate Carolyn and I would hitch our way down through Europe to Greece. We did the poor man's Grand Tour, following in the footsteps of all the great European poets and artists in centuries gone by. Among many places we took in Amsterdam, Paris, Rome, Venice, Florence, Milan, Pompeii and Athens but always ended up on a Greek island; maybe Rhodos or maybe Corfu. On the long hitch south we found ourselves sleeping under motorway bridges, in alleyways and even once in the as-yet unexcavated ruins of Pompeii. We caught rides with trucks, cars of all shapes and sizes and (it goes without saying) the classic V.W. camper vans that were so prevalent. All this introduced me to Aussies, Canadians, Americans and people of my age from all over Europe. At times we were living a Cheech and Chong movie.

But at our destination, the Greek Islands, along with other young like-minds, we slept on deserted beaches in sleeping bags or bamboo huts, had massive barbeques of fresh fish caught yards away in the sparkling Aegean, and partied until we dropped. We lived like that until late September. We hitched back.

In that parallel world most others called real, we lived through the dark days of 'The winter of discontent,' oil shortages, strikes and general greyness. For us one of the biggest disappointments was the dismal decision to join The Common Market in 1973; a step that seemed parochial and condemned our country to being inward-looking. The Commonwealth worked perfectly well and ensured us friends all over the globe. Europe was small in comparison. We students voted 'no' out of respect for those Commonwealth friends and the effects it would have on their economies. Today there is a completely different attitude; an attitude that Europe is the 'be all and end all' of an extremely big world. Times change for sure. I suppose it's a question of comfort zones.

Meanwhile we, the nation's intelligentsia, were hard at work studying. (Not). Inside the deceptively dated exterior of Leeds Student Union a huge, modern extension had been added. It was a bold, white concrete construction of open-plan seating areas and glass roofs. There were tiered, massive communal television rooms like the drawers of some giant's cupboard (left open in typical student fashion). I mention this to give you some insight into student life and to reassure you of how wisely we spent taxpayers' money.

Let me invite you to a typical Thursday night. That was the night to be there, there in those T.V rooms. The lounges were absolutely heaving.

At 6.30 came Tom and Jerry. When the name Fred Quimby came up on screen a huge roar of 'Yay. Fred Quimby.' rose from the assembled throng. After the cartoon came Star Trek with the inimitable Captain Quirk. As naff and naïve as those early series now appear, Star Trek was radical.

A long, long time before the audience participation at Rocky Horror Shows, to a man we hundreds chanted in unison, "To boldly go boldly where no boldly has ever boldly gone boldly before." There would be a momentary, deafening silence before a final 'bold-ly.'

When Quirk's crew did an away mission a new guy always appeared in the cast. We all chanted "No. Don't do it! Check your contract!" But he would ignore us and inevitably came a cropper.

After our trip around that latex and polystyrene universe we sang, "Dum dee dum dee dum dum dum dum," the intro to that other new series "Monty Python's Flying Circus."

The Python team have a lot to answer for. Those guys influenced student conversation big time. We had to get our weekly dose of new phrases and reference points to slot into our daily lives. 'Dinsdale', 'my brain hurts' 'defunct, deceased, gone beyond' are but few from a very long list. Their sketches became a part of our psyche. They would never fail to spring to mind when my life took a turn to the surreal or downright comical. The Python team were anarchic. Gilliam's animation was unlike anything we had ever seen. One sketch in particular would prove invaluable when I eventually hit the road. It was the 'Phrase Book Sketch'. In a nutshell it's a skit between a tourist and a typical Englishman. The tourist refers to the book and it delivers the most ridiculous translation, a prime example being 'My hovercraft is full of eels.' Bear that in mind as we go along.

So yes. The wonderful Full Grant system that was once in place gave me and thousands like me the opportunity to grow and spread our wings. It took a working-class kid from a council estate to the dizzy melting pot that was a 1970s university. It introduced me to people from every walk of life and social standing. I dined with the Duchess of Kent, Michael Foot and Denis Healy, I got drunk with Leonard Cohen, I lived, loved and laughed with coalminers' kids, with both hoi polloi and hoi oligoi alike. I learned that people are people, for better or for worse.

The only problem with University was that work got in the way of fun. If that isn't a lesson that prepares you for life, I don't know what is.

At 22 years of age I had completed nearly 18 years of state education. I was a B.A. Comb. Hons. with a Post Graduate in Education. Don't let that fool you. Certificates don't guarantee intelligence. They can often signify a great memory. I'd fulfilled my promise to my grandad to get an education, 'play the game and be free.' Suffice to say I had enough wits about me to understand that I could not, in all conscience, turn around and go straight back into the classroom. What did I know that was worth a fig? As far as I could see I had nothing to offer kids. I wasn't ready to be anyone's role model. No. It was time to boldly go boldly so to speak (boldly).

No Rhythm Some Blues

One sunny spring afternoon in 1975 found my friend Pat and I waiting for the Newcastle train at the oldest railway station in the world, Temple Meads in Bristol.

We were weighed down with far too much stuff in ludicrously heavy backpacks. We were armed with nothing more than passports, Youth Hostel memberships, an international driving license, our old Student Union membership cards, £200 each, a sense of devil-may-care and three key addresses. Those three were contacts in Newcastle, Stavanger in Norway and an Iranian address we would most probably never use.

It would be remiss not to mention the secret armour we carried. That was a can-do attitude and confidence enabled and nurtured by our remarkable schooling at the hands of extraordinarily dedicated teachers; women who managed to keep their patience (for the most part) with a pack of teenage girls who were too clever by half.

In the 1960s and '70s the now much-maligned Direct Grant system opened the way for brighter kids from poorer families, to reap the rewards of a first-class education free of charge. We studied and played in a huge old Georgian town house, in the poshest part of our city. Best of all, we were taken under the wings of women who had led extraordinary lives in their own right and who were incapable of even hinting that women were in any way less capable than men. Sadly, schools like La Retraite are a thing of the past.

Our only fixed destinations were Newcastle where we'd spend the night with an old school friend. From there we could catch a ferry to Stavanger. Then we'd simply take things as they came. That was it. Oh yes! We both wanted to get into Russia if we could. That was our plan, if you can call it that.

As for the meagre amount of money? We'd made a rooky mistake. The last eight months or more had been slogged out in a factory to save up for the adventure. Trouble was that after all those years of being students and all those exams, we'd spent most of our pay packets the minute we got them. Let that be a lesson!

In this modern world mobile communication is real. Back then it was a fantasy confined to Star Trek. Gap years hadn't been invented but anyway they come nowhere close to the sense of adventure we both felt that day in Bristol. I believe gap years involve planning and funding from mum and dad. What a peculiar notion.

I have often been told I'm brave. I don't know about that. I see myself as more of a classic fool like say, the infamous William Kempe. What a guy? He Morris-danced a hundred miles from London to Norwich in the year 1600; a stunt of nine days spread over several weeks. He was cheered by crowds though. I wasn't expecting any.

We stayed overnight in Newcastle. Even back at Temple Meads we'd already decided that most of the clothes we'd packed had to go. Our packs were way too cumbersome. We ditched practically two thirds of our burden and donated it all to a charity shop.

The Scandinavian ferry came as a pleasant shock. Bright, clean and child-friendly it was a far cry from the neglected, often shabby public transport we were accustomed to in Britain. It was obvious we were entering a culture that cared a lot more for its people in respect of a return for their taxes.

Stavanger came slowly into view. My old university friends picked us up at the small, thriving port and before long we were eating a meal ready for us in their lovely little apartment. Their wonderful hospitality allowed us four days to make some choices and have a stab at setting out some kind of route.

If you're going to be ill on a long adventure, it's best to get it over and done with as soon as possible. I did just that. I was sick for the first three days. Nevertheless our friends took us out on sightseeing trips and I survived.

If you want to conjure up a mental image of the Norwegian landscape you could do worse than dwell on these few words 'majestic, breathtaking, magnificent and pristine.'

We visited a nearby fjord. What can I say? Compared to the polluted waters around the coast of Britain this wasn't water! This was a monumental mirror perfectly reflecting the tree-covered, steep slopes sweeping down to peer into it and relish the splendour of their image. The impact was dramatic. 'As above, so below.'

I've asked around and I'm not alone when I say there are places on this planet that emanate the feeling of, 'a lack of people'. My body and mind pick up on it.

Norway was one of those places. It was a sigh of relief. My thoughts were no longer cramped or jostling to fight for attention. My body relaxed. The impression of space was phenomenal. There was wilderness.

All too soon it was time to leave. We caught a local bus to the edge of town and disembarked at that telling point in any adventure when tarmac road turns into almost-track. I believe it's commonly known as 'the end of the road.'

Alright, I know. For those of you who are of a less Romantic nature, more power to your elbow! You've already considered the impracticalities of hitch-hiking in that glorious 'lack of people.' We hadn't. But then whoever said Morris-dancing was practical?

There were few roads and even fewer cars. We stuck out a thumb and waited. We waited some more and then we waited. Did I mention we waited? Then we walked. But for the sensible ones? Be fair, you're never gonna meet Pinocchio, are you? We did.

He pulled up in his pick-up truck. He was a real man now, grown from a real boy, but I would have recognised him anywhere. It was possibly the funny little woollen cap-cum hat thing and the patterned braces under his hefty jacket that did it. (But his nose was long too.)

Pinocchio wound down the van's window and called out 'Bergen?' Since we had no idea where we were going, it didn't much matter where we ended up. Whatever had come out of his mouth was our destination. We nodded and got on board.

The other reason this young man merited the name Pinocchio was his obvious lack of vocabulary. For the next 7 or-so hours he counted from 1 to 1000 very, very slowly in English, German, French, Italian, Norwegian and Swedish. I think it was meant to impress us. It certainly impressed and amused him. Each time he reached a factor of ten he turned, grinned and encouraged us to join in. We didn't.

All of this numerical recitation was punctuated with 'masse sno' which even we non-Norwegian speakers could understand. He had a great way of saying it though; a sort of delight wrapped up in amazement. He did make an impression, but not the one he wanted. I will remember those two Norwegian words until the day I die.

Luckily the scenery gliding by on that coastline route was mesmerising. I was looking at some of the most dramatic views I'd ever seen at that point in my life. Somewhere after 999 in Italian we caught a ferry but don't ask me where. Pinocchio produced a huge thermos flask of coffee and kindly shared it.

We stood on deck and watched in awe. After nearly a week I realised we'd done it. We were actually in Scandinavia.

Bergen was pretty, especially because Pinocchio left us on a mediaeval wharf called Bryggen. I think that place is a World Heritage Site now but I'm not sure. If it isn't it should be. Colourful and old wooden-clad boathouses lined the quay, picked out against the mountains surrounding the town. This was a jig-saw puzzle box cover. Norway being Norway, the slopes were carpeted with pine forests and when we arrived the tall, tall trees were covered in 'masse sno'.

After fond farewells to Pinocchio (driving off on the count of about 757 in Italian again), we found the Youth Hostel. Signage is another thing the Scandinavians are good at. Here in Bergen we found a new word to describe Norway. 'Expensive.'

I imagine Bergen's changed a lot in the last 40 years. It struck me as one of those small gems ripe for tourist exploitation. For now it was almost empty with evidence everywhere of the two main pastimes around here, skiing and fishing. I hope the food's improved. The choice was non-existent, 'stodge' with or without fish. It didn't bother us much but then, we weren't the average tourist. The prices however, did bother us. They were terrifying.

Bergen had an amazing funicular railway. Two Scandinavian cousins of Thomas the tank engine trundled us up to the top of one of those slopes. From up there we had a panoramic and overall view of the beauty of this area. Majestic landscapes were ahead of us then. We still had money but we could tell it was going to be eaten up pretty sharpish. Before long we were on the road again.

This is where Norway gets a bit blurry. I think I know why. It's travelling by car and truck that does it. In a vehicle everything speeds up, you get comfortable and watch the scenery go by. I never paid attention to exactly where we were. There was no need.

We had a vague notion of getting up to the extreme north, to Narvik and across that imaginary line the world calls the Polar Circle. We stuck out the old thumbs.

There's a lot of nowhere in Scandinavia.

After nearly a whole day driving with a sweet little old couple, we found ourselves in the middle of more nowhere. This particular nowhere was land where forests and reindeer were our only companions. Towering old pines stood sentinel. The air was sweet and life felt new. We walked a bit and walked some more.

We walked and found a ring of stones neatly arranged around bits of logs, charred and dusty with charcoal. (It seemed okay to have a campfire then.) We got out our little primus stove and fired it up. There among the trees and deer we drank coffee and wallowed in freedom.

Hours later we still hadn't seen a single vehicle. Our mood soured slightly as the hours passed. A bit more walking broke the monotony of waiting and brought us to the banks of a fast-flowing river. I wasn't an outdoorsy person back then. Heck! I was a city girl at heart but there was an undoubted fascination in watching gigantic trees floating by in harmony and bumping their way down a long, river. Somewhere upstream there must be a saw mill. We were most definitely in the wilderness. Two or three nights sleeping out under the stars and I was beginning to enjoy this. We gave up on waiting for anything, at which point, a timber truck rolled and trundled into view.

Better still the trucker spoke English. He was a jolly sort of man, talkative and obviously pleased to have the company. His cab was warm and oh-so comfortable. I knew he was driving slower than he probably should have been. He was at work after all. That didn't seem to bother him because he frequently pulled over for us at stopping places with spectacular views. Funny how, given time and opportunity, people love to show off the best parts of their country. To thank him we ate his cakes, drank his coffee and fell asleep.

He woke us up at a tiny railway station to catch a train he assured us we would love. It was heading in the general direction of Oslo. That wasn't a bad move. We would need jobs at some point very soon. He insisted on buying us our tickets and told us the ride was about an hour long.

The bit about us loving this train journey was bang on. If anything, he'd understated the magnificence of this trip. I can only imagine what the journey is like in summer. Right then Norway was still in the thrall and magic of lingering frost. A zillion icicles laced the route. I for one was back in the Santa Claus grottoes of my childhood but this time for real.

Our fellow travellers made it blindingly obvious that this was a ski train. It was unique. It was a clattering, wooden old thing. That made it friendlier somehow. I had to laugh because every one of the other passengers looked like some strange hybrid of man and owl. Every one of them was dressed for skiing and every one had pale, perfect circles around their eyes where goggles had blocked the sunlight. Skis were here there and everywhere on racks, leaning against doors and under seats. The train stopped a lot. Some got off, more got on. More got off, some more got on.

Outside, through the windows, a fairyland of crisp snow whitened the pine trees and icicles had grown to 5 feet in length. They sparkled as we past them by. We were hemmed in by a white majesty.

When this little engine took a long bend I caught sight of something out of the corner of my eye. I dismissed it as illusion. The glare of all this astonishing scenery was playing tricks with my eyes. Then it happened again. This time I definitely saw something through the window to my right. It was a flying skier. A skier flew down in my line of vision, right beside me and landed with a thump. He'd just jumped over my train. When one came, more came. My head started humming 'dum diddly, dum, dum diddly dum, dum.'I know, that's a poor rendition of the James Bond theme, but you get my drift (if you'll excuse the very apt pun.) This was incredible. There were people on the planet doing this? People were skiing and jumping over moving trains? They were doing it as if it was on their way to work or something. To them it was the most normal thing in the world. Well I never.

Like I say, I have no idea where we were but I'm glad I saw all this. Who wouldn't be?

The train journey ran its course. We spilled out onto another tiny station. There was nothing else for it. We walked.

About a quarter of a mile later we spotted what could be called a road. It looked a bit treacherous but it looked in use. Hey presto! Another truck. This one was heading for Oslo. What a coincidence. So were we. Mind you, wherever he was going would have been our destination too.

The warmth in his huge cab made me drowsy again. Perhaps it was all this super-duper, crisp fresh air.

I snapped awake. Oh my goodness. If the train journey reminded me of Father Christmas's grotto this scenery was where Rudolph and his pals lived and frolicked. This was their playground. Our driver explained that we were the first ones through here after the winter freeze and told us to relax and enjoy. I think we could manage that. We did.

The neatest, most delicate, most exquisitely painted snow-scene on any Christmas card ever, was coming to life before our very eyes and we were going into it.

Pine tree branches laden with snow bowed right down as if to greet us as heralds of spring. The tall, watchful trees stretched up way over our heads. They were towering above us to make a vast cathedral ceiling of their branches; a vaulted ceiling painted in ice-blue. That canopy blocked out the sky but the trees had a better spectacle in store. Their higher, thin branches were interwoven into gaps that allowed some sunlight to cast blue- grey, patterned shadows. What sunlight got through made all of this glisten. I understood the meaning of splendour.

Only minutes before, I'd believed 5 feet was long for an icicle. This winter paradise changed my mind. These glass needles and spikes were reaching down from everywhere from great heights. They were all over, beside us, below us and ventured way, way down into the sheer drop to our right. I lost all track of size or scale. The wonderland went on and on for miles. My jaw ached from hanging open. The three of us were silent all the way through.

And just when I thought natural wonders couldn't get any more spectacular? I looked over the edge and saw something I'd never even imagined possible. There, attached to a sheet of glass (that on warmer days must be a lake) was a massively wide and totally frozen waterfall about 100 feet high and 20 feet wide.

Snow Kings and Queens lived here. Of course they did. All the stories about them came from these lands. Then I understood that this was a landscape where Tolkien's imagination had wandered too. Or had this landscape wandered into his imagination? What a ride.

Some hours later, ice palaces behind us, we pulled into an Oslo damp and dreary with its low sky lending it a brooding and ominous air. For just a second I wondered if we had somehow offended the Ice Royalty.

Time to find the Youth Hostel then and find it we did.

I didn't like the feel of Oslo. I daresay it would show a lighter, more welcoming side in summer but I felt out of sorts. Our decision was to head for Stockholm. Back in Stavanger we'd learned that summer jobs were easy to find in Stockholm. That was good enough for us. It was mid-May. Hopefully we could find work.

Every capital city in the world is more expensive than the rest of the country it sits in. Oslo was no exception. Yes. It was definitely time to get work. We weren't skint yet but we were cutting it fine.

Luckily there was a train from Oslo to Stockholm. It was expensive in our terms but weighing the cost of a ticket against the costs of food, drink and the possibility of hanging around for lifts, we opted for the train journey.

Before we left we had to have a look around the city a bit. I was glad we did. It wasn't a very big city at all and there was scarcely any traffic. A leaflet from the hostel directed us to Frogner Park. What a delight that was. It was filled with striking, colossal statues by one of Norway's favourite sons Gustav Vigeland. Enormous bronze and granite sculptures populate the massive park. Enormous bronze and granite sculptures need a massive space to live and breathe in.

Being an archaeologist Pat wanted to visit the museum and I tagged along. I waited outside having a ciggie while she took her time. I'm not much one for museums or grandeur but I'm not averse to it all, in brief stints that is. I'm probably painting a poor picture of Oslo but sometimes a mood can influence a place; sometimes a place can influence a mood. I'm not sure which way round that was with me and Oslo but it felt flat.

I was a bit miffed that we hadn't made it to the Polar Circle and Narvik to be honest but I'd get over it.

The day before we left the city the sun came out. We walked around and saw its amazing architecture. Yes. Perhaps I had misjudged it.

With food, drink, sweet things and magazines to keep us happy we set off for Oslo train station and our 18-hour trip. We didn't think out student cards would be of much use but we flashed them anyway. They got us a large discount and an upgrade. We had a sleeper carriage all of a sudden. A dash of luxury always lifts the spirit. Even more so when it comes at no extra cost.

The glory of Scandinavian landscapes kept coming and coming, sliding by like a captivating travel film but without the obligatory, irritating narrator. I made of it what I would, spotting elves, sprites, goblins and the occasional troll going about their business by lakes, in forests and on mountain sides. It was big here.

I was reading the only English book I could find at the station. I had never in my life read a modern, romantic novel. Surprisingly I was enjoying it. That didn't mean I would do it again.

I'd been told that the Swedish consider themselves more sophisticated than the Norwegians who bear the brunt of their jokes. The Swedes tell jokes about them in much the same corny old way as the English tell theirs about the Irish, the Germans about the Swiss and the Russians about the Finns. In fact they're exactly the same jokes. How does that happen? Crazy, huh?

It seems the Swedes do this to the Norwegians because their language uses a lot of compound words; words like toothbrush, sawdust and armchair for examples. I know. English does too. Most languages have some compounds but Norwegian allegedly takes it one step too far. Norwegians say hand-shoe for glove and water-closet instead of toilet. Funny because I would've thought it was the Germans who excelled at that. Maybe the Swedes don't have much contact with the Germans or maybe it's human nature to poke fun at your neighbours. Who can fathom?

Here we were then in Stockholm, another country and another Youth Hostel. The difference this time was that we couldn't find it. Outside the station we asked the way and a guy explained (in perfect English) exactly how to get there. It was smack in the centre of the city, over the bridge. We 'couldn't miss it'. I might just mention here that that phrase was to become a bit of a running joke, a prompt to laughter whenever we got lost. It is quite difficult to get lost though when you don't mind where you're going or where you end up.

We followed the easy instructions and walked up and down the river bank he'd described. This hostel was nowhere to be seen, but nowhere. Eventually we gave up and asked someone else. He laughed out loud then pointed to a ship right beside us. Oh! The Youth Hostel's a sailing ship. Duh! How stupid were we? How long did we need to be in Scandinavia to grasp that we were among peoples of seafaring nations; best foot (or galleon) forward for the tourists, eh? All jokes aside, the accommodation was more than superb.

Once we'd checked in and been told the rules, we went for a wander to get our bearings. My first big shock was to see fishermen fishing in the capital's river. The thought of pulling out fish (or of even finding any) in the Thames in the 1970s was laughable. The Thames back then was disgusting with heaven-knows-what floating around in it. This river? Like all other water we'd seen in Scandinavia was clear and clean.

On that first day we sussed that Stockholm is built on a lot of small islands and had zillions of bridges. Public transport was amazing. As yet we couldn't afford to jump on and off all the little ferry boats that island hop all day every day. It was early summer and already the parks were full of willow trees that hung and draped into the rivers and lakes they surrounded. There was a lot of green grass for a city centre and an awful lot of well-tended flower beds. This place felt good.

I ought to say something here about one fabulous, intangible reward that comes by casting your fate to the winds. It's like a free gift to be claimed by conquering the fear of cutting loose from constraints; from everything that gives you comfort and a sense of belonging. I've never heard so much as a hint of it in any travelogue or travel programme I've ever read or seen.

I can sum it up in four deceptively simple words. I hazard a guess they'll conjure up nothing more to most than an airy-fairy notion as pie in the sky as Shangri- La. At best nowadays they have become some throwaway lyric to grace a song. I'm talking about these words, 'The rhythm of life.' It's real folks. It's real.

We all talk about the pace of life or the rat-race. That proves my point. Life has a rhythm. It's a rhythm we can't detect when workaday hustle and bustle constantly beats out a very different tune for us to dance to. We dance to that to stay alive. In reality it's killing us.

The best way to convey the experience of the rhythm of life is by examples. Once you cut free and have no particular itinerary or timetable the natural rhythm becomes so evident it's unmissable. No television travel programme can show you. As realistic as those televised journeys may appear, the presenter's travels are carefully choreographed and scheduled. Being followed by a camera crew isn't cutting free. It's show business.

After a month or-so of no ties, no particular direction and no fixed abode I could not fail to notice that a day where everything was a struggle was always followed by twenty-four hours of plain sailing. It was to become such a constant that I anticipated it without question. A case in point is our arrival in Sweden.

Ship-shape

Perhaps we had relaxed into being free. Perhaps we had unwittingly been clinging to that temporary feeling of being on holiday so far. Maybe we'd arrived in the here-and-now. Who can say? But with remarkable ease on our second day in the capital we secured jobs. We simply walked into the central Sheraton Hotel and walked out an hour later as chambermaids in waiting. That was easy. That was the good news. Norway had been very costly. We worked out the cost of living here was at least five times higher than in Britain. Staying fed and watered was pricey. Our money was running low. The bad news was? We couldn't start our jobs for two weeks and we had nowhere to live. The Youth Hostel had a policy of three consecutive nights maximum. Two days in the Swedish capital had been pricey enough. Hanging around here and surviving in a big city would be stressful too. Then inspiration dawned.

Hell! We were still in Scandinavia. There was still an open road of pine trees and reindeer and we did have some basics left. We had packet food, some calor gas and our cooking stuff. What swung us on getting out and hitching north for the duration were the words Polar

Circle and Narvik. They haunted us from our previous failures and the very grand title 'Land of the Midnight Sun' sounded too enticing to dismiss. Here was our second chance.

We walked to the north of the city and thumbed. Yesterday had been lacklustre so today? Well, I felt as if it was gonna be a great day. A small car stopped almost immediately. Turns out he was going about a hundred miles north and we were welcome to join him. He hated driving alone. Also turns out he was excited about his new job up there. The only fly in his ointment or, as he put it, 'the big headache' was his small flat. He hadn't managed to rent it out.

'One man's headache is another man's music' as no-one ever said. It doesn't mean it isn't true. His tiny flat was in central Stockholm. Better and better, we thought. He went on to describe it as being only four subway stops from the underground entrance to the Hotel Sheraton. Well now there's a thing! Deal done.

He was an archaeologist. When Pat told him she was, he started making detours. Don't ask me where we went but I was suddenly up close and personal with an actual, ancient Viking boat, dug up by his colleagues. It was displayed in a massive shed of dark timber. While the two archies talked shop, I ambled around it. Good heavens! This was picture-book stuff from stories of Norsemen ransacking the British Isles. Some of those fabled warriors had rowed this very boat. Those men became real to me for the first time.

Of course, one hundred-or-so miles later, we were on our own again. Since pine trees and reindeer were part of the attraction and we'd 'been here before,' you'd think we'd have remembered there was nothing but. Not so. We'd somehow convinced ourselves that Sweden would be fuller than Norway. Nope. It was much the same emptiness. The next twenty-four hours were pretty miserable. After long hours of sitting or walking, a heavy mist fell over us. Snuggled under our huge cagoules we watched the road and waited. The joys of the occasional startled reindeer grazing by our feet and endless pine forests wore a bit thin. Not a single car passed us on the now very narrow and very isolated road. We broke open a can of cooked potatoes and put it on the burner. We added some packet vegetable soup. We slept badly that night in our sleeping bags on rough, hard ground; never more glad to see the sunrise.

Feeling thoroughly miserable we sat by the road. At last a van pulled up to rescue us. Its owner was a dear little man with an adorable small dog. Since he couldn't speak a word of English and our Swedish stretched to "I'm sorry. I can't speak Swedish," we had absolutely no idea where he was taking us when he pulled off the beaten track to turn right. This lane was narrow and much less used. This was definitely an example of 'the road less taken.' Still! He was smiling and so were we.

We came upon a small village or more precisely a cluster of wooden houses Hansel and Gretel's mum and dad built. These were breathtaking; hand-crafted from the pinewood that concealed them from an outside world. As we accepted his prompt to get out of the van, our driver went to the rear doors. Children came running from every direction. Who knew we were travelling with the Pied Piper? The little dog went crazy. The kids practically killed him with kindness.

As all this was happening, the grown-ups were coming out too. Each one carried a large log to help make a big circle. Everyone sat on them.

The dog scampered over to his master. They spent a while in the van. When both showmen reappeared they were dressed in bright, colourful jester costumes. The dog was going nuts with excitement. His tail was wagging a hundred to the dozen. He was shouting with short sharp yelps. Our driver now had hoops, bells, whistles, balls and what appeared to be skittles.

It began. The show began. The man played his flute. The dog danced. The man did a silly striding walk. The little dog flew in and out then over, under and through the man's dancing legs. When the whistle blew the dog danced on his own. When his master sang he sang along. The children giggled and cheered and clapped. Through hoops and hurdles the little dog cavorted. He even appeared to be applauding himself at the finale. Half an hour of pure magic was spent in a clearing in the woods that day.

At the very end of their show both performers took a bow. Lollipops and sweets were handed out to all the kids. We got back in the van asking ourselves if we had actually seen what we'd actually just seen. We travelled on with them, northward for another hour or more. We were standing at a roadside, dog and driver gone.

Darkness and a chill were coming on. We weren't in the least bit worried. Today was a good day.

Sure enough, we got a lift quite quickly from a charming old couple. These two were wearing wool. Let's face it. They were woollen from tip to toe. Woolly hats tied under their chins, woolly coats, knitted trousers and most likely socks and footwear of wool. The woollens were all a dark brown with crazy, busy patterns in primary colours climbing all over them. Quite a long way into the ride they pointed to a hand-painted, wooden sign announcing "Lapland."

To be honest I had no idea that Lapland existed. I thought it was a Christmas fabrication. At this moment I wouldn't have been at all surprised if Santa Claus put in an appearance. Here we were, in Lapland, apparently. The dark fell hard and fast up here. We travelled on. Another turn-off and another desolate, forest track. Our main concern was where to stay the night. We needn't have bothered our heads. The rhythm of life was carrying us. We were riding its waves. These friendly old folk were taking us to their home as honoured guests. What a home it was!

Here we were in the actual gingerbread house; the gingerbread house that Hansel and Gretel's mum and dad really, really did build but also lived in. Cross my heart and hope to die, I was wondering if the doorbell was a Jammie Dodger. Every single square inch of this astonishing house was hand-carved. Inside, every feature and stick of furniture was hand- crafted too. From the intricate fretwork of the fascia boards on the topsy-turvy roof outside to the floors, staircase, dressers, tables and chairs inside, I was dazzled by the skill, the aromas and all the love invested in this elven palace.

In no time at all the wood-burning stoves and oven were lit; the oil lamps set to blaze and a mouth-watering smell of stew cooking wafted around to tickle our nostrils. Mr. and Mrs. Hansgretel scurried around laughing, gesturing and smiling. At times they chatted away in Swedish at us remarkably loudly. It was that thing that people do when there's a language difference. There's a widespread belief that saying something often enough and saying it loudly will make understanding easier.

They were truly lovely people.

After dinner some kind of alcohol was handed out. To this day I've got no idea what it was. I do know it was delicious. The old man played his fiddle and we insisted on washing-up. It wasn't an amateur recital. Oh no! This was Grieg or some such. Magnificent.

Come time for bed and we were ushered into a very sweet and charming upstairs room. Bless them, they had sprinkled some sweet-smelling petals on the bed sheets and left a hot, brass warming- pan in the hearth of the room.

It was deathly quiet now. The lights were all out. Not a mouse stirred.

But then I'm not a mouse.

I wished I was. Damn. I needed a pee. I was so annoyed. I hadn't seen a bathroom and to stumble and fumble around would mean waking everyone up. Why now? Why me? They were so kind.

The only thing for it was to grope my way outside. It was pitch black. I could scarcely see my hand in front of my face. Every piece of wood creaked at my every move. In utter dark remoteness, even the slightest of creaks sound like a tree being felled. I tip-toed ever-so carefully. What a relief to make it out of the front door without disturbing them all. I should be able to get back in again more easily because my eyes would have adapted to the night. Maybe no-one would ever be any the wiser.

I closed the door so, so gently behind me and turned around. I gaped. I gasped. All of my surroundings were washed with blue-black but within that was a shining silver pathway painted by moonlight. My head moved slowly to look overhead. Right above me, hanging like a huge silvery-grey medallion, was a full wintry moon. The stars were magnificent. I almost forgot why I was out here. Oh yes.

Now I could make out a barn so I headed for it. It was far too cold to pee outside. The barn door opened without so much as a squeak. Phew. So far so good. It was so dark inside but I pulled my knickers down feeling pretty proud of myself for not breaking this peace. I squatted.

I yelled like the banshee.

At the second my arse was bared, two warm, rubbery, stubbly and slightly moist suckers took a hold on it. What the? Then came the very loud snort and grunt. A pig? When I squealed again, he squealed, grunted and ran off. Can you blame him?

Every light in the little house came on now. Everyone ran out to see who was being killed. Trust me, eh?

Some tots of brandy and a lot of laughter later, peace and sleep were restored.

The rhythm of life and 'going with the flow' are great expressions, eh?

I came to the conclusion, after hundreds of ups and downs like this, that if we can survive in the womb with no need to worry about food or essentials and if we can all do that for nine months, perhaps we shouldn't lose sight of our beginnings.

Yes. There are lots of things that travel writers won't tell you. They rarely describe the nitty gritty of hunger, illness, danger or the dull and draining tedium of train and bus journeys. On that note I'll fast forward slightly and share with you the philosophical observations of a Pakistani guy on a never-ending train journey from Istanbul to Tehran. After day one the water ran out. After day two the toilets didn't function. After day three there was no sign of tea-sellers or hawkers. In a rickety old carriage, on a train that redefined the word overcrowded and in the middle of the night, only he and I were awake. He stared at the badges sewn onto my backpack and said,

"If I may be saying something? When you are arriving home your friends and your family is saying 'My goodness look at the wonderful places you see and the wonderful places you go.' But they are not seeing you like I am seeing you…sitting eating bread and cheese, cheese and bread, bread and bread until it is coming out of your veritable earholes. What is the meaning of this?"

There's no answer to that, is there?

Our fairy godparents took us into Pello the next morning. They wanted to show us their only civic statue. It was of a famous skier; a son of this small town. They were so proud. We 'Ooh'd' and 'Aah'd' to keep them happy but all I kept thinking was how odd it would be to stick a skier's likeness up in my home city. The only civic monuments Britain had at that time (outside London anyway) were representations of a dour Queen Victoria or some decrepit, long-dead politician that nobody'd ever heard of. I quite fancied the idea of plonking this in a strictly 'no skiing' county. Perhaps it would look best next to Victoria with that glance thing she had going on.

With big hugs we said our farewells. They left us on that road again.

Groupies

"Remind me why we came to Narvik?" I was patting and hugging myself to get warm. There was nothing here. That's a lie. There were about twenty houses and then nothing. We were starving and cold. A quick walk around the place and we found something open. The railway station had lights on. This has got to be one of the world's northernmost stations, surely. At least they had a buffet.

The friendly woman serving (or she would have been if there'd been any people) telephoned a friend and got us a room. She handed us the address but then her son turned up and said he could take us in about half- an-hour.

A plate of dreadful meatballs with chips later and we still had 15 minutes to kill. We bought another coffee each and walked along the godforsaken platform. Who on earth comes here? Next question, "and why?'

We managed to fit our backsides onto the wooden sills of a window of another closed building. We lit a ciggie each. Now that we'd got our bearings we walked down the line to what looked like a train parked, waiting to pull out. As we reached it the thing sprang into life. We kept walking as it crawled beside us. We were about 4 carriages along and it was gaining speed. From somewhere further down the line someone shouted "Maggeeeee." The voice was attached to a body, barely discernible but definitely human because the arms were waving in my direction. "Maggeeeeeeeeee." I could not believe this.

I ran to see who this was.

"Jim. Jim." The thing yelled. I reached him. "I got on the wrong bleeping, bleep of a bleeping train. I couldn't bleeping get off the bleeping thing." There was no mistaking that voice now. An Aussie accent is an Aussie accent. As the train pulled out I was shouting "Sheraton Hotel! Sheraton Hotel!" I could only hope he caught that.

Jim was a guy we met on our first day at the Youth Hostel. We hit it off. He was supposed to be in London by now. How the heck did he end up in Narvik? Ridiculous.

"Remind me why we came to Narvik?" I returned to my original question.

"To cross the Polar Circle to the land of the midnight sun and maybe see the Northern Lights?"

"Right. Next time we have a bright idea, maybe we should think it through. If I come up with one, stop me, stop me, would you?"

Our ride arrived.

Some of you would have known, wouldn't you? You'd have known that the words 'Midnight sun' mean exactly that. The sun shines at midnight. Well, let me tell you it's not romantic. It's a pain in the butt. That's why our guesthouse provided eye-shades free of charge with every reservation. At midnight we still couldn't sleep because it was daylight outside. Still, we had high hopes of seeing the Northern Lights, right? Wrong! Think about that. (We didn't.) If the sun is always shining there isn't any dark to see these mystical lights in, is there? Call us slow but it took us two days to suss that out. What's the cliché that comes to mind? Yeah! 'We live and learn.'

So we were stuck up here in the Polar Regions and needed to get south. Who do you think we met? Well done. You got it, a Beatles tribute band from Liverpool. Who else would you expect to meet?

We met them in the one bar in Narvik. Their gig didn't go down too well. I don't think it was a reflection on their musical prowess. It was more likely the fact that there were only four customers in the pub. And that's how come we ended up chatting to them. After dossing at their accommodation that night we took up their offer of a ride to Kiruna the next day. At least it was south.

I think it was part of their rock'n'roll fantasy that they'd pick up swooning groupies. Pat and I didn't exactly fit the bill. We got on with them well enough but in truth none of them were all that bright, a bit laddish and (what's the word?) 'Chancers.' In a way we had that last one in common. We managed to travel south with them for the next eight days free of charge, down along the east of Sweden, the Gulf of Bothnia.

We had a home. Our flat was great. Above all it allowed Pat and I to have time to do our own thing.

Behind Closed Doors

The Sheraton Hotel kindly provided breakfast and an afternoon meal for its chambermaids. That was brilliant. It saved time and money and wasn't a bad way to start and end a day's work. With twenty-four rooms to attend to in six hours the days went quickly enough.

The thing about being a chambermaid was that every one of the guests in the international hotel thought you were an idiot or at best one slice short of a loaf. This was more than a tremendous advantage. It was a gift. Why an advantage? Well, it was the closest I will ever come to being cloaked. However I got treated the whole thing was hilarious.

In a prestigious hotel in a bustling city like Stockholm everything contrived to amuse. Of course I had an ace up my sleeve. I knew that. I knew the job was temporary but even still. Our allotted twenty-four rooms were always on a given floor. We were armed with a list of the rooms vacated overnight. Those were the ones that got seen-to at eight o'clock or thereabouts when our shift began. The work was routine but never got boring thanks to the guests who unwittingly provided an unending supply of entertainment.

Like I've said before, everyone agrees that when you're talking to someone who obviously doesn't understand your language, the time-honoured, tried-and-tested way to convey your message is to speak slo-wer and shout lou-der. Ultimately you reach a point where you're shouting and pronouncing one word every ten seconds then adding mime. With perseverance the method never fails, or does it? Nearly every one of the guests in the rooms I had to clean had unfortunately learned this method. All they knew was I was an imbecile and couldn't possibly understand their predicament by any other means.

They all had the same problem, to be fair. In Scandinavia, the common language used by most travellers is English. But then again, no stupid chambermaid here would be able to speak that as well as you do, right? The stage was set.

Let me give you a day in the life of Maggie the chambermaid.

By nine o'clock it was time to start tackling the rooms that were still occupied. The quicker I could get those done the quicker I could get home. I tapped on one door, peeked in and got a wave to enter from a small Japanese business man. He was obviously in the middle of a phone call because I could see the phone off the hook on the desk by the window. Gesturing for me to do the bed and the immediate surfaces around him, I made a start.

I do wish he hadn't started speaking. Oh god I wished he hadn't opened his mouth. At first I managed to contain myself. I kept my giggles at bay. After a while it got ridiculous. Was this guy winding me up? He obviously had a bad line to wherever it was because it went like this (and quite loudly)

"Yes. Yes. I am in the shitty. In the shitty! Yes. Yes. It is a velly, velly big shitty. Yes. Big shitty. Ah ha. Me also. I think it small shitty too. No. No. Big, big shitty. Are you in the shitty? I say. Are you in the shitty?"

Thank god he didn't turn round. If he had done, he would have been greeted by the image of a girl standing, cross-legged, shaking and willing him to stop saying that city thing over and over and over. I had a brainwave. The survival instinct will do that. I dived into the bathroom, shut the door and pulled the toilet flush so I could explode undetected. That was better. Now all I had to do was clean the bathroom and escape. All he had to do was keep up his end of the bargain and not say a word. Not a single word. I made it.

I hadn't gone far along the corridor when an American family walked towards me. They were encouraging (what looked to be) their eldest son to ask me something.

'Go on! Ask her. Go on.' At this point you should know, (if you don't already,) that Sweden has an incredible amount of public holidays where everything (and I mean everything) stops. It was understandable that travellers needed to know when these were. This family had obviously heard a rumour that today was one of those days. The young man approached me cautiously and nervously. That was a laugh. I kept a straight face. In fact, keeping a straight face gave me an idea.

"Good morning." He said, very, very slowly and deliberately. My face stayed blank. The ruse was working. The rest of the family encouraged him with

"Well done. Well, go on. Go on. You're doing great."

"Is today?" He looked at his family for support. "Is to-day-a-pub-lic-hol-i-day?"

Well, I ask you. What was I supposed to do? I lifted one eyebrow and looked puzzled. He came at me again but louder. He tried a new tactic.

"Hol-i-day? Hol-i-day?"

Clever, I thought. Yep, that'll do it. Missing out the verbs will help. Yes I know, it was wicked but it was fun.

"To-day." The whole bunch joined in and turned up the volume. "To-day-hol-i-day?" We had quite a chorus thing going on now.

How long could I keep this up? The mother got an idea. I have never actually seen anyone try to mime the word holiday before. It was mind-boggling. I have to give respect where respect is due, she put her heart into it. Very strange.

I cracked, my face crumpled and I started to laugh. The dad said, "Look guys. She'll never get what we're saying. Let's go down to the lobby and ask."

"No. It's not." They stared at me. "It's not a bank holiday today." I said it all painfully slowly and deliberately, mimicking them. They did have a sense of humour because, after the initial shock, they burst out laughing and the shouted in unison,

"By God! The girl's a Brit."

Believe me! You'd be surprised to find out what people who present a classy exterior get up to in hotel rooms. Some of it came as quite a shock. I was party to some guilty secrets and some vile and quite disturbing habits. It all came in handy. How? When those persons decided to be downright rude or even abusive I smiled, stared at them innocently and waited. I waited for the realisation to register; the realisation that I knew and they now knew that I knew that they knew I knew. Oh the power! In the three months of working there I never had any problems.

Just before finishing time I was pushing my cumbersome trolley down the last part of my corridors when I was grabbed by a Chinese man standing in his half-open doorway. He grabbed my arm quite roughly and snapped at me,

"Hao Yu Gaw Eh Niho?"

My thought was, (as anyone's would have been, right?) "Uh?"

Yes. He had learned English by that same old method. Much louder and slower this time he shouted, "Hao..........Yu.......... Gaw.......Eh.....Niho?"

My second thought was 'O..........kay.' I lifted up a towel from the trolley and held it out to him.

"No....ho!" He shouted even louder. This time the emphasis had fallen on the 'ho' bit and I began to suspect that this was a separate word. It was possibly the object of his desire. The strange dance began. I held out serviettes.

"No.......ho!" The 'ho' was definitely bearing the brunt of his wrath. His face was getting redder and redder. The blood vessels in his cheeks were reddening; the veins in his neck stiffening. I held up a pillow,

"Ho!"

I held a spare toothbrush aloft,

"Ho!"

A flannel, a floor-cloth, a toilet roll and everything I had on my trolley was offered. In fact, I ran out of things to suggest. There wasn't much I could do. I shrugged and went to walk away. He was stomping with frustration and anger.

At this point he looked back over his shoulder into his room. Someone inside was obviously asking if he'd managed to get his 'ho'.

"No! No.............."

I heard a very loud "Why noh'?"

His next answer cracked me up.

"Oh! Stoo-pid grill don't spick Ingrish!"

And we wonder how wars start, eh?

A Peek behind the Curtain.

As that chambermaid I acquired a lot of reading matter. It's one of the perks of the job. People leave all kinds of things for chambermaids to keep or dispose of. I picked up the usual shampoos and conditioners, a lot of Swedish coins and even a very posh dress. I sent it home to my mum in the U.K. It fitted perfectly and she kept it for best. My favourite find was a Swedish to English phrasebook. I got curious. I suddenly had a burning desire to find out what phrases a Swede could possibly need urgently on a visit to London?

When I flicked through it to see what phrases were deemed crucial, I laughed until it hurt. What could they possibly need to look up? How about this one?

"Excuse me, where can I hire some jodhpurs?" or this priceless gem? "Wait a moment please. I will have to look this up in my phrase book." (Yeah…the hilarity of that one kind of creeps up on you!) Thanks again Pythons.

By summer's end our months of work were over. We had a stash of cash and were raring to go. Finland here we come.

You can imagine how all of the phrasebook stuff plays into a scene I was about to star in on the set of Helsinki railway station.

We were trying to locate exactly which train was going to Moscow. We had always hoped we could get into Russia but the Iron Curtain was very iron back then. It had taken some effort to get this far. The last two weeks in Sweden were spent going from pillar to post (or more accurately embassy to embassy.)

Apparently, the only way into Russia was to be part of an organised tour. Of course we had a problem with that. Eventually we were given details of a mixed group of young people who were on a package visit. The said group would be in Moscow at the same time as we could possibly be.

Every country involved demanded a visa. Denmark wanted confirmation of arrival times and date; Russia wanted confirmation of the dates on our Danish visa and Sweden needed Russia to confirm that it would have us in the first place. It was Catch-22 but it was a laugh. We couldn't get a visa because we couldn't get a visa.

Surprisingly the Russians cracked first. It meant travelling into Russia by train from here in Helsinki and somehow meeting up with this group. All we had was the name of a hotel as a rendezvous point. The rest was up to us.

We had taken a six-week crash course in Russian back in the U.K. (just in case) but let me tell you. If you ever consider learning Finnish? Don't!

I'll give you a clue why. On a tram in Helsinki I looked at the back of my ticket. It was covered in typed print. In all of that print there were only two sentences. Each of those two sentences had only six words. Nearly every word was more than fifteen letters long. I did ask about it but, whatever the linguistics, it was still indecipherable.

So where are we? Oh yes- Helsinki railway station. It's early evening; we're tired and beginning to feel more than a little wary of what we're getting ourselves into. The scene was daunting.

The concourse was quite big but not that busy. We could see Cyrillic lettering over one section of the platforms ahead. To find the one to Moscow was the mission. Unfortunately, we had to get past Akilina the Hun. We called her that because Pat (who'd obviously paid more attention to Russian classes than I had) said Akilina meant powerful. In this woman's case that was an understatement. She was sitting on a hefty wooden crate, her big hands plonked firmly on her knees. Her expression was a severe one. She was built like the proverbial brick... you- know-what. If her size and demeanour weren't scary enough, the uniform clinched it. One of us had to ask her for our train.

Pat was shy. This one was on me then. I psyched myself up and walked across to our nemesis. I was doing my best Gary Cooper in 'High Noon' walk. Then I folded. Actually I crumpled. Dammit! I'd slipped into a Python sketch. Come on. I was seriously going to ask "Where is the train to Moscow?" This was surreal.

We all know what the compulsion to laugh does when confronted by the stone wall of a deadpan face, right? Absolutely! It increases exponentially.

I did a sharp, soldier on parade- type about-turn and walked back over to Pat. I smoked a ciggie and told myself to calm down. I could do this. I could do this. No I couldn't! My second attempt was even more pathetic. Just a few steps in and I so wanted to know the Russian for "Where can I hire some jodhpurs?"

By now Akilina had us in her sights. She was looking a bit quizzical. It was an improvement. Her face was still frightening but quizzical was definitely progress.

On my third attempt, I got swept up in an old spy movie feeling; one of those where I say, "The weather has taken a turn for the worse." (or some such) and she counters with, "I hear it's nice in Paris this time of year." In my head there's that deep, rounded Russian intonation running with her words.

Every time I tried, my face melted and the trembling kicked in. I fought to swallow my giggles and keep comedy at bay.

I had a stroke of genius. I grabbed Pat and we grabbed our bags. Why didn't I think of this escape sooner? All we had to do was act nonchalant and thrust our tickets and travel documents at the female mountain.

Mission accomplished. We found the right train. The Leo Tolstoy was to carry us to Moscow but it would take some 14 hours or more to do it.

The Leo Tolstoy was not like it is today. Our compartment was, well, oh I'll just say it, wooden. We had booked it exclusively for us. We were to find out that didn't mean a thing. There weren't any bench seats exactly. There were four bunk beds with thin mattresses and no bedding. The top two on either side folded up against the walls.

Pat and I browsed over a map to see where we'd be going but we were pretty tired so at about 9 o'clock we crawled into our sleeping bags, fully-clothed. The old train rattled along and rattled us to sleep. Just at the point of going deeper, the old wooden door slid open with a clatter. A handsome young man in uniform walked in as if he owned the place. Who knows? Perhaps he did. Still, it was a bit of a shocker; seemed like we were sharing with him then. Biggles wanted to socialise.

We climbed out of our sleeping bags. It wasn't long before he produced a bottle of vodka.

Stop here while I fast forward to 2018 for a moment. Last week I read a post on Facebook that announced "Scientists discover that alcohol improves the ability to speak foreign languages?" Really? What took you so long folks? Not enough field work?

I discovered that more than 40 years ago on this train. Our Russian words magically came back. They were random but they came. What the recent scientific findings don't tell you however is that later (when the booze wears off) you haven't got the foggiest idea what you actually said.

Nonetheless, in the following hours we three took part in the most insane game of charades I'm ever likely to witness. Our travelling companion did some excellent mimes. He did being a pilot, having a wife, two kids and a dog. This said dog may have been a Rottweiler, an Alsatian or an aggressive poodle. Did I mention the vodka was strong? At one point he was reduced to crawling on all fours to explain something. Who cared? We laughed ourselves silly.

Who knows when we fell asleep again? It didn't matter. A loud thumping and a familiar door-rattle jumped us all awake. It was black outside. What?

We heard the unmistakeable, rhythmic thunder of jackboots marching through the wooden train. 'Oh! No!' A familiar face. Akilina was back. She was here, in our carriage. She was already supporting fistfuls of passports and shouted for ours.

We surrendered them and filed out into the long corridor to join every other passenger being ushered off the train.

Now, I am of the generation who lived through the JFK assassination, the Cuban missile crisis, the worldwide-shared nightmare of the bomb and the whole Cold War thing so naturally, I prided myself on being a free-thinking, reasonable grown-up who was not about to become paranoid by simply crossing a border. In no uncertain terms, it turned out, I was deluded. I was paranoid right now.

We had no idea what was going on. It was spooky (as in spies not ghosts).

On a desolate railway platform in God- knows-where and in the dark (in more ways than one) we watched gobsmacked, as dozens and dozens of Soviet troops unceremoniously ripped our train apart. Every plank of every carriage was uprooted; every nook and cranny searched. For what? We never knew. We gaped as the army reassembled every bit. We got back on as She-Who-Must-Be-Obeyed handed us back our passports.

Was there any point in trying to get any sleep? Strangely our young pilot had vanished. It occurred to us that he might have been a plant. If he was, then this must have gone down in his memory banks as the most peculiar assignment he ever had. I would love to have been there at the de-briefing.

Very early in the morning Leo Tolstoy arrived at Moscow Central station. This was real then. Through bleary eyes we stepped off the train. My mind screamed at me,

"Oh! Hello! Watch out! Wake up! What's this?" and then "Welcome to the 1940s sunshine!"

Have you ever stopped to consider how amazing the human mind is? Mine stores memories in picture form and, in any strange new situation, it scans for a comparison. I think it's trying to be helpful. I might be sitting drinking tea near the ancient ruins of Troy and my mind goes "This is a bit like Wales" and I go "What? No it's not. It's nothing like Wales." Okay so sometimes it gets it wrong. In this instance though, it was spot on. Here I was with no script or suitable costume, thrown onto the busy film-set of an old black- and-white movie.

The next reference point my mind threw up was 'an away mission in Star Trek.' This was a time travel episode for sure. Okay. So now I'm Ohura and 'boldly going boldly where no boldly has gone boldly before." I could handle that.....boldly!

The exit was straight ahead. Sunlight was flooding into the huge station. I had a hell of a hangover and I was hungry but Treky time-travellers never fail. We had a hotel to find.

Picture this if you will. Standing in the vast entrance archway, we were confronted with Moscow's early morning rush-hour. Streams of people were inches away in a swarm, scurrying to and fro as workers do. This traditional ritual is upheld in cities the world over. Just beyond the stream was a traffic jam. Traffic lights were halting proceedings on a main road. In the queue at the lights were the most random of vehicles. An old cart from a Constable painting was piled high with hay. Behind it was a cumbersome 1940s delivery van. Following behind that was one of those 1940s, World War ll, open-backed troop-carriers featured in old war films and documentaries. Yes. In the back of that truck, (on two opposing benches) sat five or six stocky soldiers, helmeted, stock still and face to face. They were gripping their rifles, perched upright in front of them.

Despite trying to take all this in, my mind was frantically trying to focus on what I had to say to one of the scurrying masses. I had to go up to one and say, "Excuse me, please can you help me?" Then show them the name of the hotel. A doddle.

I was just about ready. I stepped forward to approach a young woman. I had the Russian words on the tip of my tongue when, the traffic lights changed. Oops! A pop-up moment! Red Square popped up in front of my very eyes. Red Square was right in front of me.

Seriously, Red Square was across the road. Think of something you'd define as huge. Got it? Now multiply that by at least 100 and you're coming somewhere close to the absolute, ridiculous enormity of the place. It had those onion-shaped, fancy painted towers and everything. Onion-topped spires, multi-coloured and sitting there right in my line of vision and just over the road.

My head was scrambled. Oh for a phrasebook!

I stared at the passers-by, back at Red Square, back at the pedestrians, back at the square and back at the people. My head thought we were in a central seat at a Wimbledon final. It came up with some Russian at long last. What it came up with flipped me back into Python sketch again. I got the giggles. What the?

Just when I thought every single word of Russian had deserted me, what did my mind come up with? One phrase. One single phrase. What was that? Was it something I could use right now? I needed something I could use right now.

Alright. Alright. Whose bright idea was it to teach this to anyone? I ask you. How or when on earth could it be of any use? In what possible situation even? (It was certainly not here and definitely not now.) Yeah, that'll be right. I'm gonna walk calmly up to one of these pedestrians and casually announce, "Krass-nee- ah ….. ploss-chad…… vuv….. sien-tra…….. Moskva." *

*(Red square is in the centre of Moscow.")

We'd arrived. Best find a taxi before I got sectioned.

Knock Knock

If I'd ever doubted the power books have had on my mind, all doubt left me in the taxi from Moscow central station that day. My mind kept giving me images of - Alice in Wonderland. As we drove to the hotel address I understood why. I'd swallowed the tablet labelled 'Shrink me.' I was in a dinky toy watching everything sliding past. The everything loomed out of all proportion and became enormous beyond belief.

I was in shock but didn't know it. There again, that's a sure symptom of shock. The sense of watching an old black-and- white movie stayed with me. It played itself out, projected on the car window. I struggled to work out if I was the star, an extra or just a cinema-goer, aghast and stuffing popcorn.

The nickname for Moscow is The Big Village. It was easy to see why. The traffic was an odd mixture of tractors, carts and cattle trucks mixed with the heavy and lumbering cars reminiscent of Sunday outings with my dad and various uncles back in the 50s and 60s. Then there was the odd motor bike and sidecar. These were vehicles Rommel would have felt perfectly at home in, doing that salute thing they all did. Being tiny, the enormous multi-storey and Stalinist apartment blocks were stacked up around me like childhood building blocks. Every now and then a huge square cropped up. Like a small part of some massive chessboard abandoned by unseen giants it sat, overgrown with trees and bushes.

On those chessboards decorative pieces were still in play. One was possibly the modern equivalent of a knight? It was the biggest space rocket ever cast in shining titanium. It was hundreds of feet high and stretched ever-upward. The plinth alone was gigantic. It left the rocket on top looking as if it was already in the stratosphere.

I'd entered Russia determined not to see it through Western eyes or jump to hasty conclusions based on an upbringing of propaganda. It wasn't easy. My mind kept leaping to judgement. It was telling me that scale was being used in a determined effort to squash individualism; to overwhelm the individual with a show of the authority of an all-powerful State? My alternative was to consider the plight of the Russians for hundreds of years. They have been constantly beaten down by less-than-benevolent rulers. After all it was only 30 years or-so since the end of the Second World War. Millions of their young men had died in brutal conflict with Uncle Adolf. It was a century or-so since Russian men and women had so bravely struggled to win a revolution only to have it stolen from them by some all-knowing smart-asses. Perhaps this monumental architecture and street-furniture were examples of Civic Pride. By the time we arrived at our hotel I'd settled on a combination of both.

They say that travel broadens the mind. I'll go along with that but with caveats. There has to be interaction of some kind, either with new surroundings or with the people of different cultures. There has to be a mind to broaden in the first place.

For now? We were here. It was early morning and we were thanking our lucky stars for our perfect timing! Against all odds we'd managed to get to the hotel just in time for breakfast.

There are some rare and glorious instances in life when you get a chance to see yourself as others do. One such moment was our sudden intrusion into the group we were joining at this strange hotel. You could see by their faces they'd been expecting English ladies and were suffering under the illusion that we'd be well-groomed, slightly prim and definitely proper. Poor things!

It must have come as quite a shock when two young women (looking more than slightly the worse for wear) plonked themselves down at the long breakfast table, blind to anyone or anything other than food. Hunger will do that. All niceties get slung straight out of the nearest window. We couldn't believe that we and breakfast arrived at the same time.

Everyone had just that moment sat down. Plates of food appeared. Pat and I lunged forward, made a grab for our hard-boiled eggs, tapped them on the table, peeled off the shells and took huge bites. We swigged a glass of black tea down in one. Only then did we realise the others were deathly quiet. Around us everyone was shaking out a napkin and gently tapping one egg with a nice little spoon. They were staring at us with a look that said 'uncouth'. We'd definitely arrived.

Gallons of tea kept coming. It was a strange breakfast. It consisted of delicious black rye bread, soured cream-cheese, boiled eggs and believe it or not, a huge bowl of plain spaghetti. What the heck? It was food. We waited until the others were leaving and picked up their leftovers. We knew what it meant to go hungry and we couldn't stand waste. With our stomachs silenced, our bodies allowed us to take in our surroundings.

It's tricky to describe spaces and places in Russia. Like I said, think big. Nowadays when I see Putin entertaining some foreign dignitary or other my head shouts "Oh yes! Those rooms! That furniture!"

Everything is too big. It spreads down from the public megastructures and civic statues to the width of the roads, hotels and individual rooms. They're all too big. It seems like there isn't enough furniture to fill any of the living spaces. Carpets that would be huge anywhere else shrink to doormats. Wooden panels are stuck randomly on walls just to make the place look lived- in and they fail miserably. It seems like some bright spark has said, "We need some soft furnishings" and hung or nailed vast pieces of net curtain in the strangest of places to try to blur the utter starkness of the chasms. Huge ornate chairs become dolls' furniture and, despite all best attempts, you are left with the feeling of being in a mausoleum; insignificantly rattling around in a massive space, feeling lost.

Our room was, how do I put this? Oh yes! It was wooden. No, seriously. It was wooden from floor to ceiling. Let's face it. It was built of varnished planks. It was big. In one corner there was another enormous wooden box. I opened the creaky door warily. It was a bathroom. We jumped on the extremely hard beds, set the alarm and as soon as our heads hit the pillow we were gone.

We woke up in time for more food. If you let it, life will toss you a pleasant surprise or an unexpected gift at the strangest of moments. It's a delight when it happens. Over dinner we discovered that we hadn't just paid for a ticket in and out of Russia and a hotel room with breakfast for thirteen days. Living with the extortionate costs in Scandinavia had made us blind to one thing. Our money went further than we thought. We had inadvertently paid for all of our evening meals, a night out at a hotel with cabaret, several guided tours around the city, three days in St. Petersburg (including train fare) and a night at the Russian State Circus. With all the hullabaloo of getting here and getting visas we hadn't thought to ask about details. We never saw all that coming!

Back to that platitude 'travel broadens the mind.' Sometimes there just isn't. There just isn't a mind to broaden. One of those times came up after dinner. In our group were three eastern Europeans, four young Americans, one Danish girl and us two Brits. After we'd eaten our evening meal one of the young American guys came up to me and asked, "You guys just come in from Scandinavia?" I nodded.

"Disappointing, huh?" He said it as if we'd automatically agree. Assuming that, he didn't wait for an answer but added, "I did Sweden. Never saw one reindeer."

"What d'you mean you did Sweden?" I wasn't quite sure what that actually meant.

"I got an Air-Pass. I fly where I want around here and fly out again. I spent a day in Sweden before here. I did it." He emphasised the 'did'.

Those were the days when, long before the European Union, it was possible for us all to buy rail passes for flexible travel across borders but an Air Pass? That was a new one on me.

"Whereabouts in Sweden?" I was still trying to give him the benefit of the doubt.

"Stockholm." He said casually. I looked at him, thought for a minute and decided this conversation wasn't worth pursuing. He carried on regardless. "Never saw one damn reindeer." I was sorely tempted to tell him we'd met Pinocchio and the Pied Piper but any hopes of he and I communicating had vanished.

We decided to leave them be for a while and go outside to suss out our immediate surroundings. We wanted a walk.

As we got to the entrance our tour guide stopped us. "There is no need to go out alone." She smiled sweetly.

"No need?" I thought it. I bit my lip. I wanted to say, "Lady! What's need got to do with anything? There's no need to be here in Russia in the first place. Need? Need?" but I didn't. "We just want some fresh air." We convinced her we'd be fine and she let us pass. Hey! What possible mischief could we get up to?

The way she approached us struck me as a bit weird. 'Stop it!' Here it was again, that paranoia thing. We sat some way down the street and smoked a ciggie.

Perhaps we were seeing the little episode through those prejudiced Western eyes again. Perhaps the famous Russian hospitality we'd read about demands they look after our every need and it's not control at all. We settled for that, for now at least.

It wasn't long at all before two young blokes came up to us and asked if we'd sell them our jeans. This was a turn-up for the books.

Their English was good and we explained we'd love to but we were travelling and only had one pair each. Difficult though it was for them to believe, they believed us in the end.

"Do you want come with us to Youth Club?" They asked.

"Why not?" Pat and I signalled to each other by facial expression. Off we went, into the land of the giants.

Like I said, 'What possible mischief could we get up to?'

I'd scanned my mental diary. Just as I thought. Nothing planned for the rest of my life. My mind hiccoughed. It had stumbled on an exception. 'Near future. Day unknown. Russian State Circus, Moscow.' I could cope with that.

I've said it before but I'll say it again. The human mind's a wonderful thing. When it's uncluttered from the usual useless stuff, it functions as it should. Travelling gave me time to muse and surmise a lot more often. The mind's designed to create and absorb new settings and ideas; solve problems and even has an alarm-alert system fitted. It can even record the soundtrack of events for effective recall. Inexplicably, at that moment mine reminded me I'd stored a really annoying song. I didn't even want to acknowledge it for fear of having to replay it. It was too late. The stupid song was playing on the Scandinavian ferry when we first left Britain. It turned up again in the apartment block in Stockholm. A neighbour kept playing it. The thing had a knack of just being with us in the oddest of places. I tried to skip over it now. 'Um. Where was I?'

Our new guides Alexi and Dimitri were leading us merrily along the streets of Moscow. With a sudden sense of mild panic I realised we had no idea how to get back to the hotel or even the name of it. "Hotel. Hotel!" I said a bit too loudly. They both laughed. After a minute they got my point. "No problem. One hotel for tourist. No Russians." They both laughed like drains as they mimed one of them being dragged by the collar.

"Really?" I asked.

"Really." Came the reply.

My musing mind threw up the name Darwin. Right there, walking through the Moscow streets with two complete strangers and my mind says 'Darwin'. Why? It was most likely because of all the gestures and mimes going on with our language barrier. Actions speak loud and clear. I don't ever remember anyone ever teaching me that a pat on the stomach indicates being hungry. But it does and it's international. Think about it. There are millions of signs and gestures we all know, every man-jack of us.

I've never had much time for Darwinism but seeing this body language it dawned on me that at some point we all communicated with gestures. Personally, as a language teacher (if I was pushed) I'd have to say my preferred method of conveying something to a non-English speaker is definitely mime.

So we understood. First off we were going to get them both something to eat. Up until now the streets had been pretty empty. What hundred-or-so people we passed were dwarfed by everything so a hundred people seemed more like ten. My mind was scanning everything and picking up on it all. There was absolutely no litter. There were no litter bins. I supposed this was evidence we weren't in a consumer society. No junk food or snacks. No thoughtless buying for buying's sake. That realisation led to 'Oh! There's no hoardings, no billboards, no advertising for anything anywhere.' No sooner had that thought struck me than "Hey presto!" there was a hoarding of sorts. Twenty-or more enlarged photographs of um 'people.' These, we were told, were The Workers of the Month. Even today, when I see similar mug shots hung in fast-food outlets, I cringe.

A similar practise arrived in Europe years later under the American flag. I found it demeaning and somewhat insulting. Honestly? They take your picture and pin it up in plain sight to illustrate how much money you've made for them? A very peculiar concept. Flattery will get you a long way, I guess. We stopped and stood in front of the installation. We waited for a passer-by to take a photograph of us. I knew we weren't heading for a burger joint or a fish 'n 'chip shop but nothing could have prepared me for the Workers' Café. Right outside it, a huge feat of civic engineering was under way. A swarm of workers, male and female, were building a fly-over and a road tunnel. They were burrowing away as if there was no tomorrow. What struck me was the size of the women builders. Did you ever see those naughty and very British postcards of the '50s and '60s where the henpecked husband is a weed and his wife an enormous battle-axe? Those characters were here my friends but they were building a road.

Before we entered the café the lads whispered, 'You are Russian' then reverted to ape-speak by putting one index finger up to closed lips. Silent we would be then. We went inside. A chunky counter stretched along the length of the right-hand side of the space. The entire interior was tiled in stark white. I was struck by a huge, white ceramic weighing-scale with its silver scoop-bucket and its weights stacked up beside it. If I could come up with anything comparable I would have to say a butcher's shop in the 1950s. Behind the counter stood five more of those burly women; their hair tied back by means of small head-kerchiefs knotted at the nape of the neck. Behind and in front of the women was a bewildering array of steaming cauldrons, stacks and stacks of white ceramic and identical bowls and other pots with ladles.

We sat at one of the tables on the left. Dimitri gestured for me to come with him to the counter. I know. I thought it odd too but I agreed. I wouldn't have missed this for the world. This was some experience.

In the West our usual first step is to order but not here. There was no need. There was only one meal on offer. It was a type of workers' stew. The first woman only needed to know how many people were eating. Once she knew that, she set off the chain reaction. She placed two bowls on the open surface and put a huge dumpling in each. The first bowl was placed on the scale. She and the second server weighed and checked it. This co-worker added a ladle of cabbage and potato. This was weighed. A third added a meat portion. This was weighed. A fourth added gravy. Yep. It was weighed. Both bowls went through the same process until it got to the fifth woman who took the money.

What can I say? Make of this what you will. Everyone is equal? Quality control? No swindling? Big Brother provides in fair measure? The same to each? I was bewildered.

All in due time we set off and arrived in a back street where three knocks on a strange door gained us access. I kid you not. A tiny wooden hatch slid aside and two eyeballs scanned us. Oops! That paranoia thing again.

First impressions of the inside weren't good. It was all a bit shoddy, outdated and sparse. However, the atmosphere was relaxed. We caused quite a stir. We were bombarded by handshakes and introductions.

After a lot of Russian banter between themselves some guy held up two bottles of beer. He handed them to Pat and I and announced "Eenglish Beer." I doubted that. Someone had printed off pictures of a very young Queen Elizabeth and pasted them onto old bottles. We smiled and took the beers.

There was a very old television with a portable aerial on top of it; a table and chairs; a radio and a makeshift pool table. After a few Queen Elizabeth beers someone dragged us to sit by the T.V. Watching telly wasn't exactly what we had in mind but their laughter and enthusiasm coupled with "You must see. You must see" convinced us to give it ten minutes or more. An old Betamax recorder was tugged out and a video slotted in. The show began.

I cannot even begin to explain how totally surreal it was when "Fawlty Towers" started to roll. It was bootlegged and overdubbed in Russian. Can you imagine seeing the quintessentially British John Cleese talking in Russian? I was giggling. When they realised we got the point, we were shown whole sets of that series. A guy whose English was brilliant had turned up and asked, "You understand now that the English and Russians have same sense of humour?" That comment has influenced my attitude towards Russians ever since.

With the same bloke acting as translator now, things got a lot easier. Questions and answers from both sides flew back and forth. We learned more about Russia in that one evening than we could ever have hoped to by sticking strictly to a tour.

There were special hotels for foreign visitors and special shops. Wherever we went we would never be among the Russian people. Everything was carefully controlled to create a good impression. Most people were poor. Food and products of all kinds were scarce or never available. We would see queues everywhere for everything.

Seated around that table, watching and listening to their banter and the translating I noticed a habit they had.

When someone was hogging the conversation another would knock loudly three times on the table. At that point the talker would laugh, stop talking and hand over the reins. I kept noticing it so I had to ask if that was just something they did amongst themselves or did it mean anything. "Could we do it?" They all split a gut laughing.

"No. It is better you do not." He did the threefold knock. As he knocked each time he said out loud, "K. G.B."

As all this was going on, our translator started rolling a joint. Seeing the look of astonishment on our faces he explained. "It is okay. In here you can smoke." That was okay for him to say but after the K.G.B. thing we weren't so sure. Anyway, the last thing I wanted right then was a joint. But, my grandad always told me to go and live, make memories and make stories to tell. I thought for a second and laughed. My thoughts ran like this.

"If I smoke this, one day I'll be able to say, I smoked a joint behind the Iron Curtain in the '70s.' I may even write it in a story one day. I took the joint and a few tokes. It was time for some music.

Out came the old red and cream Dansette record player with the clunky cream arm and needle. Out came a collection of 45s. I use the word 'collection' very loosely. They had a handful. After a considerable debate they chose one.

Unbelievable. No. That stupid song was here. 'Everybody was Kung Fu fighting.......'

My mind apologized "Sorry. I thought I'd erased that!"

We sang along anyway. That damn song! The stuff of nightmares.

Several games of sort-of-pool and a lot of laughs later, it was time to leave.

My head was swimming with all the new information and images of people in Torquay hotels speaking in fluent Russian. My God did we all laugh a lot.

It was somehow decided that the guys would get us a taxi but we would have to make our way to a specific place. So, a little the worse for wear and decidedly stoned we walked out into a Moscow under darkened but gloriously coloured skies.

We walked. There were an awful lot of plaques everywhere. I asked about one on a wall, "Lenin slept here." I asked about another plaque, "Lenin gave a speech here."

I could see a pattern developing here. I could do this. I took over.

A little too full of good cheer I touched a bush and said, "Lenin had a pee here."

It was when I sang out that "Lenin smoked a joint here" that the boys hushed me and were quite happy, I think, to shove us into a taxi and give the cabby instructions. They paid him beforehand with some money we had and hugged us in a farewell.

"Remember us!" The lads yelled as the door closed.

Then, as if to hammer home the point about the Russian-English mutual sense of humour thing, they sang out "Everybody was Kung Fu fighting, those boys were fast as lightnin'."

Small Expectations

The following few days were spent getting to know the others in this group. Truthfully it was more a question of getting to know how to avoid them. Alexi had been right when he said "Eastern Europeans? Never speak. Americans? Never stop."

The three wise men from the East never separated. They walked with their heads bowed and wore black from head to toe. The concept of youth seemed to have eluded them. As for the Americans among us? They were (all but one) an embarrassment. The concept they struggled with was 'guest'. We settled for two friends among this motley crew: A tall young Swiss-American called Guy and a Danish girl called Helena. We should've guessed from the start they were cool. They were both travelling alone. We didn't know it then of course but in these two allies life had again handed us exactly what we needed. Guy was soon to give us a second (and very welcome) encounter with Russian people at home. Helena was to provide us with a gorgeous place to stay when we arrived in Copenhagen after this present adventure. It's funny how things have a habit of working out just fine, if you get out of your own way.

We were a little underwhelmed by prospect of a planned outing to a department store. A department store? Be still my heart! Still, if the Russians were proud of it enough to want us to visit, we were up for that.

If anyone was expecting Harrods they were in for a shock. Our trip to the Workers' Café prepared us to expect the unexpected and our two Russian student friends warned us about queues. It was a taste of what was to come. That elusive and almost mythical notion of full employment in the West was alive and well here. It meant it took five people to sell you a bowl of stew. We arrived at the prized Gumm store just off Red Square.

There were cordons with accompanying queues and two workers manning each. This was the same at every step of the way on this shopping experience. It started at the front door just to get access. Inside we were confronted by eight queues and cordons depending on what department we wanted. Then, you've guessed it, once inside a department, three or four more cordons and queues narrowed down which section of which department you could access. Then, presumably because we'd by now learned how to queue without killing anyone, we waited to actually touch the products. That left a queue to hand over a purchase, the wrapping queue, the lines for the bill printer, the money taker, the receipt giver and then the supervisor who checked all the others' jobs before handing you your item. Nearly two hours to buy a scarf? Yes indeed. Still think full employment's a good idea?

After those two long, laborious hours of this ordeal, the tour guide asked,

"Do you want to buy something else?" I so wanted to say that I had some stuff I wanted to do before I died. I've never queued so much, so often and been handled by so many people so slowly in all my life. The café had only been a glimpse or a type of warning sign. I obviously hadn't fully taken the hint. Still, tonight was the big night! Circus here we come! Not!

Back at our hotel Pat and I were informed there'd been a mix up. Instead of the Russian State Circus we had tickets for the Bolshoi Ballet instead. Now, I know that culture is culture but I wasn't raised in a home where opera or ballet were much admired. In fact they were the subject of ridicule. So, as far as I knew, I hated ballet. In my mind it was something that posh people did. Of course I'd never actually attended any ballet performance. What's prejudice for? I accepted the surprise invitation graciously. After all, it was a free ticket. It couldn't do any harm.

With my only pair of jeans washed and dried and a clean t-shirt, I got on the bus. It was only when we pulled up at the gates of the Kremlin that I pinched myself. No-one had mentioned the theatre was inside the Kremlin. Now I was excited. Who gets the chance to go inside the Kremlin for goodness sake? Is it just me being a bit slow at times or is there anyone else out there who experiences times when two facts you know don't actually fit together until a cosmic hammer hits you over the head and makes the connection of the two glaringly obvious? It's called putting 2 and 2 together. Here for instance. I knew that kremlin meant castle but I never suspected there was one behind that awful brutalism of its exterior. Totally unprepared, the penny was about to drop.

In and in we drove. This was thrilling. When we got off the bus we were deep in the bowels of the huge Kremlin. Long winding corridors were leading us to somewhere.

Gobsmacking Pop-up book moment!

I literally gasped. My mind was blown. We stepped from the gloom of a hallway into the most fabulous and glorious Baroque theatre imaginable. We were back in 1776.

That's when this was built for Catherine ll. Yes, that Catherine, Catherine the Great. Trust me on this. It was exquisite. I'd been in a few late-Victorian playhouses in England and the Old Vic in Bristol which is quaint but this?

This was ravishing. Not only was it plush, (with its gold and ruby décor) but it was palatial.

This wasn't built to house the plebs. This was grand but kept an intimacy. Perhaps its narrowness and sheer height made it intimate. This place was built to host and entertain a few close friends of a queen - old Cath to be precise. The royal box for her majesty wasn't so much as a box but a small sitting-room and it wasn't near the front. No. The royal sitting- room was directly opposite the stage. On all sides, radiating out from that room, were layer upon layer of boxes up to the highest of heights. The more humble amongst the aristocracy were seated in the auditorium. Up and up and up it went to the domed ceiling. The chandeliers were something else. It was impossible not to feel enveloped, cosseted and inspired by the space and the spectacle.

This whole ticket-swap thing had been such a rush we had no idea what the Bolshoi were about to perform. My programme told me 'Anna Karenina.' Was that even possible? Was it possible for ballet dancers to perform such a novel? All I had ever imagined were people prancing around in white tutus. The lights dimmed. The atmosphere was electric. Even a barbarian like me could tell that we were about to experience something very, very special; something extraordinary.

That night is an ecstatic blur. It has settled in my memory as a feeling. Yes, there are splendid images attached but this was a spell (a word I use wisely) that changed my life. The whole performance was the most magical of pop-up books.

I'd read the novel but seeing Anna and her lover Vronski dance at a ball in this setting?

The stage- sets mirrored the very setting we were in! We were in this. I was lost in it.

I recall standing in the intermission, scanning the other patrons. It was strange and oddly ironic to be standing among Moscow's glitterati wearing my jeans and a t-shirt. For an instant I felt I was betraying our new student friends who could never afford a night like this. Ironic because, in a way, that's what Sovietism's about, isn't it? The plebs having access to what the knobs have always had? I didn't feel at all awkward or out of place. It made me smile.

When I used the word glitterati I may have given the wrong impression. No-one seemed to be extravagant. This wasn't 'dolled up' as I understood it. As I checked them out, the word 'Sweet' came to my mind. They put me in mind of the oysters in Lewis Carroll's 'The Walrus and the Carpenter.' Here those oysters were, 'All eager for the treat. Their coats were brushed, their faces washed, their shoes were clean and neat —" I liked these people.

I'll try to convey the scenery on stage; the drama and the splendour of it. I'll have a shot at describing the scene in the book where the scandal of Anna and Vronski (her lover) comes to the attention of the gossiping masses one night at the opera. In between sets some unseen stagehands had somehow altered the backdrop into tiers exactly mirroring the ones we now sat in. When the curtain went up we were there, in that audience. We were the ones doing the prying. (Correction) I was prying.

Ballet dancers, male and female, lined these on-stage tiers. The lights focussed on them. They were holding a long cloth of gold with tassels along its length. Their grip on the cloth made it dip and rise to mirror the decoration of the boxes and balconies out front. Suddenly we were fully included. We were all in the same place. The stage and front of house merged. I felt complicit.

Throughout the performance, the costumes were gorgeous: From the grandiose colours of the military to the dazzling ball gowns or daily dress of the women. And the end? The final climax?

The houselights went out. We were plunged into sudden darkness. From our abrupt, enforced silence we heard the distant sound of a train. It grew louder as it came nearer. A light appeared on a back-cloth, centre stage. It gradually intensified. It got bigger. The chug, chugging sounds of an old steam locomotive slowly became a deafening roar as that one beam of light grew ever brighter. We could smell the unmistakeable smells of an old steam train. A loud, heavy hiss then steam shrouded the stage. In that circle of light we spotted the silhouette of a solitary figure. A blinding blast of light made us flinch. Deathly silence. Blackness. We had all, to a man, gone under that oncoming train.

"What was THAT?" My heart and soul gasped.

"That," my higher-self answered me "was a full, all-singing, all-dancing, display in glorious colour and surround-sound of what lies beyond your expectations."

Wow. Just wow.

Going Underground

Package tours don't hack it for me. Thankfully back then they were unheard of. There weren't any cheap 'no frills' airlines. The peoples' hero Freddie Laker had tried his best since the mid-sixties to make air travel more accessible to us plebs but had met with nothing but strong resistance from the Powers that Be.

After many months of total freedom this tour felt restrictive. It was true we hadn't needed to use our three-knock code since the youth club but I still felt as if I was being watched. I felt we were being steered away from contact with any ordinary Russians. The overall feeling this tour was giving me was like my feet (used to flip-flops and sandals) were suddenly squashed into proper shoes; shoes worn under duress; shoes I wanted to kick off at the first opportunity. So, that's what we did next.

The Eastern Europeans still didn't mingle. I sometimes wondered if this fortnight was their holiday of a lifetime; something they'd saved up for for years? I hoped not. The naive Americans were best left alone. Their loud comments of derision after every single thing we experienced made us cringe. That just left we gang of four. Guy, Helena, Pat and I. We had allies now.

Museums and palaces are great up to a point. I was all palace'd out. 'Seen one, seen 'em all' kind of thing. After a while the gold dripping from everywhere, the luxury and the brazen flaunting of wealth turns beauty into ugly. My eyeballs feel under assault. I made the most of these cultural visits by paying attention to the jaw-dropping skills of the craftsmen and artisans who had made it all possible. It's okay to visit a single palace on a fortnight's holiday but after several? They all become a blur in my memory bank. The sheer 'look how rich we are' of it all sends my mind into muse mode. I couldn't help but think that grand cathedrals, churches and palaces are nothing more than repositories of the wealth squirreled away by the Toffs. They're display cases for their plunder; plunder they got from the people they governed and sought to control.

Take palaces for example. They started to scream at me that the people who once rattled around in them were once those kids who had posh dolls-houses. The furniture is so twee and uncomfortable looking. My dolls-house? I made furniture out of matchboxes, glue, fabric and scissors. Which kids got to have the livelier imagination, I wonder?

No, I wasn't a culture vulture. I was more like Adela in 'A Passage to India.' Even though I didn't like myself for it, the inner me was nagging 'I want to see the real Russia.' Daft when you think about it. There never is such a thing. Nevertheless I wished for it. At least the organised mini-bus got us out and about. It served its purpose. After a long walk through one more rambling pile we contrived to get lost. The gardens were extraordinary. Guy offered Pat and me the opportunity to silence my Adela voice. He was going to visit an ex-professor of his who'd mentored him in Switzerland. Did we want to come along tomorrow night? Um, let me think. Yes! Wish granted. Now things were looking up.

The next day we were taken to one of those shops that Alexi had mentioned. This was strictly for us foreigners. I felt disgusted and embarrassed. Sure I went in, but the Russian eyes peering in at us through the large windows got to me big time. This was wrong. In here there were no queues. There were luxury goods and expensive tourist souvenirs, wonderful craftwork, duty-free smokes, liquor and artworks. I hoped this was an economics thing, a way to get foreign currency circulating. Roubles were not accepted in here. Even still, to display such treats to your own people and make them unavailable, seemed cruel. I didn't buy a thing. My mind was on our up-coming adventure.

Back at the hotel Guy called us aside. It was all arranged. Dinner was at 7.30 and the apartment wasn't that far away. He had directions. It was about a ten minute journey on the subway then a short walk. "We'll leave at about 6.30." He said it casually but the numbers didn't add up. "Why so early?" I asked.

"Ah!" he said, smiling. "I'm told we're to get on and off at as many underground stations as we can." I looked at Pat and tapped my ciggie packet on the coffee table three times. Pat nodded and tapped her knee three times. Okay, so we were both sniffing the return of paranoia then.

"Why?" I could feel that James Bond spy feeling looming.

"The Prof. tells me the Moscow underground is well worth seeing."

Okay. Okay. Here we were, back with that Marlena Dietrich kinduh spy-conversation-password thing going on again. I started to smile.

"What's funny?" The poor guy asked.

I wanted to say, "My hovercraft is full of eels" because whatever I said was gonna sound like the next part of a password sequence. Hell! I had to say something.

"I can't imagine any underground station being that worth seeing. That's all."

"Well. Apparently they all are. If we leave an extra hour we can find out."

We all agreed to the arrangements and Guy got up to leave,

"What did this professor teach?" I only asked that as a throw-away line.

Walking away, he turned back and said calmly, "Nuclear physics" and was gone.

Pat and I looked at each other and without saying a word we both knocked out a complete drum roll on the table like a couple of kids.

"Uh. Oh!" I said, in an exaggerated sort of way.

"Uh. Oh! Indeed." Pat smiled.

"Are we still going for it?"

"Damn right."

Paranoia does strange things to an otherwise completely rational mind. For the next few hours I watched mine grow. What my mind did was compose two conflicting narratives and then run through them. It ran the sane version first and then the paranoid one; constantly comparing the two. It ran like this,

'O.K. So you've been invited for dinner. What's the big deal? You trust this Guy fellow. He seems calm about the whole thing. You wished for this anyway. You wanted to meet more Russians. O.K. So you're taking an extra hour and gonna hop on and off at as many underground stations as possible to see how amazing they are. Nice of the man to be so thoughtful. Anyway. Lots of people study nuclear physics. It's no big deal."

The paranoid version went more along the lines of "This Guy's dodgy. His eyes are too close together. You're his cover. This professor's up to no good either. What secrets are they passing? Metro-hopping as sight-seeing? My arse! It's to shake a 'tail'. Russian nuclear physicist? Run!"

We got to the entrance to our first subway and went in. The escalator was so steep we were sliding slowly out of a ceiling, down and down into something or somewhere. On that moving trackway I noticed there wasn't a single advertisement. Lower and lower down we went and then it came into view: Absolutely mind-blowing, in- your-face beauty. This wasn't a subway station. This was a work of art. We were standing in an Art Deco masterpiece; light, airy and bathed in a golden-yellow hue. No hoardings, no rubbish or dirt to be seen. Pillar after pillar shape lined either side of the chequered and highly-polished floor. I honestly felt I ought to take my shoes off. The pillar mouldings were in pairs and were alternating small and large. The larger pairs seemed to be leading up and down to unseen and intersecting platforms; the smaller were decorated with stained-glass panels of astounding colours and lights. As we stood waiting for a train, I stared through a pillared gap opposite me. On the far side of the track the design on the wall matched the missing part made by our archway. When I stood to square myself and stand facing the gap, head-on it disappeared. It was a trompe l'oeil par excellence. Extraordinary. From the archway we never saw the whole train. The carriage doors were level with the gap and we stepped in.

Maybe the voice of paranoia would stop blabbering now. This physicist bloke meant what he said. I wouldn't have missed this for the world. There was even more to come. Station after station proved astonishing. Every station had incredible artwork on its walls and some had monumental bronze sculpture. Many had depictions of the glorious revolution done in that massive, forceful style that is uniquely Russian. Some stations had remarkable wrought iron-work on their walkways and more than one had golden chandeliers. Yes, chandeliers in a tube station! And all the while I realised how wonderful and refreshing it was to travel this way without once being bombarded by advertising.

After that trip through living art, we really didn't care how the rest of the evening went. Whatever happened would be a bonus. We came above ground and walked straight onto the film set of 'The Bourne Identity', you know, the block after high-rise boring block of workers' apartments on stark, windswept streets. Stark wasn't a powerful enough word for this. I remember thinking that if I were these people in these blocks I'd pack up and go and live in a subway. But this was Russia.

I was wrong about feeling paranoia earlier. I now knew I'd only played around its edges. As long as that voice of reason can present an argument, paranoia hasn't got a grip. Here, now though, paranoia wasn't a mental discussion. It went whoosh as it washed over me. Paranoia is a feeling.

Every solitary figure was lurking and staring. Every one of the people we encountered averted their eyes a little too fast for my liking. My reason abandoned ship. The short walk was a million miles. All eyes were on me. Eyes that I couldn't see were on me. What was that guy doing up on that roof?

At long, long last we arrived at an older style high-rise. Guy was checking over his shoulder (I'd swear to it) as he mumbled something at a box on the wall and the door clicked open. We were in.

There was a spy-hole in the front door. Why oh why did it have to be called that?

Hugs and Russian greetings filled the cosy apartment. I never knew Guy could speak Russian.

My reason came back momentarily with 'Will you quit?' and magically I obeyed. I began to relax and get my head together.

Three people greeted us; a middle-aged man, his wife and an old man. The apartment was dinky. Perhaps it appeared smaller because of the lovely handmade covers and cushions draped all around. The colours and patterns were busy.

The apartment wasn't the square that the outside block led me to expect. As we entered, light was coming in from a window to our left. This window was in an annexe of sorts; an annexe large enough to fit their dining table, already spread with gorgeous smelling food and set for six. They'd gone to a lot of trouble to welcome us. Guy saved his biggest hugs for the middle-aged man who was obviously his ex-lecturer. There was genuine affection between them. Meanwhile the woman and old man ushered Pat and I into the miniscule dining area and started pouring drinks. I noticed the green, chenille tablecloth that reached to the floor. It was exactly the same as my granny's. Suddenly my granny was in my thoughts. I was safe.

Two things happened the instant I recalled my gran. The first was that I suddenly understood where my aptitude for languages came from. The second was that the old man had a light in his eyes that wasn't there before. The languages thing came from memories of a sturdy, wooden-cased, old wireless in my grandparents' room. I would twiddle the knobs and listen to odd, fascinating 'Weee---err---wee---ow' sounds until I tuned to some far away and remote language. I wondered if I'd found Russian at some stage to make me think of that now. The light in this old man's eyes showed a connection we had, he and I, to that bygone age of radio. Here was a man with so many experiences, so many stories untold. His eyes said 'I wish I was your age again.' I sent a message back. 'I want to know where you've been and what you've witnessed.' It all happened in a flash but it was real.

Food kept coming and coming. It was a veritable banquet. For those of you who don't already know, I can tell you that most sane people of this world (exclude the Brits and the Irish) indulge in alcohol as more of a food supplement. None of them would dream of drinking heavily without food to hand. Here, in this odd place, I was about to learn how the Russians do it. We each had a shot glass and a tumbler. The shot glass was constantly topped up with vodka that had to be downed in one. That had to be followed immediately by gulping down the tumbler of fruit juice. Then came more food. The process was repeated over and over.

The result was my gentle and gradual descent into total and unashamed drunkenness. To cut a long story short, Grandad and I ended up under the table. Like kids in a makeshift tent we chatted away with no problem at all. Who needs language classes? This was the culmination of my personal research into how liquor and foreign language abilities are inextricably linked. This was the absolute proof. Like a finely- tuned old wireless our minds 'wee-errrred and weeeee-owed' until we tuned in to each other and understood every word we said. My god we laughed.

There was suddenly some interference on our private frequency though. After our first hour and at thirty-minute intervals ever since, their old landline rang. When it rang the room fell silent. 'No-one there.'

Now, at the table over our heads, we could hear the hubbub of the others chatting more seriously. Their tone had changed. After three hours of merriment the strange phone calls had become more ominous and of genuine concern.

"Time to go" the strange Physicist barked. This sounded serious. When the old grandad and I extricated ourselves from under the chenille cloth, we could feel the mood of the evening had deteriorated. The scientist and his wife looked worried. Me? I was out of it.

It was decided that we needed a taxi. A taxi was called. A taxi arrived.

I fell asleep that night asking, "What just happened exactly?" But then it wasn't the first time and wouldn't be the last.

Back to the Future

This was odd. According to our trusty old map we were retracing our steps on a train heading back towards Helsinki. It was okay. It was even funny. We were young with all the time in the world. What did it matter? It was about 8 p.m. when we'd boarded this train to St. Petersburg. You'll never guess what the train was like? Yep. You're getting the hang of this now. It was wooden. If Henry VIII had done his best to strip England of its forests to build a fleet, he was a novice compared to these Russians. I was seriously worried about their forests if they kept this up.

Not only were we going backwards but we were going the longest way about it. There were trains that could do this journey in a couple of hours but our overnight excursion was to be a 12- hour stint.

We had no Russian Biggles to play charades with this time. We were all paired up and bandied together in a group. Our carriage had two berths separated by an awkward little table. Looking back perhaps the Cosmos was getting us in training for some exceedingly long and cramped train journeys to come. For now, we remained ignorant.

If we had been sensible (heaven forbid) we would have at least tried to get some sleep. We weren't. We didn't. We broke open our unused Swedish playing cards and the four of us played a lot of cards. Most of the night was spent chatting about the differences between England, Denmark and America. Contrary to popular (and very probably future historic) accounts, Denmark came out as the most advanced and forward-thinking of them all.

Helena took photos of us, we took photos of her and someone took photos of us all. Since our spy adventure Guy, Pat and I had a curious bond, but that Moscow escapade was never discussed. We played at cards and at being grown-ups, I guess for far too long, into that rattling old night.

Some twelve hours or-so later we got to St. Petersburg. Did I mention that I was already palace'd and museum'd out? Thought I did. Well that, my friends, is not a good state of mind to be in when arriving in St. Petersburg. This palatial city is full of just that. It must be cool to get there as your first introduction to Russia and go 'Ooh! Ah!' and 'Gosh!' on cue at relevant attractions but me? Nah.

I was temporarily excited by the very name of The Winter Palace. I was half- expecting a palace of ice with Omar Sharif and Julie Christy driving past in a magnificent sleigh while they looked dreamily and forlorn into each other's wide eyes. Surprise! Surprise! That didn't happen. That would have put us in Hollywood. This was Russia.

I did get intrigued by a gargantuan column in the square outside said palace. I kid you not. The column stands 48 m. (145 feet) high and weighs 600 tons. (There was a city guide next to me) That's big, huh? Yes. Although I was tired of being dwarfed by massive stuff, I do remember that piece of engineering as being something extraordinary. It was a monument to Alexander 1st who defeated Napoleon. All the more extraordinary was the fact that it's not fixed down at all. It just remains upright by virtue of its own weight. But wait for this, the most remarkable thing is that it only took 2 hours to erect. That was in a time long before they had any gadgets and machines to do it. 'Hang on a minute lads!' I thought. 'I think you're not talking to each other on some very important issues here. I mean. Why not look up the paperwork on this and maybe swap notes? You can solve the riddle of Stonehenge and oh-so much more.'

I wasn't only sick of being dwarfed by big architecture I was getting irritated by it. I realised how lucky I was to be born in a country where everything is comparatively tiny and twee. What was the life-long effect on morale and on the mind of living in a place where civic buildings shrank you into a feeling of insignificance? Did that apply to America? North and South? I wanted none of it.

Strangely St. Petersburg has been stored in my memory with the colours of pale blue and gold trim. I don't know why. Perhaps most of the massive buildings were painted like that. I can't recall. Like I say, for palace read 'blur'.

Somewhere there are photographic flashes of a few notable moments. They may be haphazard but they're there. I am standing inside St. Isaac's Cathedral and distracted by the presence of a few wandering Orthodox priests. My intellect tells me they speak English but I'm not sure. Then I overhear one of them conversing with a man in a suit. When they finish I approach the priest and introduce myself. We shake hands and I say "It is good to see freedom for religion here. I did not know." He was pleasant enough, smiled and was about to reply when the man in the suit stepped in between us and the Priest disappeared. What did that mean? I'll leave you to draw your own conclusions.

Very soon afterwards I became aware of a few people standing under the extremely high dome and craning their necks to stare up at it. I walked over. I was soon craning my neck too. My eyes were following the line upwards of a pendulum about 300 feet long. It was fixed at the centre point of the dome and the plumb bob weight almost reached the floor. I looked at that floor again. We were standing at the edge of an enormous type of clock face picked out in the integral tiles of the old floor. But this was a clock-face the likes of which I had never seen before. It was massive too. So very gracefully the pendulum swung; so slowly too. It was rhythmic and mesmerising. I looked around and spotted wooden upright boxes full of what I hoped were leaflets. Perhaps those pamphlets would give me a clue about all this. I was right.

This type of clock is called 'Foucault's Pendulum' and, to cut a long story short, it was designed by Leon Foucault to dispel any lingering doubts about the rotation of the earth. Apparently "it started a cultural shift in our fundamental understanding of how our universe works." I read that this very pendulum was the biggest and highest example in the world. Now why didn't that surprise me? I loved it. I felt surprisingly privileged. I could have watched it for hours. To stand directly in line with this thing and to see it coming directly at me was mind-changing for some inexplicable reason.

To write this memory I looked up the details of this clock. I was saddened to read that it's no longer there. It was put into storage in the vaults at some time in the 1980s. That's the thing I suppose. I wish I could take you back to the times I'm describing; times when you could be one of only three or four people standing mesmerised and watching such a magnificent machine, be practically alone in Pompeii, walk up to and touch the stones of Stonehenge or sleep out on a Greek beach for weeks. There are so many of my experiences that are no longer possible due to the sheer numbers of tourists and the threats they present. I hope I'm giving you a glimpse at least of what once was.

Our little party joined me. Heaven only knows what they'd been up to. They had a moment to stare at the pendulum and then we were off. Call me a Barbarian but ten minutes into the world-famous Hermitage and I left. I was still coming to grips with having seen evidence that we're all hurtling through space. I guess I was literally and figuratively reeling.

Our basic little hotel was cheap and cheerful. The staff were more relaxed than the Muscovites. Perhaps that's the nature of capital cities. They brought us sweet-smelling lemon tea at every opportunity and were more than kind. Up early enough we soon embarked on a boat trip on the river Neva. It was a joy to be travelling by boat again. All in all St. Petersburg is pretty. Perhaps we only saw those canals and parts of the river that were clean and those parts of the city suitably spruced up. I couldn't forget the cleanliness of Moscow underground stations though so I doubted my own doubts.

It is a strange city. I can't be the only person on the planet who picks up the feel of a place. My sixth sense picks up on ancient spaces and I felt nothing here. A bit of brain racking and I remembered my history. It would feel new, wouldn't it? As marvellous as this façade was, it was all a reconstruction. Who could forget the horrors of the interminable siege of Leningrad in World War ll? This was the place. It was destroyed. That one-upmanship of old Adolf presaged his ultimate demise right here. I understood. This city is comparatively new. I had to laugh at the brochure. There was an exact date for the original city, May 27th 1703. The Americans among us couldn't understand why I was saying this place was quite new.

On this, our last evening in Russia, we were off to some sort of show or cabaret. The inside of the hotel where it took place was a flashback to Moscow. We were again in a room that was far too big for the tables set for us all. Tonight it seemed we were among other Russians on the many other tables. This would be fun.

The food was, to be polite, basic. It did its job. We drank vodka with the fruit juice to hand. The music and dance were absolutely amazing. Everything was going so well when....the Americans in our group decided to get patriotic. This was so embarrassing that I wanted the floor to open up and swallow me there and then. Over this loud, powerful and energetic Russian music our Americans started singing 'Home, home on the range' at a volume to compete with the entertainers. As soon as this started Pat and I moved. We scooted over to a table of Russians near the stage area and were welcomed with open arms.

Perhaps we had made ourselves conspicuous to the entertainers or perhaps we just deserved what happened next. It was a treat. The dancers dragged us up onto the floor and there we were dancing with Cossacks. That brought the house down! It even put a stop to the dreadful American singing. A good time was had by all.

The following afternoon we found ourselves at St. Petersburg airport waiting for a flight to Denmark. By now Helena trusted us enough to spring an invitation on us. It was settled. We were about to stay at a commune in the suburbs of Copenhagen. Next hurdle safely negotiated. If what we had gleaned was accurate Denmark sounded as if it was about ten or fifteen years ahead of Britain in lifestyle and attitudes. Soviet Russia was in the 1940s, Britain in the '70s so Denmark must be in the 1990s. We were going back to the future. Back to the future? Piece of cake!

Hold Ups

When you are living a life scheduled by a regular job there's a need to get as much done as you can in your free time. Even the slightest hiccough in all those best made plans is stress personified. When you have no such cares a hiccough can be entertaining. It proves there's no point in making the perfect plan in the first place. It seems funny that you thought you could. Why on earth should life comply with your hair-brained plans?

So...we were sitting in St. Petersburg airport. For such a huge city the airport was tiny. Rightly or wrongly I assumed that not many Russians could afford air travel. I knew from Alexei that not many had passports. Whatever the reason, the holding area was the size of a small living-room. But it wasn't as comfortable.

Shamefully it took us a while to realise that we'd lost the Eastern European contingent of our group. Just goes to show how little we interacted. Anyhow, they were magically vanished, never to be seen again. From the large window we could see our meagre luggage being loaded onto the plane. Unbelievable as it sounds now, it was a small plane with propellers. When did those eventually become a thing of the past? No matter. We were so close to the plane we could hear the airport workers talking and shouting to one another.

When it was clear there was some kind of delay we were given cups of lemon tea and a biscuit by way of apology. And when did that become a thing of the past? We were understandably distracted by the trays of free food on a far table so got a fright when there was an almighty bang from the direction of the plane.

To a man we ducked. Travelling left us pretty much devoid of international news but we'd all heard about the Palestinian Airline hijacking earlier in June. That news was difficult to avoid. No sooner had we ducked than there were three more bangs. Nerves were frazzled.

The Russian staff flew into a flurry. Eventually we heard them cackle, chortle and belly laugh. One of the young Americans was singled out and taken to a different room. We guessed we could sit and drink some more tea. We had no idea what was going on until we were led to the actual boarding gate. There, red-faced and red-suitcased was the young idiot. His suitcase was frothing and dripping. He had taken into his head to purchase and pack four bottles of extremely strong, red Russian beer. In all the bouncing around and tossing here and there of the offending bag, the bottles exploded. Who would have thought they could go off with such a loud bang though? We boarded and waited for him to clean his bag as best he could. He boarded, settled down and we were off. We literally left Russia with a bang.

Whether or not the last clock I saw in that airport was stopped I don't know but it distinctly said "12.00." The flight was just over two hours and passed without incident. It was a little odd to be handed out caviar, spiced biscuits and vodka as our in-flight snack. Caviar may be an expensive treat in the rest of Europe but here they were dishing it out as if it was going out of fashion. I could get used to free shots of vodka though. When did that become a thing of the past? Several free shots and a cigarette later and we were ready for this commune Helena talked about so much.

The reason I mentioned that clock? As soon as we got into Copenhagen air terminal there was another clock. It blew my mind. It said 12 o'clock. What? The flight was two hours and Copenhagen was an hour behind St. Petersburg. Maybe it was the vodka but I couldn't get my head around the maths. I gave up. I just accepted that in many ways we had never been to Russia. It was like the universe was saying "Okay. You've been on hold for a while. You can come back in now. Welcome back to 'Time'." It made me laugh. (Did I tell you the vodka was strong?)

Individual Tastes

There was no getting away from it. The minute we got off the plane my mind breathed a deep sigh of unexpected relief. We all felt more comfortable in our own skins. Paranoia was nowhere to be seen or felt. We waited for our bags to come through and chatted about the red beer incident. It was one for the old mental scrapbook for sure.

The normal sized luggage began to filter through on those incredibly annoying belts. Pat, Helena and I could see that for some reason our backpacks had been set aside and were going to come through last. No sweat. We stood back to allow the other passengers enough room to do that crazy song and dance routine they all know. "Me. Me. Me. Mine. Mine. My suitcase is the most important thing in the world."

We got wind of something being amiss. First came the sounds of shock, followed by noises of people being extremely disgruntled. We had no idea what was going on. We wandered over to have a look. Every one of their suitcases was unlocked and tied back together with rough string. All kinds of things had gone missing; cameras, souvenirs, jeans and t-shirts. In fact anything that was difficult or impossible to get hold of in Soviet Russia was gone. There was nothing to be done about it. We three looked at each other and realised we'd had nothing worth nicking. We didn't even have locks on our luggage. That signalled it wasn't worth breaking into.

Our backpacks made an appearance. Here they were perfectly intact and untouched. What could we say? We left all the other folk to it, made our escape and headed for a taxi-rank.

The Danes, like every other Scandinavian, speak perfect, fluent English. There wouldn't have been a problem. Helena gabbled away to the driver in her mother tongue. It was great. It was great to be in Denmark and instantly thrown into a lively conversation in the native language. In many ways it was easy to get the drift. After months in Norway and Sweden and a background in German the sound, rhythm and actual words were familiar.

First impressions of this pretty city were calming. Its quirky streets and buildings looked tiny and quaint after weeks of monumental architecture. The Scandinavians are and always have been way ahead of the rest of the world in attitudes, laws, social care, education and 'green' issues. As we wound our way out into leafy suburbs we had no idea how advanced some of those attitudes were. There was something Helena had forgotten to mention. It wasn't because she was going to break it to us gently or that she had forgotten. It was that she took it so much as a matter of course and so commonplace. The rural old mansion of a place that we pulled up at (with its long secluded driveway and gorgeous plants, flowers and ancient trees) was a Lesbian commune.

In the 1970s Britain we had left behind this was unheard of. If such a thing existed (and perhaps I had led a sheltered life) we had never heard of it.

It would take a lot to shock either Pat or me by now but we were shocked. It wasn't the Lesbian bit, it was the 'this is perfectly normal' bit that came as shocking and a strange hint perhaps of things to come. I personally don't give a damn about anyone's sexuality. It's none of my business. We were shown to our rooms; two small guest rooms that were stunning in their simplicity. In fact, the house was a treasure. It rambled around wooden staircases and quirky corridors that led to rooms of all different odd shapes and sizes. Every room was flooded with summer light through large sash-windows framed by antique wooden shutters inside and out. This was a house that the Romantic artists and writers of Europe could have lived and thrived in and would have relished.

This house was old. It was solid. The main focal point was the enormous country kitchen. Back then I had never been in a kitchen with a huge Aga. Nothing else would have done it though. If the Aga was enormous then the hand-carved, plain- wooden table and chairs was absolutely massive. Helen pointed out that all eighteen of them could sit around and eat together here. The elegant French doors at the far end led the eye and soul out into those luscious rambling gardens. How lucky were we?

As a welcome home for Helena and to greet us two, a feast was to be held outside later that first evening. After a much-welcome shower we unwound and drank coffee; mooched around outside and offered to help with all the food preparations. When our offer was declined, we sat out on a big garden swing and wallowed in the shade of the gorgeous trees with the soundtrack of glorious birdsong. Russia and its suppression of individualism was a million, trillion miles away; a dream perhaps?

More and more of the household came home from work. Gradually they came over to chat and get acquainted. Like I say, their English was perfect.

To walk out into that garden in the early evening and to see the feast laid out for us all was beyond memorable. After weeks of black bread, boiled eggs and pasta for nearly every meal just the sight of it made me feel privileged. When they said feast, they weren't joking. The garden tables weren't big enough for the whole gang. Two had been dragged close together, within hearing and chatting range.

As the warm summer evening wore on, the wine kept flowing. Guitars and flutes appeared and singing started. We ate our fill of fresh bread, local cheeses, different salad concoctions, fresh meats, fresh vegetables, fruit salads with cream, chocolate puddings and cakes and pastries. The list was endless. Of course we had to share our stories straight from Russia. Story-telling is always the best part of dinner parties and Viking feasts!

When I finally got to bed that night I clearly remember thinking "How can one little planet provide so many, totally different lifestyles and cultures? Being human never gets boring. That's the truth."

And then....just as I was drifting off, the kid inside me popped up with

"Hey! We're in the land of Hans Christian Anderson now. This journey is something else."

Friendly old girl of a town

That inner kid who bounced me to sleep the night before, bounced me awake on our first full day in Copenhagen.

The waking feeling was 'Dust off any mental cobwebs, throw a virtual hat in the air and breathe in this seaside feeling of freedom. Taste the salt in the clean air.' Scarcely anyone I know has been to Copenhagen. I have no idea why. It's a joy.

My impressions of this enchanting city were bound to be coloured by the ten previous days in Russia. I felt free and so very alive the minute we arrived. My mind kept saying "Thank you, thank you."

The inner child stayed with me as we walked and bussed our way around the city. I expected to see a huge banner at any moment saying "Welcome to the Real Toy Town." No wonder the fertile imagination of Anderson thrived here.

We had come from the land of soviet giants; fierce, all-powerful and menacing. Now? We were in the land of elves and goblins, a world where imagination can flourish. Maybe there was the odd giant or two lurking somewhere but he or she was most definitely benign.

I knew a bit about the great man Anderson. I knew there no point in looking for his house because he never owned one. From humble beginnings he grew to be a wanderer, preferring to travel around, have experiences, meet people and collect stories. The kid inside me so wanted to be a writer. Perhaps I was following in his footsteps? Nah! That was presumptuous.

The girls in the commune left a gift for us with the breakfast placed ready for us. How sweet was that! We had a city travel card each. Denmark being Denmark we could travel anywhere at any time on any bus, metro or local train; hop on and hop off wherever we chose. Sweden had transport pretty much sussed but here was the most efficient system of public transport I'd ever witnessed. Even the Switzerland and Germany of many years before were outclassed. The bus came every three minutes exactly when it was supposed to. The metro was equally as efficient. It made sightseeing a pleasure. And oh boy! was there a lot to see.

The best way I can think to describe Copenhagen is to ask you to cast your mind back to the first time you ever saw and walked around one of those miniature, model villages that still grace some quirky towns in Britain. Like I say, in Russia we were shrunk by all things gobsmackingly huge but here we shrunk of our choosing. We were kindly invited and magically enticed. The colourful old merchants' houses (narrow, tall and centuries old) lined the quays. They were a higgledy-piggledy collection, leaning on each other for support and painted in bright colours. In the harbour tall ships like the stuff of childhood dreams, bobbed gently up and down. Smiling people strolled and chatted along the cobbled streets and stopped to drink strong coffee in glorious sunshine at welcoming bars. Where was Russia now?

I realised the 2nd World War had left this magnificent architecture alone, unlike in my own country where Uncle Adolf obliterated most of it in the major cities. How wonderful European cities must have looked before the Luftwaffe came a-calling.

For hours we walked around aimlessly. We could have taken advantage of tourist leaflets but it wasn't our style. It was always much more fun to bump into something splendid and totally unexpected. The inner child loves surprises.

One such surprise popped up in a very narrow and old main shopping street. We looked casually to our right and there were toy soldiers in their little wooden, striped sentry boxes. This was a royal palace and these were the Danish royal guards. To all intents and purposes they were like the famous guards at Buckingham Palace. They wore the big busby hats but their jackets were blue. The palace was tiny. These were the guys to be placed on Christmas trees for sure.

I couldn't tell you anything about the geography or layout of this magical city. Were we in the east or west of it? It didn't matter. We hopped off a bus when something took our fancy. In 1976 tourism was generally for the wealthy. Somehow we were right there among the visiting posh folk. It was great. I couldn't help but think of those privileged, wealthy few who did the proper Grand Tour back in the 17th and 18th centuries. I'd done the poor man's version way back in the very early '70s but was that what we were doing here too? The thought tickled me. It made me want to jump for joy.

The Danes are remarkable people. Every single one of them we met spoke perfect English. The tour guides, policeman, café workers and bus drivers spoke an English often better than most English people. There was a wonderful friendliness; an openness. There was none of that feeling of "Why don't you speak my language" often aimed at tourists today. The Danes are comfortable in their own shoes. They have a strong sense of owning their country.

I have a strange relationship with major tourist attractions. Like the fool William Kempe that I referred to earlier, I am destined to stumble onto them by accident. It wasn't any different here. We were licking big delicious ice-creams and sitting on a low wall by the sea. The waves were gently lapping over the rocks just below us and sounded wonderful. We were so engrossed in the ice cream that it took longer than it should have done to spot a statue to our right. Yep! We were eating ice cream in the company of the Little Mermaid. No idea why but my first ungrateful thought was "She's too small." My second thought was "You doughnut! Pray tell. How big is a mermaid exactly?"

In less than an hour I'd say, we got more evidence of how advanced the Scandinavians truly are. In the centre of the city there's (wait for it) a whole new town. It's called Christiana. For this we needed tourist guidance. A leaflet explained what on earth Christiana was about.

Freetown Christiana was founded in 1971. It is a vast society within society; is anarchist and makes its own rules and laws defined by a simple list of do's and don'ts. Like any small town it has every necessary facility but so much more.

We ambled in. There were homemade, ecologically-sound houses and workshops for craft and trades people including blacksmiths and glass-blowers, spinners and weavers. Everyone had a bike. There was a live music venue and a vegetarian cafe. There was a huge market and wonderful parks; playgrounds and art galleries. In brief the whole place was alive with alternatives to the mainstream way of doing things. I couldn't get my head around this widespread anarchy being allowed in the middle of a capital city but it was great.

That first day we took it all in. We soaked it all up.

Not only was Copenhagen wondrous after the feeling of Soviet suppression but it made us reflect on the rest of Europe and Britain in particular. The Britain we had left was troubled and grey; the people perpetually at odds with a government they did not trust or have much in common with. Class structure still had a grip (and still does). Here in Denmark there wasn't even an inkling of that. When we got on a bus it was like "Here is Hans the bus driver. He speaks perfect English and is happy." I always assumed when I was little that Toy town was like that. Everyone just did their jobs and was happy. Isn't that still the impression we give to our kids in their scheduled T.V programmes today?

No wonder most kids get disillusioned very early. In Britain they learn all too soon to know their place.

After a long and thought-provoking wander around this storybook city we made our way home. Tomorrow was another day.

"Time for tea." The lovely ladies said chirpily.

"Tea it is then," said the children from far away.

"Tea it is," sang the birds in the lovely gardens around the big old house.

Kindness

After that first day in Copenhagen I sat in the exquisite gardens with time to reflect. There's a quote from my favourite Persian poet Rumi that goes something like, 'Step out and the way appears.' There was no getting away from it, evidence of just that littered our journey so far. The ease with which we got a job in Stockholm; the way an apartment appeared when we stuck out our thumbs to hitch north in Sweden; this commune and a chance meeting with Helena. There was a pattern of some kind of wish-fulfilment going on. I would have to be blind not to notice. It was a long time since we'd left England and we had met with nothing but friendliness and generosity.

These girls were insisting that we stay as long as we wanted. There was no way we were going to abuse their kindness. We had nothing suitable to give them as a thank you. We'd brought with us a whole bunch of silly English souvenirs, pencils and pens with local English names on them; key-rings with London buses on them, that sort of thing. We gave them as thank yous to the people who befriended us on our way. This was trickier. These girls had everything.

I ran into the house and got my small sketch pad and tiny watercolours. I was thinking that maybe a painting of a tiny patch of their garden would do the trick. An hour- or-so later I'd finished: an impression of dappled sunlight over some simple daisies. Tomorrow we could buy a frame.

We had no idea of our next move. Germany was on the border but the thought of travelling through it wasn't exactly thrilling. The south of that country is the prettiest part but I'd visited twice when I was younger. Our rough aim was to get down to Greece and do some island hopping. That seemed a long, long way off.

Over dinner we talked about what else we should see in Copenhagen and outlined our very sketchy plans. That is, no plans at all. Pat and I had a chat about money. We were doing okay. The universe seemed bent on preventing us from spending much. Still some more wouldn't go amiss. We dreaded the thought of working again just yet. There were miles ahead of us and places to see and enjoy.

The following day in the city centre I spotted the main post office. The chances were slim but I took it in to my head to check and see if anyone had sent us any post. One of the great things about the Russian insistence on schedules was that we actually knew when we were going to be in Denmark. In Stockholm I'd contacted home and given a Poste Restante address and dates. Poste Restante was an international service for travellers to access mail. I was not really expecting anything but sure enough Pat and I both had post! That was exciting.

In response to our money worries? Out of the blue the Swedish government had sent us a tax rebate! Every single penny (or Krone) we had paid in tax was refunded. It was a lot. The other envelope for me was handwritten. I squealed with delight. It was from my closest friend ever. It was from Chris. He was a fellow loony from Post. Grad. days and the brother I'd never had. I hadn't seen him for two years. 'Could we meet him in Amsterdam?' That was a no-brainer. We were heading for Amsterdam.

Our day had taken a brilliant turn. We decided to just live it up that day and be proper tourists. Copenhagen had an amusement park the Tivoli Gardens. We felt like kids again going on all the rides and the huge Ferris Wheel. We stuffed candy-floss and played all the fairground games. We laughed and screamed ourselves silly.

We found the houses where Christian Anderson lived and wrote. We went in palaces and museums. We treated ourselves to a slap-up meal in an exclusive waterside restaurant. We found a shop that sold picture frames and bought new t-shirts and essentials.

All in all, a great day was had by all. We didn't have a clue how to get from here to Amsterdam but it didn't matter. I was so excited at meeting Chris. I was trusting Rumi.

To this day I don't understand how we got a boat from Copenhagen straight to Amsterdam. Look on any schedule and there's no such ferry. It had to have been someone in the commune who knew someone who knew someone who.....!

On our last morning we felt sad to leave. With a mountain of fresh sandwiches, treats and drinks we gathered our possessions. Helena rang for a taxi to take us to the docks and we said our farewells. We handed them my painting as we got into the cab.

At the harbour a huge ferry- boat was waiting but no-one seemed to be boarding. We were standing at a gate looking confused when a guy in naval uniform came over and asked, "Amsterdam ladies?" The words were sung in that lovely Danish lilting-English that inspires confidence and engenders warmth. He walked us up a gangplank and led us to the very front of the ship on the upper deck. He showed us a wooden seat that was attached to the huge funnel and said, "Sit. Sit. Have a nice journey but stay here." Then he put one finger up to his lip in a shushing gesture, grinned, winked and left us alone. There we stayed for the whole trip; our own little private area with a glorious view. Not a soul bothered us; not a ticket inspector in sight. Somehow, without spending a cent we had the most amazing views of the Kiel Canal and slept out beneath the stars.

"Thanks for the tip Rumi."

The Agony and the Ecstasy

Amsterdam was a doddle. A taxi from quay side to Chris's hotel was no problem at all. We booked in. I can't adequately describe what happened when Chris came down to breakfast but to show the make of the man he didn't bat an eyelid and went to sit at a different table, nodding across to me casually with "Morning." and that broad, mischievous smile. Then we both simultaneously stood up and went "Waaaaaa!" and hugged each other.

Let the fun begin. Thank heavens I'd explained to Pat that when Chris and I are together all kinds of weird stuff happens. That day proved it. We three set off prepared for anything. We were allegedly only going for a walkabout around Amsterdam but Chris and I knew that things could always, well, take a turn. We took sleeping bags, food, drinks, a change of underwear and oh…the proverbial toothbrush.

The first thing on the agenda was to go to the central railway station and get some tourist info about trips that might be worth a shot and train timetables. There we were, innocently standing chatting when a man starts ushering us onto a train. My co-conspirator and I made eye-contact, raised our eyebrows and silently communicated 'Shall we? Yeah. Why not?' We followed the direction of his pointing finger. We were soon huddled in some kind of tourist group; some travel party all speaking German. I touched one of them on the arm and in my perfect German asked, "This is the outing to…?" I pretended to be fumbling for something in my pocket but I deliberately hesitated so that she could clue us in. She took the bait nicely. "To the islands. Yes."

I looked back at my friends, cocked my head in the direction of the train to say 'Let's go'. Three giggling interlopers boarded the train for the God-knows-what islands. This was fun.

As luck (or Rumi) would have it, we sat slightly aside from the others and whispered like naughty school kids so as not to get caught out. We were just getting into enjoying the scenery and the humour of it all when, after about an hour, the train stopped and everyone got up to clear the train. At first we saw it as our way to escape detection. Surely we could get off here, have a look around and get another train back. No such luck! This was quite literally the end of the line. It didn't go any further, no track, no station, only the water's edge. I still don't know where this was or if it actually exists. We decided we'd discovered one of those mythical places that only appear once in a thousand years.

We stood in line with everyone else. A boat appeared and we all got on. It could not have been that long a trip because it was still early afternoon when we disembarked. Somehow, as they boarded a coach, we hid and ended up alone on a strange island.

We found a beach and made a camp. We played at rock-pooling and acted like kids do on a beach. Suddenly Chris chuckled and ran like a madman into the sea. He was hell- bent on retrieving something. We watched him wriggling and fiddling with something black in the water and what do you know? He waddled out of the sea as a demented penguin. He'd got hold of an inflatable penguin abandoned, left to float and get slightly tattered. That was it. For the next hour or more he was possessed. He became that penguin. We laughed until we cried.

By campfire light he and I caught up with the two years we'd missed. Chris can tell great stories but we were armed with a few of our own. By that fire we were Vikings just arrived in Valhalla; storytellers from legends; pirates swept up on strange shores. As night fell the whole thing turned magical.

We lay there, three strange companions washed ashore by the tide, come to rest under a huge canopy of stars. As we gazed we saw, for the first time, the orbits of satellites, regular and repetitive. When the eye detected one it detected a second; a third and more and more. Personally I fell asleep as one of those satellites.

I can't speak for the others but I have my suspicions.

Have you ever woken up on a beach under hot sun with a mouth feeling like the inside of a bird cage? Ever been woken up by that sun beating down on you and wondered where on earth you are? No? Well, you haven't missed much but in my youth it was pretty much par for the course. It must have been the few beers we drank before spiralling off into unknown galaxies in paroxysm of giggles. Who knows what struck the killer blow?

Sometimes, thinking back. I wonder if any of this stuff ever actually happened to me and then? Then I find a very old photograph of Chris as a plastic penguin and my mind goes, "See! I told you so." But I don't have a photograph of what we saw next that morning. At the time it surprised us so much that we just lay there, staring in amazement (hangovers and all.)

We stirred at pretty much the same time. We all very gradually remembered our insane journey to this island. Chris being Chris, he snapped right into the day with, "Did I have a good time?" through half-opened eyes and with a distinct tinge of 'Oh God I'm thirsty' to the rasp. His humour was always contagious and soon we were playing at being pirates cast ashore upon some desert island for our sins and in fear of encountering the natives who may or may not have bones through their noses and a huge cauldron waiting ominously on a fire. He shushed us into silence and crawled up the nearby slope (S.A.S style) and beckoned us to follow. We played along. As we peered over the ridge we saw it!

There is no way to adequately describe it. We were overlooking a campsite like no other before or since. It was the size of a small village made up of inflatable everything. These were serious campers my friends, serious. No such thing as canvas tents here. Oh no. The camping accommodation was inflatable and was two-storey. Little ladders were placed on the ground to climb upstairs. That was not the best though. Every little rubber house had its own garden earmarked around it and staked out. You guessed it. There were little inflatable walls dividing one family from another; just enough room out front to create a garden.

The gardens had gates! In the gardens? Yep, blow-up easy-chairs and collapsible tables. Most had a television. They even had rubber mats at their front doors. This was unbelievable. It stretched on and on. When we gawped at new houses being pumped up further along we got so engrossed that we were totally spooked by a man who popped his head out of the house very near us. We slid back down the slope and asked each other "Did we just see what we just saw?"

Our conversations deteriorated into wondering if they had blow-up sinks. Inflatable water? Inflatable ideas? Inflated egos?

The mind boggled. Very quietly we washed in the sea; ate stale sandwiches and drank warm water from plastic bottles. Any idea of exploring this place had gone out the rubber window. Who were these people? Why would you go to an island for a holiday and create exactly what you had left back at home? Okay so it was a rubber copy but what the? After a lot of suggestions thrown into the mix two were preferred. 'A middle-aged Midwich Cuckoo's Nest' or 'NASA's secret Cloning Project for Lunar Development'?' We settled for a film set. It's a funny old world.

We did our best to make ourselves look human. We took a very long route around all of this trying to fake it. The task was to act as if we'd been staying among them all in rubber world all along. There was no choice. We sat near the small jetty and hoped that all this to-ing and fro-ing happened daily. Sure enough the tugboat-ferry-thing turned up and a line of perfectly groomed and well-turned out rubber-loving tourists filed on; dragging us in their wake. Hilarious looking back.

We fooled ourselves that we were expertly blending in but to be honest we were wrecked and we looked like it. Still, we did our best to keep up the façade. It was only when Pat chided Chris for talking a bit too loudly in English with the words "Sh. You'll make us conspicuous!" that we took a look at ourselves and cracked up laughing. That was okay.

By then we had negotiated the boat ride and were on the train almost at Amsterdam central. In that grand old station Pat and I purchased two tickets for the Magic Bus to Athens at the princely sum of £8.50. That was gonna be rough but what the heck! More to the point it was gonna be swift.

It was agreed that the next few hours were a write-off. After some food and coffee in the welcoming lobby of the little hotel we took showers and crashed for as long as it took.

Afternoon saw us leave the hotel to see what we could see.

Way back in the mid-seventies Amsterdam was pretty, quaint, clean, orderly and surprisingly empty of foreigners. The E.U. would take some years yet to open its borders and immigration was still something very few people even considered as a topic worthy of discussion. Amsterdam, with its canals, narrow walkways, cascades of flowers; quirky waterside architecture and general devil-may-care attitude was as pretty as a picture. It could pose for the cover of a jig-saw puzzle box without even trying. With brightly painted houseboats draped in flowering plants, its many bicycles, friendly coffee shops and open-hearted culture, it was a town more than welcoming. There's something about places where water is at its heart. They breathe.

We stuffed our faces with large sandwiches of fresh bread and strange tasting cheese outside a pretty waterside café. We were sipping from bowls of frothy coffee with a touch of brandy. Life was good. Pat and Chris wanted to see Ann Frank's house but I'd seen it years before. I wanted to visit the Van Gogh Museum. It was my perfect opportunity. My intuition (normally so calm and quiet) was screaming at me to go alone.

I made my way to the museum. At that time it was only some two or three years old. I was practically alone inside. I was beginning to register a pattern between myself and world-famous places in this world. They were there just for me. I took it personally.

There are people in this world who listen to music or view art concentrating on the wondrous, mind-blowing skill of the maestro concerned. Those individuals listen for the juxtaposition and counterpoints and major-thirds (whatever they are) or stand nose to canvas with a painting to inspect every brushstroke and be awed by the very mastery. I understand there's a place for that. Not me! I'm a heart person. Music and poetry and art move me deeply or they don't. I would have to be blind not to notice the skill of the great masters who captured realism but then there is.....a Vincent.

I began at the beginning. Of course it wasn't. Every artist has tossed hundreds of failed attempts in the bin; torn them up in frustration but as best they could the curators had placed Van Gogh's paintings in chronological order. I stood well back. When I view a painting on a wall I see it as a hole; a window into the artist's world at the very moment it was captured. When that world view comes from love and genuine emotion I trust the artist enough to walk in. My imagination takes me there.

From painting to painting my eyes watched the light; my spirit felt its warmth and hope. For a few initial paintings me and Vincent were fine. Then, as I sidled onward to the next insight, our world view dimmed. It dimmed ever-so slightly at first but over the next few windows darkness began to win. From heights of joy of sun-drenched fields we found ourselves in ever- darkening rooms and landscapes, and under heavier skies. We were confronted by dismal self-portraits. When I thought I couldn't take any more I squinted. I was afraid to go into the next painting. "Hooray!" There was a dim light up ahead. Lighter and lighter the next few shone. We were dipping again. Our emotions were on a crazy, out-of-control rollercoaster; a runaway train.

In an hour and a half I flew, I soared, I faltered, I dipped, I plunged. I caught myself and took to the wing again. At his last desperate painting I felt utterly exhausted. I burst into tears. I was drained. Here he left me. He surrendered. He gave up the ghost.

It wasn't only the artwork. It was the realisation that, through all this, the man had held onto a brush; held on for grim life. Bravery doesn't even begin to describe it. He was mentally ill and he knew it. How could he not? But somehow by way of a huge desire to show and share his passion for and with the world, he managed to keep hold of that brush.

What power of spirit is that, to endure and master, to reach out from beyond his grave and reach me?

I went out into the garden section of the cafeteria and bawled my eyes out.

I got so into the darks and lights of my being. I sat, head in hands, oblivious to everything around me. I yelped. Chris sneaked up behind me, put a hand on my shoulder and leaned forward right into my face. I saw that big smile of his and with that lovely, kind voice he whispered. "Did you have a good time?

He had switched the light back on.

"What next?"

We strolled around Amsterdam to the beautiful, floating flower market. Not far away was the area known as Jordaan where artists and poets lived in the 16th century. Now there was nothing but dilapidated courtyards. Nowadays I believe this whole area has been rebuilt. Later we watched the tourist boats chugging peacefully along the million canals. Why not? We hopped on board.

A distorted megaphone was growling at us. Travelling by water on one of these cruises is probably the best way to get an idea of the age and traditions of this sweet city. After a while though, facts don't matter and everyone has a tendency to switch off and just enjoy the scenery and the ride.

One highlight was the announcement that the 'rear end of the new post office sits on its hundreds of piles.' Hmm. What an unforgettable and unfortunate turn of phrase that was. It made a lot of people on the boat snigger and wince at the implication.

Our days in Amsterdam were fun-loving and carefree. I laughed so much I often had stomach ache and had to walk away. It would soon be time to move on. Pat and I had some serious thinking to do. Before that though, late one night, we just had to pay a visit to the infamous Red Light District.

I believe this district has been transformed now but then? It was unbelievable. Street after narrow street was lined with shop windows turned dramatically into small living-rooms where prostitutes sat plying their wares (for want of a better word.) It was extraordinary. As I walked and unashamedly stared, I fancied myself as a Toulouse Lautrec. I wanted to sit and sketch what I was seeing. I didn't. We kept moving. One prostitute caught my eye. In her mock room she sat on a rocking chair; her legs sprawled wide open but, unbelievably, knitting. The steely look in her eyes contrasted so vividly with the motherly craft of knitting that I was spellbound. To this day I know that, when her eyes met mine, we understood each other. That sounds crazy but it's true.

I don't think I will ever forget that walk around. Eventually we made our way out of the area and found a restaurant to have our farewell meal together. It was crowded enough. I somehow ended up on the edge of a table that was occupied by one serious looking young man. Half- on and half- off the table I was sharing with Chris and Pat I talked to him- with some difficulty. It was noisy all right. It's not my style to ask a stranger 'What do you do?' The answer never tells you anything about the person. This time I did. His answer was exciting. "I write for a magazine."

I can't speak for you but for me? Back then I idolised anyone who got their writing in print. As soon as he said it I built him up to be a Dickens, a Hardy, a Trollope or a George Eliot. 'I am not worthy' was the feeling (if you get my drift.)

"Really?" I asked, wide-eyed and star- struck. "What magazine?"

He slid over and seemed to deliberately half-swallow his answer. "Sorry?" I prodded. He did exactly the same again. It was like the words slid reluctantly out of the side of his down-turned mouth. In my blissful innocence I genuinely believed he was being humble. Unfortunately he'd met a true fan who wasn't about to give up.

"What? Say again?" I kept on at him. I took a large gulp of my wine.

Then he said it. Oh my god....talk about a grimace. My face buckled and contorted. I couldn't laugh at him. That would be rude. Shaking and almost choking to death I turned away sharpish to grab a serviette and hold the wine in. Well. Wouldn't you have laughed? His illustrious career centred around that prestigious magazine 'Steaming Hot Holes.'

More of a Feeling

How on earth can any of us who were having the time of our lives in the '70s convey that overwhelming sense of freedom we enjoyed? Some of us have managed to hint at it to younger generations by our lifestyles and open-mindedness. How on earth can we convey what it was like to queue at a phone box down the road to make any call at all? Or explain that when the first house-phones were installed they were often party-lines; lines shared with another family or two? Come to think of it anyone who took any time off after university was seen as a bit of a fool or an outsider.

Then of course there's the matter of clunky cameras that needed specific shops to buy specific rolls of film. After a week's wait your pictures were developed. We had no cameras watching us in the streets. That belonged in the fiction of Orwell.

Stonehenge stones were caressed and climbed over; the Colosseum was a place that you walked straight into and nosed around in. Dozens and dozens of stray cats were your fellow explorers. You could turn up at Pompeii and be the only one there. You could get a bus overland from the UK practically all the way to Kathmandu and Tibet.

It was a world where travellers were mostly backpackers or the stinking rich who did most of their travelling by expensive air travel or cruised around the Med. sipping cocktails at every stopover. That suited us. We rarely bumped into them.

Today I read something posted on the ubiquitous social media. Someone was complaining that Brexit was no laughing matter. He would no longer "be able to travel freely across borders or be able to live or work elsewhere." I suppose it was as late as this morning when I realised the younger generation who know nothing but the European Union are quite ignorant of the world before that cumbersome organisation.

Crossing borders back in the '70s was usually a case of sitting for ten or fifteen minutes while a guy walked up and down your bus or train, checked your passport and, if you were lucky, stamped it with an exotic stamp as a souvenir. Russia and Israel were exceptions but I believe they still are. Getting a fistful of strange banknotes was fun. From the artwork on their notes you could get a feel for what kind of people you were among. Anyway it was a rite of passage, a clear sign that you were abroad. The ease of travel? Nowadays a forty-minute flight from Ireland to the U.K takes four hours, allowing for the compulsory two hours beforehand and all the paraphernalia.

In the world of 1976 the Middle-East was not a hotbed of terrorism; we in the West had not bombed those countries back to the Stone Age; Americans were thought of as a bit loud, very naïve and quite amusing but definitely not hated. It was comparatively safe for two young women to stick out a thumb and hitch-hike through the whole of Europe. We were young. Like most young people we had no idea how fortunate and free our generation was or how soon those freedoms would disappear.

For three long days and two nights non-stop, (except when someone was brave enough to shout 'Toilet!') we travelled in a ridiculously hot, sticky and ultimately smelly bus that eventually spewed us out in Athens. That was the Magic Bus.

I'd been here before in our student holidays but a hike up the hill called the Acropolis was always a must. Athens was hot, dry, dusty, noisy and polluted even then. In the heat of a Greek summer it was not a place to stay in for too long. Like most capital city inhabitants, the Athenians are not really representative of Greeks as a whole. They can be snappy and irritable and more than a fair share are out to rip you off. Who can blame them? Living in the chaos and temperature of that place would be enough to make anyone tetchy and want to get their hands on as much money as possible so they could get the heck out of there too.

It probably didn't help that backpackers made it quite obvious that they were off to the Islands (the exact place the Athenians would be if they didn't have to cater to the backpackers).

We settled in to a cheap and cheerful guesthouse near the Acropolis, had a cold shower and went out to have a meal. The glorious prospect of days spent island-hopping was in our grasp. Camping out on fabulous sun-soaked beaches under the stars and lulled to sleep by the lapping of the warm blue, crystal-clear waters of the Aegean. Damn right our spirits were high.

The Acropolis was practically deserted. It was well past midday but still scorching. For the first time on our travels a hat was essential. Sun lotion? No. I told you. Think '70s. We did not give a damn about health and safety. Sun lotion? That was what posh folk bought and used.

Everyone must surely know that the huge structure of the Parthenon is at the top of quite a steep climb. That means 'sit down for a minute when you get up there.'

My favourite parts of the structures up here are the Caryatids on the Erectheion (a temple dedicated to Athena and Poseidon). For those of you who don't know the word it describes the female stone figures who serve as pillars to support a flat bit of the building. Karyati were apparently the women of a Peloponnese village. The reason I love them is, the first time I saw them, I dreamt about them the same night. In my dream they came to life still standing in place. As I looked at them in the dream they could each turn 360 degrees without losing hold of their burdens. As they turned they opened a hidden door. A slab slid back and I was invited in. Unfortunately (or fortunately) I don't remember if I went in or not but the dream has remained with me to this day. Now I was here to pay them my respects.

We wandered around for a while and looked out over Athens. We left.

A taxi to the main port of Piraeus was cheap enough. It wasn't hard to get the times of the ferries heading out the next day for Mykonos. We needed a good night's sleep in any other position than was possible on that awful, long, long bus ride.

After a wonderful breakfast we were off. A couple of hours later and we were in the Passenger Class area of a rather big old chugging ferry, bobbing about on the bright blue sea. I had to laugh at the classification of Passenger Class. There wasn't any other class. Everyone was herded on to the open, sunken deck of the old boat. A massive white canopy tied up around the edges was our only protection against sun, sea, wind and rain.

So much has changed in the many years gone by but, if you do go on a Greek ferry, take a look at the back of your ticket. I hope the wording hasn't changed. Check out the list of exclusion clauses in the event of an insurance claim. Made me smile. They pretty much covered every event that could possibly occur to anyone ever on a boat, in Greece, in hot, cold, freezing, sweltering weather, torrential downpours, an earthquake, volcano eruption, hailstorms, flash-flooding and tsunamis. For good measure the Greeks added "or personal injury, sickness (new or old)" and then came the coup- de-grace "or any Act of God." I guess they don't accept any responsibility then!

How breathtaking is Mykonos? How enchanting it was back then. At the small harbour the old-style windmills that characterize this island, stood, tattered maybe but magical nonetheless. Here it all was, that wonderful blue and white of the painted buildings that proudly reflect the colours of the national flag. This was a time long before tourism had demanded more construction. To the right, as we disembarked, was a line of lean-to shacks, their roofs thatched with a thin layer of bamboo. Inside them and spreading on to the pathway were displays of stunning calico cotton outfits in stripes and bold tasteful patterns. Sandals in the making with flat soles and a toe thong were to be seen as their makers sat, inviting us to sit and be fitted for a new pair. An old hand lathe was busy. Local craftsmen chatted, making wooden ornaments and the like for wealthy cruise-ship passengers who appeared once a week.

These locals had seen and met enough backpackers to know that money was scarce. They smiled toothless smiles and shouted out a 'hello'. They were more than a little surprised that Pat and I walked over to buy sandals. We bought cotton tops, flowing skirts and stopped to share tea and chat. I love the Greeks

The travellers' grapevine on the ferry rumoured that Paradise Beach was the best beach to be on right now. We headed that way. Only a short walk from the shopkeepers at the water's edge and we came to the main shopping area. When I say 'area' it was a row of stone, brightly whitewashed shops with tiny windows. Their frames were painted blue of course. Small outside tables with wicker upright chairs said, 'Make yourself at home'. I think there were no more than four such shops, looking back. They were the original fishermen's cottages. One was a pottery and souvenir shop, its shelves lined with brightly painted tiles depicting characters and tales from Greek legend and myth. There were wall plates and wine jugs painted much the same way. Next door to that was a small café that smelt delicious. Along from these were a small bakery and a grocery store.

I remember standing and letting my shoulders relax downwards. I remember just staring around me. There is something about the light in Greece. There is something about the stark, sharp shadows it casts. There is something about how the bright sun dances on the crystal blue water forever glaring down from an enormous sky of childhood paint-box blue. With basic supplies in hand and having changed into our cooler, cleaner clothes we set off for the walk to Paradise. That's funny.....

I could've sworn I was there already.

Paradise

It's not difficult to imagine the natural beauty of an unpolluted Greek beach; its soft, fine white sand in stark contrast to the turquoise blue of the Aegean that laps at its edges. What is most likely more difficult to imagine is that it was fine to sleep out and camp on any Greek beach for as long as we travellers wanted.

This particular beach greeted us with a roughly painted wooden sign "Welcome to Paradise." By the time we reached it, Paradise Beach had a longstanding tradition of young travellers gathering there. As we turned the last sand dune, a pristinely clean beach stretched out before us, dappled with strange little handmade bamboo shelters just large enough for a body to sleep in.

A first scan and my enduring visual image was of a strong, young man standing some way off shore on a low rock. He was black and brandishing a makeshift spear. He looked for all the world like a Maasai warrior peering into the sea and fishing. The reason this image sticks in my mind is that he was so sun-tanned his black skin had turned blue. It was a blue that shimmered like mother-of pearl or a merman's scales catching the sun's rays.

As for the assembly? Memory tells me we were about sixty in number. Our ages ranged from eighteen to the ripe old age of twenty-nine or early thirties. We were an international bunch. We were

Americans, Aussies, Europeans, Africans and one or two intrepid South Africans. We were transitory. Unlike Pat and I, for some Mykonos was a destination. Some were doing Europe and stopping here for a few days or weeks. Those who saw this as their destination were extremely organised.

Everyone slept in their own little bamboo hut; a simple rectangle, easy to construct. Like I say, there was just enough room for a body to sleep in it and store belongings. The huts provided much welcome shelter too, against the searing heat and ever-present sun. As some folk left, others arrived. Luckily for us there were two ready-made huts abandoned and ready to use.

Set back from this scene and some metres beyond the dunes was an old Greek building. It served as a café of sorts. There were always a few people loitering on its front, open porch. There were three rooms for hire but unsurprisingly they were always fully booked.

I don't want to give the impression that the beach was crowded. It wasn't. Each and every one of us had respect for another's space and the little bamboo constructions were spread out far and wide. Nonetheless we all mixed. The longer term residents had systems in place to make life here run smoothly and still maintain a sense of carefree fun. With the help of locals, fresh water supplies arrived daily by truck at a minimal cost. The same truck took rubbish away regularly and came in handy for help with entertainment and transport around the island when walking was too much of a drag.

It always amazes me how practical people get things done in the most extreme environments. Only a few days in and we learned that by chipping in as much as we could afford, we could share in the nightly barbecues where fish caught only an hour before (by the fishermen amongst us) were griddled on a large open fire. Fresh bread from the town was always in ample supply. From time to time the youth of Mykonos would turn up with cheap bottles of Retsina to wash this all down with or to drink later as we sat and watched the sun slowly set into the sea.

And so the lazy days went by. Wake up with the sunrise. Walk twenty yards-or-so into the warm waters of the Aegean for a swim. Eat dried bread from the night before and sometimes get invited for coffee along the way. Chatting, swimming, socialising, walking, swimming, eating, drinking, laughing and going to bed beneath vast and star-stained night skies. It was a hard life.

From time to time and without warning a disco arrived as the sun was setting. In super quick time an area was marked off with large bamboo screens, unloaded from a battered old truck. Within the hour a generator was providing fairy-lights strung up all around the perimeter and a brighter standing lamp lit the interior space. We had a stage, decks and amplifiers. We chipped in for the cost of their fuel and time and had ourselves a party. It went on long into the night and everyone was in fine form. I guess it was the first-ever outdoor event like that that I'd ever had the pleasure to experience. The memory comes flooding back as one of pure joy.

In less than an hour after the last music there was nothing. There was no sign of what we had just witnessed. Were these the precursors of raves? Probably. I hope there's no blame attached to any of us who had that lust for travel way back then. Occasionally I feel sad that perhaps we started it all; the travel en masse; the package tour; the inundation of these peaceful, empty islands by so many uncaring and thoughtless people. Were we part of the destruction that mass tourism was to bring? Were we instigators? Maybe it would have all happened anyway.

On that subject there were clues though even then. The close-knit community of island dwellers meant that a grapevine was inevitable and efficient. We soon learned not to go down to the harbour for supplies between certain hours on a certain day each week. Why? On that specific day one or possibly two small cruise liners would stop off on their tours. We heard that everything quadrupled in price for those visitors. Word had it that it was their own fault. Over the few years of a pattern developing, the tailors, shoemakers, potters and food-sellers had heard these visitors comment all too often that everything was 'so cheap.' Even when the prices were quadrupled these tourists thought they were getting a good deal. Who could blame the locals for making the most of it? I believe (and expect) it's much the same today.

A walk into the old town of Mykonos was quite arduous in the heat but well worth it. I have never been one for setting myself apart from the local inhabitants in any way, shape or form. If you have not made friends with anyone living in the place you are privileged to visit, "What kind of a guest are you?"

The richer folk had been coming here since the 1950s of course. There were not enough of them to detract from the age-old charm of the town. The ancient architecture in narrow, winding streets was blindingly white in the sunshine and highlighted with the characteristic blue on its woodwork. And always there was the awe-inspiring backdrop of a big and clear blue sky.

My most treasured moments are the days I walked around Mykonos on my own. I would bum a lift from the beach and just land there. I had the advantage of looking ordinary; certainly not wealthy. I also had the advantage of being one of the very few who ventured there alone. The Greeks (ever friendly and welcoming) opened their hearts and homes to me. I don't think there are any words to conjure up the feelings that washed over me in those wonderful little streets. There were scarcely any tourist shops and no exploitation. I carried my sketch pad and pencils in my shoulder bag and whenever I could I sketched the people who gave me tea or who wanted to meet me. I gave them the drawings by way of a thank you. To kids I encountered who bubbled over with curiosity I handed out cheap souvenirs from Scandinavia and watched their faces light up at their newly-acquired treasure. I picked up a few necessary Greek phrases and made a lot of the locals laugh at my childish attempts at their language.

Here are some of my scribblings from a very old notebook of those bygone days.

"To wander up and around thick whitewashed stone steps; to stand and stare at these old, tattered windmills picked out against the sea; to stand aside in a street where I can stretch my arms and touch the houses either side; to let an old lady (head to toe in black) squeeze past with her prized donkey fully laden; to sit a spell and play backgammon with old men who watch as women work; never to ask questions but to observe and know that I was here. That I passed through."

Back at the place officially known as Paradise someone suggested taking a walk over to the next beaches. Funny how you can live somewhere and it never occurs to you that there are similar beaches just around the corner. Anyway, the next beach along was called Super Paradise. Here the rich and famous held sway. They swanned in with their fancy yachts and posed up on deck alongside all the other yacht owners doing exactly the same thing. We didn't fancy hanging around there but someone said there was a beach a little further on from there that we might find interesting. I was up for that.

Me and two lads from Wales decided to make the hike. Rather than take much money with us for food we visited the beach front café and ate a hearty breakfast. We fell chatting to an obnoxious American guy who was thankfully about to leave the island. I mention him because somehow he laced our food and altered the course of my day completely. For now, we set off across the dunes to Super Paradise and beyond.

Day Tripping

Between the white sandy beaches on this side of the island were scraggy sand dunes and nothing but those sand dunes. Any grass there was had a hard time surviving but was managing. The sand was scorching hot from very early morning and to walk in sandals wasn't easy. We three (two Welsh guys and little old me) left Paradise and headed for Super Paradise. We had no idea what lay beyond and didn't care.

Some ten minutes into the walk the guys were discussing 'if they should tell me.' Once you've caught wind of a notion like that there's only one outcome. I told them to 'spit it out.'

Seems they had taken L.S.D before and recognised its effects on them. They knew that some people didn't get any effects at all and were hoping that was the case with me. They reckoned the idiot in the café must have spiked us all. 'Great.' Like everyone else who lives on planet earth I'd heard all the horror stories about Acid. They raced through my mind right now. I calmed myself down and knew that this was all out of my hands. An old song from the '50s that my mum would sing came back to me. "Que sera, sera."

Anyway I told them,

"Nothing odd is happening up till now at least." But then I had an afterthought and I added, "Apart from the fact that I've just walked out of Paradise with 2 Welshmen."

I walked blissfully on. It must have been about 500 yards away. Something in the dunes caught the sun. It glistened and flashed for a second. I left the rough path and headed straight to the spot. I felt magnetised and, despite the object refusing to shine again, I walked straight to a lost engagement ring and picked it up. When I got back to the lads they were cracking up. I showed them the ring and they laughed even more. "No effects then? Presumably your eyesight's always that good?"

Hmm. In all of the propaganda I'd been filled with about Acid, no-one had mentioned it can heighten (and I mean heighten) your visual senses without the infamous weird hallucinations. Trouble was, now that I suspected I had it in my system the fear factor set in. If you've been with me so far on this whole adventure, you'll know I'm a thinker. That's not a good or a bad thing. I just am. In strange or bizarre circumstances I know that my mind searches for a familiar reference to see me through and help me cope. If ever there was a time I needed that it was now. Me being me (with a university degree in literature) it's not surprising I take things literally. Writers have saved my sanity more than once. It's so comforting to know that someone else has been there and lived to tell the tale. Right then. I popped the ring in a small concealed and zipped pocket in my cloth shoulder-bag and eyed my two companions. Which one was Samwise Gamgee and which one Smeagol? I couldn't tell. Was I on my way to Mordor?

The acid dissolved time. It stretched it out of importance. All three of us were on the same island, the same dunes and heading in the same direction but we were definitely not in the same reality. I relaxed and put 'Lord of the Rings' back on its virtual shelf. More amazing things were at hand. I became the sky. Sky and sea –blues, silver-white sand and splashes of green grass blades warped into the sky where they met at my horizon. A heat haze I'd somehow not noticed before painted the sky into Vincent's swirling waves. I laughed and laughed and laughed until my stomach ached. He really had drawn me in in Amsterdam. His vision was playing out before me. After an eternity we reached Super Paradise. The beautiful people pranced, lolloped and posed. I considered handing the ring in at their beach café but it occurred to me they couldn't be trusted. I thought better of it. For a while we sat on the café veranda and sipped water and coca cola, each of us together but worlds apart.

We walked and walked and walked on. It was obvious we were near another beach. Squeals and beach sounds clued me in. I was dying to get into the sea. There wasn't much of value in my bag but I had to wear the ring for safe keeping. My body felt panic. I was standing in front of a wooden sign, knocked together, roughly painted and nailed to a post. I got a gut punch of raw fear. "WELCOME TO HELL."

Tripping self: "So this is Mordor. Go invisible. Put the ring on! Put the ring on."

I slipped it onto my finger as we made our way down the short, sandy slope to the beach.

"Who knew?" I just kept saying that over and over to the guys and laughed my socks off. I was absolutely helpless and no-one was taking a blind bit of notice of me. No-one. The beach was busy. A hive of busy people doing what busy people do. Couples were playing that bat and ball thing; a few men were playing Frisbee; some were flat out soaking up the sun; others were reading or chatting. Along the shoreline small rowing and paddling boats bobbed about with their owners in tow. I picked my way through the insanity to the café where a second sign said, "Clothes must be worn in here."

This was a nudist beach? The extraordinary and hilarious thing from my new perspective? Every single one of them was male. I was the only woman here in hell. Gaydom and nudity weren't my problem. A girl has to get her priorities straight. I was in Hell.

I was 24. I had quite a curvy figure. The size of my bust was always a source of embarrassment. Here? I could dance naked, scream and turn cartwheels and no-one would even notice. I simply did not exist. The ring worked.

My fluidity of mind kept spilling into mental side corridors where dregs of religion went 'Boo!". This is hell then! Invisible with no interaction for ever and ever because I'm female?

The brighter, freer spirit of me kept laughing in spasms. It whispered "You have to admit it's pretty cool to be invisible. The sense of freedom's amazing. Self-consciousness is gone. You don't have to be naked to lose your inhibitions. Everyone here is doing it for you."

What? Why is everyone running to the shoreline? Why are they prodding the water with sticks? People were running out of the water like stuck pigs.

I ambled over to see what all the fuss was about.

It was a Hitchcock film. It was "Invasion of the Giant Jellyfish."

I stared and stared at these remarkable and elegant creatures. The colours inside them were extraordinary. I could see straight through them. The thought occurred that they and I had a lot in common right now. I got the giggles again. A dreadful pun popped into my head. I had no-one to share the joke with. I had no idea where the Welshmen were so I laughed at my own joke and boy did I laugh. It came from the overall silence while they all tried to fend off jellyfish with sticks. It was "So jelefish'in does kill the art of conversation." Maybe I remember that so clearly because I had to keep it to myself.

What can I say about the rest of that day? Eventually we got back to our little huts on our patch of Paradise. Then the worst part of this trip kicked in. It wasn't terrifying or scary in the least. It was just interminable. I was dog-tired but my closed eyelids became cinema screens where I watched bright animated films with colours swirling that played out a replay of my entire day. That lasted all night.

It ended when I at last dozed off at sunrise.

The morning brought thoughts of moving on and of island hopping anew.

C'est la vie.

Bygones be Bygones

A new day then and it found us sitting kicking our heels in the now familiar old port of Mykonos town. We were at a rickety old table outside the only café sipping tea with a great breakfast. The timetabled ferry to Patmos was due any minute. It did feel good to be on the move again. All we knew was we were heading east. East was a big place. Every step was taking us closer to Turkey and, if Mykonos was anything to go by, further back in time. It was an exhilarating thought.

Was there ever a time when travellers to foreign shores thought better of taking snapshots of or depicting the people that greeted them? The answer is yes. To this day I feel it inappropriate sometimes. Hopefully we were about to visit places as yet untouched by commercialism, consumerism or in fact the modern world as we knew it. To snap away with a camera would be intrusive. I stashed my box Brownie further down in my backpack. From now on sketching would have to do.

Before the ferry arrived, an old Salt with a weathered and deeply-wrinkled face came and sat beside us. After a few words with the woman who ran this place he smiled at us and she translated to ask us if we wanted a lift.

It should have dawned on us that, in a seafaring nation like Greece, hitch-hiking would be done by boat. It hadn't. It came as a delightful surprise. He was heading for an island called Naxos in his small fishing boat. We had absolutely no idea what Naxos was like but we did know that Chronos (Time) once hid from Zeus there. Now, if Time could hide away from God there? It was a no-brainer. There couldn't be a better recommendation. In no time at all (excuse the pun) we were aboard a little blue and white boat bobbing on the ocean blue.

I would love to be able to tell you how amazing that trip was. To be honest I stretched out on a wooden bench-seat, snuggled up with my head on my pack and let the gentle swaying of the turquoise, clear waters of the warm Aegean lull me to sleep.

A strong breeze on my face and body woke me up. Our smiling captain used charades to explain this wind was called the Meltemi. It was more than welcome. The sweltering heat of the islands at this time of year could be overpowering. If Naxos had the added benefit of this wind then so much the better. As we got closer it was obvious the island was much bigger than either of us had imagined. Coming in by sea it looked much more fertile too with forested areas and even mountains. That was unexpected.

We pulled in at what could be called a harbour but only because it had several small working boats moored by its beach. We jumped out before we reached shore and waded in; our jeans rolled up to our knees; the backpacks skirting the water.

Here we found nothing but smiles, greetings and hospitality beyond belief. There was never going to be any accommodation for tourists here. Obviously tourists were an unknown entity in this part of the island. Rumours of rich foreign visitors (if there were any) would most probably reach these folk via the boatmen or traders but seem like far-fetched fables to them. Pat knew some history. In the 19th century the island had been feudal. It would have had a strict class system. At the top were nobility or masters; next came the traders or business folk and at the very bottom were the harbour people. They were the poorest of the poor. It seemed as if, (in this village at least) not much had changed in the meantime. Fishing and farming had at least given them a way to keep body and soul together.

So here were two young girls washed in by the tide. Their small beach was not a beach for the idol to lounge on. It was covered in coarse nets spread out to dry and all the trappings of the fisherman's trade stacked up in various states of disarray. Posts hammered into the sand held strings of drying octopi. Salty air and the unique, pungent smell of all things fishy were strong enough to taste.

Our first encounter with the people of Naxos was in the shabby but welcoming shack-cum-café set back from the water's edge. There sat those ubiquitous old Greek men playing their backgammon, smoking, laughing and sipping Retsina. We were greeted as if we were royalty. They plied us with whatever they had to offer. After rather heated discussions (with we two clueless mariners just watching) the gang commandeered our map. We explained where we hoped to go. They then excitedly took it upon themselves to work out our itinerary. When they were done they let us know what we were doing, where we were going, with whom and when.

Apparently we had the rest of today and a full day tomorrow here before a cousin was heading for Patmos via Ios in his own boat. After that we had a chain of connections or cousins hopping and taxiing us on to Leros, Kalymnos and eventually to Cos. Payment, they insisted, was out of the question. These boats were going that way every day with or without us.

As if all this wasn't enough, our ferryman now led us away to a small semi-derelict cottage-style house not far from the small harbour. He gave us the huge old door key. It was fabulous. Inside, the thick old white-washed walls held the large room cool against the blistering sun. The bare floorboards made the living space look huge. From first glance it was obvious that someone used this place from time to time. It was clean and it was sparse but we wouldn't have exchanged it for any fancy hotel or posh villa for all the tea in China (or all the goats in Greece.)

We settled in. By that I mean, we unrolled our sleeping bags and placed them on the squeaking old sprung beds. We dug out our small but adequate camping cooking equipment and flung open the huge window and its long, tall wooden shutters. Outside was a neglected garden with fig trees and grapevines tangled, overgrown and perfect. A goat helped himself lazily to whatever he fancied. Beyond the garden was the astonishingly blue sea. With a water supply, a camping stove, a working outside toilet and shower we were in the lap of luxury. Food shopping was gonna be fun.

Like any small, rural community anywhere in the world, everyone knew everyone. News of their esteemed guests had spread. Everyone smiled and waved and kids went crazy. Despite a million offers to come in and have tea, drink a beer, eat we managed to get salad stuff; tomatoes the size of large apples and goat's cheese that smelled as if it was made only minutes earlier. We even found some candles. With other ingredients, fresh bread, eggs, bottles of water and local wine, we ambled back home. With our booty stashed in what appeared to be a pantry, we went out for a poke around.

If you haven't been to this part of the world you should know that the architecture (both rich and poor) is gorgeous. It's quirky at times. In the hearts of these old villages narrow streets twist and turn to defy the modern car (if one ever appears.) Some streets turn at sharp right angles where a car would have to bend in half or reverse. Outside in the narrowest of streets, old wooden upright chairs are perched by a door or window for neighbour to chinwag with neighbour. Flowers thrive and splash colour hanging from small verandas and window boxes below. Sturdy trees grow out of walls and crevices and defy the need for moisture. There's a kind of comfort in it all.

We were scooped up by a cart tugged reluctantly by a donkey and taken off to see ancient ruins that are nowhere on anyone's map. The jolly old farmer took us to see his land and in a field near his house he knelt and wiped away some top soil. There, after an old leaking bucket of water was tossed, a fabulous Roman mosaic magically appeared.

How amazing is that? To have that kind of thing just hanging around right outside your house?

We walked our feet off. Naxos was jam-packed with history. Everybody and his brother had captured and ruled this island at one time or another- Thracians, Mycenaeans, Rhodians, Ptolemies, Spartans, Persians, Romans, Turks and who else but the Venetians? They got about a bit! I'm sure there are more. We saw temple complexes, the large temple on the peninsula, churches, Venetian towers, ancient statues and even some broken amphorae just tossed aside and lying by the roadsides. We were given rides to mountains, valleys, caves, beaches and woodland. Eventually we got back to our palace.

Imagine if you will, that night on our slightly dodgy veranda. Like royalty we sat, as the remains of the day gave way to the black velvet cloak of night over the sea just beyond; a cloak made threadbare by Chronos himself; its small holes revealing the silver-golden glow beneath. That was how, it seemed too me at least, that Time the Magician himself was creating for us this illusion of a million stars in the Cycladean sky.

We sat and stared, gobsmacked with our lit candles perched and flickering all around the wrought-iron railing. We ate. We drank wine. We sat back. We 'ooh'd' as we counted the shooting stars diving into the warm Aegean over the hidden horizon. How far away were the grey city streets of Britain with its low skies, its industrial unrest and its taking-for-granted of these glorious stars?

Lying on that bed I began to wonder about myths, legends, old books and old tales. This place was as the Greek myths said. Time was hiding here. It was nowhere to be found. There is a kernel of truth in all of those ancient stories. Most people dismiss it all. I remember thinking that when my mum used to put things in a 'safe place', she could never find them again. Yep. The Greeks had put their truths in a safe place – their myths. I slept like a baby.

Kos We Could

"Oh my god!" sums it up. That sums up everything that came at me as we bobbed and bounced our way into a small bay on the island

of Kos. It was like a gust of wind swept over my mind and threw open
all the shutters; lifted all the blindfolds of my Western upbringing.
How? Why? It was everything about that first glimpse. Yes, there was
the all-too-expected shack-café set back from the shoreline. Yes there
were the same old guys drinking and chatting but hey! The castle to
their left glowed in the morning sunlight and there were palm trees
everywhere. Not far inland was our first glimpse of a minaret. We
were so close to Asia we could see it, feel it, smell it and taste it. The
revelations came thick and fast.

The castle had seen better days as a fortress but by now I could
recognise Venetian handiwork anywhere. Perhaps this edifice was the
one that tipped the balance but I got it! The Venice I'd visited a few
years earlier gave my modern mind the impression of a small, quirky
little island city; ridiculously spectacular and elegant yes but small and
insignificant. Now I realised these Venetians had been everywhere and
boy could they build. Of course they could. Who else would construct
a whole city on a chopped forest of pylons sunk into the middle of
the sea?

Then came the realisation that this castle of the Knights of St.
John was built by the same ambulance brigade I knew from childhood.
Both the importance of Venice and these guys had shrunk over time.
They were the Knights Hospitalers and that meant the origin of the
word hospital and a whole lot more. The next bolt out of the blue
was 'Hey! If you were Chronos (Time) hiding from God way back
on Naxos, what would you do? 'Answer- Stand still'. Yep! Time had
been standing still throughout these fabled islands. Time seemed to be
holding this island in his hand, in suspension. Then I saw that palm
trees to me meant exotic. They were what had always been missing
from all those nativity scenes of my youth.

If there was a fortress here then we must be getting close to the
pesky Turks. Visions of the Welsh border flashed through my mind.
All those castles represented clashes between two different cultures.
Here was the first inkling. Before we got out of that little boat I
reached for my notebook and scribbled, "So many clashes happen
because we know we all live on the same planet but forget we live
in different worlds." I was excited at the thought of moving into a
different world. Who wouldn't be?

'Greeks will be Greeks.' Someone famous should have said that but I'll say it just in case. 'Greeks can't help being helpful'. No sooner had we had breakfast than we were whisked away in a rickety old car to a beautiful guest-house in the centre of what appeared to be the capital of this island of Kos. Capital sounds a little too grand for the quaint and picturesque hub of activity before us but apparently capital it was. It was also a feast for the eyes and welcoming shelter for a body and soul.

Two young foreign women in town were impossible to miss. What else could they be looking for but a place to stay? We were led up a flight of those typically Greek, chunky, dazzling white and wonky outdoor steps (practically moulded to the side of the old two-storey building.) We took possession of the key to one of two rooms for rent. Traditional outdoor steps are wonderful throughout Greece. Abandon any ideas you might have of steps having to have sharp, crisp edges. Gone are any sign of clean-cut angles. These curvy things are done by hand.

Unburdened of our rucksacks, showered and freshly clothed we couldn't wait to go exploring. What a place it was. After a very quick peek at the castle we put it to the side of our plate for later. It was big. A nearby alleyway was overflowing with flowers. It had odd little corners packed with upturned amphorae, stuffed with flowering geraniums. With these corners came an absolute 'must'; wooden chairs tucked in at any angle to sit on and watch the world go by. This alley led us into a courtyard square.

There in this haven of greenery and comparative calm an enormous Plane tree stole pride of place. A brass plaque (aged and tricky to read) told us that Hippocrates taught his students under this tree in the 5th century B.C. It was unlikely that this was the actual tree but a section of it that looked ancient was protected by a makeshift wire frame. Who cared? Now we were walking amongst the ancients again and my soul sensed it.

The shops in this market area were laden with delicious fruit and vegetables and (a million years after I should have done) I realised where Kos lettuce comes from. Just like a King Edward potato back home it had never occurred to me that either King Edward or Kos had anything at all to do with the naming of these fruits of the land.

The shop fronts were rickety open stalls. It wouldn't take a geology expert to suss that this island had suffered earthquakes. The ubiquitous crazy paving of Greek Island streets (grey slabs of all shapes and sizes held together by a white filling like icing) dipped up and down in waves that seemed to actually flow in the shimmer of the summer heat haze.

We found a small stall selling stationery and newspapers. There we found some old copies of the Hippocratic Oath and snapped them up as souvenirs. Heaven knows what happened to those. No matter. When I revisited Kos some thirty years later I replaced mine. Anyway, compared to other islands this was a veritable hive of activity. We stumbled upon a bike rental shop. Now you're talking. Before long we were away.

There wasn't any traffic to speak of. The freedom felt glorious. We headed off along the one main stretch out of the town that swept under the castle bridge. Within minutes we were cycling along a road with a ditch running along either side. You can't imagine how strange and how oddly satisfying it was, to see hundreds upon hundreds of bits of ancient Greek and Roman statues, pots and columns up-ended and tossed aside, just lying there, just like that. The enormous hand of the Emperor Somebody-the-Second (or Third) reached up to us as we gaily cycled by. 'How the mighty have fallen' took on a completely different meaning, I can tell you. So what? This was Greece. This was an island. They had too much of that stuff to worry about.

After some acclimatising and a good bit of broken antiquity giggling we started to notice and look at the fruit trees around us. Fallen apples, lemons, oranges and figs were strewn all along the roadside. We stopped to peel and eat some. We stashed some for later. It was glaringly obvious that this island was packed with stuff to do and see. We needed a plan and somewhere to stay for at least a week. Our friends at the shore had told us it was about 25 miles long and 5 miles wide and now we had bikes. As luck (yeah right!) would have it, a fellow cyclist pulled over to join us. He was Matt and he was an Aussie.

In no time at all (perhaps time should have a capital T) we were off-road, freewheeling down a side lane that eventually led to the sea. It was lined with fig and orange trees and smelt delicious. Not surprisingly, now and then, the odd and enormous limb or two of some antiquated God or Goddess reached out from the undergrowth in a forlorn attempt at reclaiming past glory. That was remarkable (if not weird). Half way down this track was our destination. Although ribbon-development was still some way off in the future, here were the beginnings of a modern bungalow; its roof in place; the front of the ground floor structurally completed and with a makeshift kitchen and bathroom for the builders.

Matt's story (who knew or needed to?) was that he was hired to look after the place until the Greek owners from Athens returned in the late autumn. Meanwhile he got lonely and decided to share his luck. Yes. Of course we would stay.

And so began our two week stay on Kos. We shared this palatial residence with six young guys from New Zealand, Australia and the U.S of A. Suffice to say that the parties and the barbecues we had were out of this world. During the day? Pat and I had our own adventures.

It is something else to cruise into town on a sunny day and have as a landmark a slightly neglected Roman Forum to your left. With bottled water we explored the huge ruins. Why water? We'd learnt that lesson from our farmer in Naxos. Here too no-one paid them much heed.

Over the days we cycled out to the Asclepeion named after Asclepius, the Greek god of Medicine. It is enormous. When we were there excavations were not completed but we still felt overawed by the sheer scale of this Healing temple where modern medicine is said to have been founded. It stands in walnut groves and pine forests and is simply beautiful. Heaven knows what it must have been like to come here as a patient back then.

From people we spoke to we learned we must go to a mountain village called Asfendiou. Apparently a visit there would conjure up the magical diversity of this small island.

Sure enough we cycled and hiked our way there some days later. That was extraordinary. There were only 100 inhabitants in this gorgeous little village but the most amazing thing was its feel of an Alpen settlement. Pokey, climbing narrow winding streets with dinky houses twisted and turned, with the people sitting doing every kind of craft or simply shooting the breeze. Here was a completely fresher and clearer air. The view from the end of this village was unbelievable.

In our remaining days on Kos we bathed in thermal pools that sprang from nearby rocks on empty beaches. We swam in the warm Aegean whenever we felt like it. We said hello to wild peacocks that roamed free in a vast forest nearby. We walked around the castle and dined out in quaint, isolated tavernas. We drank too much Retsina and laughed 'til we cried before cycling home slightly drunk on that one (as yet unused) main road.

And every night we free-wheeled down that lane; picking fruit as we went and saying goodnight to the disembodied Worthies that lurked in our foliage. How could you tire of that feeling? Tire of those perfumes of sea and fruit? Cease to be fascinated by those priceless antiquities and above us, practically dropping down to our feet, those magnificent stars? You couldn't. We couldn't but Turkey and Asia beckoned.

Confused? You will be.

You very probably learned, like me, that Father Christmas lives at the North Pole and like me, you assumed everyone else goes along with that. Think again.

I was standing in a very humble dwelling on the edges of a remote village near Assos in Turkey. Outside, the heat was blistering. Inside, the cool relaxed both body and soul. Something about the decor made me think of that fellow Santa Claus. Simple it might be but every inch of this tiny dwelling was filled with soft furnishings that had been handcrafted, lovingly sewn and embroidered by the very timid woman of the house. It was lush, gorgeous and simply exquisite. Everything was handmade. Bench- shaped seating in rich velvety fabric stretched all around the tiny room, hugging the walls. The edges were laced with tassels.

Wall-hangings stole the imagination. Roughly-woven and multi-coloured rugs were scattered over the stone floor. The stitching of the rich colours and intricate patterns of the upholstery was in burgundy reds and ice-blues with gold threads and beading chasing the designs. Here and there odd fragments of mirror had been sewn in to twinkle magically. All around us were tremendously thick, whitewashed walls made of heaven-knows-what. There were no straight edges in here. It was an almost cave. It was an igloo of sorts.

My mind scanned for a comparison to help me acclimatise to the very unfamiliar surroundings. I knew it could mislead me but on this occasion at least it wasn't far wrong. It threw up Santa Claus. I was convinced this was his sitting -room; somewhere he could comfortably slough off his boots and wriggle his toes into those ornate pointed slippers usually associated with the likes of Ali Baba. And strangely the Turkish Father Christmas link wasn't far off at all

Our grinning host and his wife were insisting that we all three sit and take tea. A small coffee table was encouraged to fit between our lavish seats and soon held a magnificent brass samovar. The charcoal was lit and we waited for tea. We watched as our hostess filled the small table top with various sweetmeats and snacks, quite obviously made especially for us. Their smiles were better than any Christmas present.

Okay. So what am I doing in a tiny village in the middle of nowhere? Sorry. Turkey? when I was in Kos a day or-so ago? You have to rewind. Just like this text, things didn't always take the most expected or direct route. Welcome to our world back then. (I'll get back to the Santa thing later.)

If you look at any map you will see that Kos is a tiny distance from the West coast of Turkey. It should have been easy and definitely would have been more practical to hop on a boat and go across at the shortest crossing. No. We could not find anyone who wanted to take us across. Perhaps customs or passports were involved? Who knew? Since we never had any plan to speak of, it just didn't matter. We were sitting in the café in Kos harbour and considering going all the way back to Piraeus (the main hub of Athens) to catch a commercial ferry across to the next continent.

Do two girls get more opportunities more easily on this kind of trip? It's something I've often wondered. I will never know the answer. As 'luck' would have it (and I had no idea what that word meant any more) a young guy in his early thirties-or-so plonked down beside us and asked us where we were going. Good question. He laughed himself silly when he heard our answer. "East."

His story was that a brand spanking new, bright orange convertible B.M.W (that he was pointing to) was his. Introducing yourself by way of meeting your car first says a lot about a person but hey! He was Turkish. His English was remarkably good. His name was Deniz. (Memorable because thereafter we referred to him as 'Menace'; a joke he found hilarious but had no idea why.) He was making his way back home to Istanbul but on a round-of-about sort of sightseeing trip. That we could relate to. If we had stayed on the Magic Bus from Amsterdam we would have been in Istanbul a very long time ago. The 'scenic', unexpected detour route was always much more fun.

So, did we want a ride? Now, being on the road gives a person a heightened sense of a stranger's intentions. An antenna flips up, spins at a hundred miles- an- hour and rapidly scans to detect possible danger. It's all done in the blink of an eye. One look between Pat and I confirmed we both felt the guy was safe. Our next dilemma was that Istanbul seemed an awful long way away and almost in the opposite direction from where we thought we were heading. The Menace left us alone to have a think.

As far as we both felt, this guy just liked the idea of driving around with two girls in the back of his prized possession; his open-topped Beamer. Seemed logical; the kind of image to complete a young buck's fantasy. Yep. We agreed he seemed harmless. In for a penny? Well actually, no! He wasn't even asking for that much. It would certainly be a great (and cheap) way to see more of Turkey.

When a clunking and slightly rusty ferryboat pulled out of Kos harbour that day, among its freight were a shiny Beamer and three carefree passengers. (Two of whom had absolutely no clue what awaited en route to the fabled Istanbul.)

For now though, it seemed we were heading for the port of Kusanasi via a short stopover at the island of Samos. A map on the wall behind a makeshift coffee dock on board showed us the place was only about 26 miles long and 8 miles wide. There was a narrow mile wide, stretch of water called the Mykale Straight separating this island from mainland Turkey. We could see it was remarkable. It was mountainous.

For the uninitiated traveller the sound of being on a ferry in the Dodecanese may conjure up all kinds of fantastical notions. Stop right there. Below and above decks both had their hazards. Neither was life-threatening but neither would ever be included in any fantasy or brochure for that matter.

Below deck the grinding of the engines wasn't deafening exactly but loud enough to get on my nerves. Forget for a moment the crowd of swarthy men eyeing two (clearly foreign) young women with intentions best unknown. Above deck? In five different sorties to get air I met as many captains. Yes. I did laugh a lot and no I couldn't keep a straight face. What tickled me the most was the captain's hat that mysteriously had the same dark coffee stains in exactly the same place just above the peak.

Each captain would sidle up to me and (after the first one I knew the script) say, "Hello. I am your captain. Would you like to see my quarters?" Fair play, they'd learned the proper jargon right enough but 'really?' I did come away wondering how many times or even if ever that ruse had worked and when they would figure out they needed a new chat up line.

When we chugged into Samos harbour, the very few cars on board were allowed to drive off for the duration. It was surprising but meant Deniz could give us a quick tour of this incredible little island. If memory serves me well we had a couple of hours.

I didn't know Pythagoras was born on Samos, did you? He was. There again Epicurus and Aesop were born here too. Deniz had scooped up a handful of leaflets from a small building in the harbour. According to those there were a lot of cultural celebrities from Samos. Shamefully I didn't recognise most of the others. I did of course recognise the Olympian Goddess Hera. Apparently this island was hers.

The Menace showed off his Beamer on mountain tracks and up and down slopes covered in a million grape vines. There wasn't anyone to show it off to but what the heck? In contemporary parlance it gave him the feel-good factor. The island was absolutely burgeoning with fruit, flowers and vegetation. We stopped every now and then to take in the glorious views. There is absolutely no image on earth as dramatic and astounding as the view to be had, high up on an island that rests in the turquoise, green and sparkling waters of the Aegean. Every time I experienced it, I understood absolutely why these islands produced some of the world's greatest thinkers and poets. To have their minds and spirits lifted and refreshed every morning waking up to this? That's quite simply mind-blowing and certainly enough to make you come up with an interesting hypothesis or two.

The whole of Samos is dominated by the huge peak of an extinct volcano at its centre. That explained all the lush vegetation I guessed. Most likely it went a long way in explaining the live- for- today attitude of these islanders who were forever smiling.

We had time to visit its ancient capital, unsurprisingly renamed Pythagoreio. What would Greece be without its ancient ruins, marking time and putting us squarely in our place? Here in Pythagoreio was a sprawling complex of a temple dedicated to the goddess Hera. There it was, plonked not far from the old, dead city. I liked to imagine that this temple once stood right on the coastline, perhaps pushed inland by receding sea levels? But I knew nothing about geology stuff back then. It just seemed right somehow. It just seemed in keeping with the Greek talent for creating the striking and the spectacular visual image.

We sat to drink iced- coffee outside a ramshackled roadside café. How could we not feel privileged? Just a stone's throw from this shack, but 14 centuries away, a guy called Eupalinus defied gravity and a mountain by digging a two-ended tunnel underground to serve as an aqueduct for this very place where we sat. It's now rated as one of the eight wonders of the world and quite rightly so. That day we three ogled at its brilliance. We three were alone. Yep. The Greeks weren't half-clever!

Oh! I nearly forgot. I was gonna tell you about Father Christmas, wasn't I?

Explorers

I mistakenly believed that setting foot in Asia for the first time would magically and instantaneously transport me to the land of the Arabian nights, Ali Baba and magic lamps. I got a grip. Reindeers in Stockholm syndrome was not something I wanted to catch.

After a visit to a bank in Kusadasi port to change Greek Drachma for Turkish Lire, we set off. Here I was in Asia. In Turkey East clearly does meet West. You would have to be blind not to see that. Like the Greeks though, the Turks couldn't give a fig (and they've got more than enough of them to spare) about rushing or what the time is.

The east meeting west bit was happening in my mind too. In no time at all we were driving in relative speed and absolute comfort not through the story books of my childhood bedtimes but through the pages of the Bible. It made me think. It made me question what I had been taught as a kid and why. It made me think about stories and how they travel.

Moving by car definitely did something to my brain. I was in the landscape but outside it at the same time. Alien images flashed by like film, my mind and eye catching what they could and magically drawing the future towards me rather than me walking towards it. That's a poor description but valid nonetheless.

I sat back, smoked a ciggie and succumbed to time travel; soon back in among the biblical women. In scattered villages these veiled ladies battered their laundry in fast- flowing streams and on rocks that were seemingly designed specifically for that purpose. Every one of them dressed like the Virgin Mary, chatted and laughed as they slapped their fabrics on riverside rock and wrung them as best they could before laying them out to dry in the sweltering heat. How delicious must those clothes have smelt? In the fields bullocks and donkeys did farm work long since overtaken by machines in my world. I had to pinch myself to remember this was 1976 but what did that mean? Ask one of those women and her answer would be 'Now.'

So much for Arthur Scargill and his coal miners, dole queues, riots, protest marches, trade union squabbles, oil prices and the petty bickering of politicians back home then. That nonsense was nothing more than a bad dream that as yet, had not been dreamed by these fortunate people.

My philosophical side was enjoying itself too. It produced another 'Eureka' moment when I realised why the Bible never made sense to me. These were the landscapes its stories belonged in. These were the missing bits from that entire Nativity-scene thing: Fig trees, date palms, donkeys, mangers, the veils that were the appropriate costumes and the three wise men. They all fitted here perfectly. Here, growing on trees were the exotic fruits we only ever had in quirky packaging at Christmas time. Christianity had brought an alien God into Britain. It wasn't in my blood or my nature. The more I thought about it, the more I realised that all of the fighting between Christianity and Islam, Turks and Europeans, Israelis and Palestinians, the whole lot was the result of a domestic that started in this East. It was a brawl that had spewed over into, well, practically everywhere. Stranger still? It was all over a story.

Were these people poor? Good question. My answer was no. They had riches we had long lost. They had that innocence we now crave and cling to as a remnant of some fabled Golden Age.

On and on and on the scenery carried us. It swept us along the marvellous coastlines of unpolluted seas where ruins of past great civilisations proved time and time again the futility of earthly power and greatness. I loved it all. I had absolutely no idea where I was apart from 'here'. That did me nicely. Thank you very much.

We stopped.

We'd arrived in small village or town called Didim. I was warming to Dennis the Menace. He'd turned up unannounced at some old friend's house after not seeing the bloke for ten years or more. I liked his style. The way things had been going for us, nothing surprised me anymore. This long-absent friend was not only still living here but was at home.

Ushered in to the comfort and beauty of a relatively well-to-do home we sat and watched as Deniz explained our presence, and as food kept appearing like something in that nonsensical song 'The Court of King Caractacus.' Before long, a huge table was spread with a banquet of unrecognisable delights. Since we had no idea what any of it was there was no point in being picky now was there?

Usually my eyes were everywhere but now my ears took over. This was the first time I'd had a chance to listen to the music of the Turkish language and to try and pick out some sense to it. 'Thank you' was the sentiment most repeated. 'Yes' and 'No' were easy to decipher. Body language and context will always point you in the right direction as far as language is concerned.

'Thank you' was 'Teşekkür ederim'. 'Yes' was 'evet' and 'yok hayır' was 'no'. It didn't take long to notice that a nod of the head here meant no and a shake signalled yes. It's one thing knowing that but quite another trying to do it.

After no more than 5 minutes of listening, I was using all this. This was much to the delight of this lovely young family who laughed at and applauded my absolutely dreadful attempts.

With bellies full, a middle-aged cousin stole us away in a beat- up old pick-up truck and, without so much as asking, proudly took us on a quick tour of his neighbourhood. Folks! How amazing would it be to have visitors and just whisk them down the road to a deserted, pure-white sandy beach lined with palms and show them your local temple of Apollo? There it was framed by that glorious blue of an Aegean summer sky. I know. I know the locals probably take it for granted. Turkey had so much of this. It wasn't precious. It was fabulous though.

Deniz decided to stay on for a week. Consequently, it was decided we should visit a small fishing village called Bodrum, a place Turks loved and a must-see. By now we had given up on using a map. Somehow the idea of having a set destination (that had once seemed so normal) sounded absurd. The very next day we set off with an arrangement to meet up with Deniz back here in about a week's time. Sounded like a plan but we didn't actually care if it didn't work out. Why worry?

The men of the family gave us a lift to a tiny, tiny village not far from this Bodrum, high up above a small bay.

We got passed like precious contraband to a man who was our transporter. We waved goodbye to our hosts for now and caught sight of our new means of transport. This very important man owned donkeys and soon we had five of them in a train. Our rucksacks had one each and so did we. Our guide had his own.

He led it by its halter and later rode with us. Before we got going I decided it was time to don my small headscarf that I bought in Red Square. Slowly but very surely, we set off at quite a steep angle, downwards, downwards and around and around then down some more; down the dusty, rocky track to our own Shangri- La.

At one point we stopped, dismounted and caught sight of our destination way below. Unbelievable. On its own small island out in the picturesque bay a sandcastle-shaped fort evidenced those ubiquitous Hospitalers again.

I guess, without even knowing it, I must once have wanted to be a heroine in a Rider Haggard novel. I realised that now. In my mind I made a mental tick gesture of 'got that', as we climbed back on our steeds and rode on into Bodrum.

There, in its one street, residents came out to wave, smile and greet us. Some welcome, eh?

What was it with this world we were in? It seemed determined to treat us and to treat us free of charge. We were about to spend a week among people who didn't want us to pay a dime for anything. They couldn't do enough for us. They changed my life for ever.

From that very first moment the residents of this idyllic little fishing village began planning where we would sleep and stay. Every household wanted to have their turn; to have the honour of having these two young white women as their guests. How did we know this? We knew it because we met Hanuk and Zeki. They were the only other two tourists right then; engineering students from Izmir who were thrust forward to help us because of their brilliant English. That night, apparently, there was to be an outdoor feast in our honour. Then we would stay at that house.

Bodrum was absolutely gorgeous. The castle guarding the small harbour was enormous. It sat out on the promontory that defined the bay. Say 'castle' today and we think of a tourist trap. Not here; not yet anyway. It sat there like some feature in a pleasant park, a place to rest, sit and stare out to sea while on a pleasant stroll.

There were no signs here, no fees and no real indication of renovation either. To me it appeared to be just as it had been left hundreds of years earlier.

The tallest of palm trees embraced this little haven that was nestling in the steep hills surrounding the bay. There was only one street and very few people wandering about. Those we did see went about their daily chores un-hurried, only stopping now and then to chat to anyone who passed by.

One side of this roughly-paved and narrow street was lined with ancient high walls too high to allow a glimpse behind or beyond them. Once in a while a gateway allowed a tantalising peep at a hidden house or courtyard tucked away behind it. The opposite side of this dusty track was the commercial side; small shops that baked bread;

where shoemakers repaired and made shoes; a store that sold basic groceries and every trade necessary for a small village was represented. Across the divide, electricity cables and the telephone line were strung haphazardly marking the arrival of modernity. I suppose the dusty yard loosely called a bus station, at the end of this short thoroughfare was a hint of what was to come too. The buses were old with huge tyres most definitely adapted for the one road leading in and out.

In quirky little curious doorways women sat weaving rugs on looms that hadn't changed in design since Noah was a boy. Men and women both wove every type of basket down by the harbour, to the sound of the quietly lapping clear water. Laid back doesn't express how slowly this place went about its business. That word business is itself misleading.

On that first afternoon we had the sheer delight of walking into the street's only café-bar. The outside was bedecked with vines and gourds. It kept its secret well. Step inside and there was no back to it at all. We were standing at the bar on soft, white sand mere yards from the warm sea. This, it was obvious, was the hub of Bodrum. How unbelievably welcoming it was. How unbelievably friendly they all were.

As evening fell on that first night, we were taken in through one of those mysterious gateways and ushered into a courtyard. Seemed this was quite an occasion. The locals began to file in with everyone in high spirits. I can't even pretend to have words to conjure up that night for me. There are times when feelings are indescribable. 'Joy' comes close.

There, in that old place, we thirty- or-forty people mingled. We mingled under a spectacular blue-black sky studded with stars. In the centre of the yard a huge bonfire spat and sparkled, casting tiny specks of red glowing fire dancing and spiralling upwards in that calm air. That air was so sweet. The trees rising above us released all kinds of fantastic aromas into the heady mix of meat turning on a massive spit and cauldrons bubbling with fat in which potatoes fried and sizzled. In the large, outdoor bread- oven flatbread was cooking. The soundtrack was the lilt of their native tongue and a muted collection of their unmistakeable music. We were treated like visiting royalty.

Our week continued in much the same vein. Every night we were hosted by a new family in a new, wonderful garden. Every morning we breakfasted outside in the bright sunlight left alone to our own thoughts but wanting for nothing. There was nothing that could repay these gentle, kind people. By way of repaying them I made a promise to myself that, from this moment on, I would be as welcoming, helpful and kind to any stranger I met who was in need of food and shelter on their travels. To the best of my ability I've kept that promise.

To put it mildly our days were spent leisurely. The heat was exhausting; too exhausting to do much. We visited the old fortress a few times. I will never forget looking down over the inner walls and there, in the deep, wide space that separated this from the outer walls, was the most enormous pile of broken pieces of antiquity. If Kos had a surplus of ancient Roman and Greek bric-a-brac, this place took the biscuit. The heap was 7 or 8 feet high in a ditch that ran all the way around this tower. Extraordinary. For the first time ever I had some sympathy with those old European explorers who'd robbed away treasures way back when. It wouldn't have seemed like theft. It would perhaps have seemed like preservation or an expression of their passion for such treasures left uncared for by native peoples. I have to confess that when I spotted an Emperor's marble finger nearby even I was tempted. Alright, alright so it wasn't exactly the Elgin marbles but my conscience still wasn't having any of it.

We swam and lounged about on the beach. We walked. We chatted to our now friends Hanuk and Zeki. We ate great fresh food, drank Turkish fresh coffee, learned more Turkish and exchanged ideas. If we'd had more time we could have taken them up on their offer to visit Patara. In the other direction was Myra too, where the Bishop of Turkey, the 4th-century St. Nicholas was born. Yes folks. I got there in the end. Santa Claus isn't Scandinavian. He was once the Bishop of Turkey.

It came as a pleasant surprise when, on the morning of our seventh day, a four-wheel drive made it through on the only road in. Out popped Deniz.

When I left Bodrum it was with promises to meet up with the guys in Izmir someday. It was also with tears and an aching heart.

Me and Zeus

The Gods of Olympus no longer governed this part of the world of men. That much was clear. It was still within their reach though. I imagined Zeus, bored and at a loose end, turning out his cupboards and dragging out a perfect, toy model of this rocky coastline of Turkey.

His delicately crafted layout was showing signs of age and a lot of the buildings were badly destroyed; old temples once so splendid lay in ruins among the many dinky cypress trees that covered the slopes.

On a whim he rummages around on a future shelf of his cupboard and comes across his soon-to-be-favourite little car; an orange, open-topped Beamer. It looks as good as new. He toys with it. Then he wheels it along the winding roads and into a dead-end at Bodrum before dragging it back to whence it came to take it on a tour. A bit shocked, he stares at three tiny figures inside it. They must have fallen out of something else but it amuses him. He stares at them again, this time more particularly at the little woman in the back.

I'd asked for it. After all, when Deniz collected us early that morning I was well aware that the next few days were out of our hands. I believe my actual words were "It's in the lap of the Gods."

I have no recollection of the specifics of the route we took. Car journeys do that. The Menace was on holiday. Wherever he wanted to go was fine by us. I do remember having that theatre stage- set feeling. After all the magnificent and oh-so different peoples and landscapes we'd experienced, and after going under a train with Anna Karenina, it was impossible not to bear in mind Old Billy Shakespeare's words, "All the world's a stage."

The backdrop to this particular set was the now familiar bright blue, cloudless sky. The stage itself was criss-crossed with light- grey drystone walls sitting on a sandy soil speckled with gravel. In and around all this the theatre crew had stacked the dark greenery of exotic trees in almost-forests on slopes brought in to provide some depth. We upped and downed through and around them.

Then of course, there was always a tantalising glimpse of the Aegean far below, popping in and out of view. From high up I could see the levels of its clear waters with their incredible shades of deepest blue-turquoise and the almost greens of coral and sandbanks hugging the shoreline.

Oh hello! We were skirting around Kusadasi again. I realised we were going back on ourselves. Was I worried?

On the stage a few extras were wandering here and there to make all this look lived-in. A lot of goats, some cows, oxen, chickens and the odd dog or-two added a nice touch of realism. Deniz pulled over. He broke my reverie. He signalled for us to get out and take a look. Sometimes life blows your mind. Mine was well and truly blown. Just below me, stretched out at my feet, were the far-reaching, sprawling ruins of mighty Ephesus. Good grief! It was big.

From our raised vantage point I could see the entire ground plan and appreciate the sheer size. Its ruins were yellowed and creamy, bathed in the late morning sunlight; its many pillars casting sharp shadows along avenues and walkways once well-known to the people going about their ever-so important business here some 21 centuries before we arrived just now.

This city was gigantic. From where I stood, the dishevelled amphitheatre stole the show. It was simply enormous. In its day it could hold 25,000 spectators. Yep. This hill gave us the best possible introduction to Ephesus. There were no queues, no tickets for admission and very few visitors. This was the '70s, remember?

When we drove down to it and walked around my mind couldn't take it all in. Of course I could tell this was once an incredibly important and prosperous place. It stretched way, way back through time. The apostle John wrote some of his letters here in 90-100 A.D (merely recent history for Ephesus). He was buried here. He wasn't the only one apparently. St. Paul lived here in the A.D. '50s. Did you know he was a Jewish-Christian? Neither did I.

When I read about those two stalwart Christians being Jewish-Christians my mind went off 'on one' again. Here we were, standing in the footprints of these two renowned story-tellers who lived when Judaism and Christianity were still joined at the hip. Somewhere along the line that mutual storyline took an unforeseen twist.

Being in Ephesus and confronted with two of the Bible writers I had to keep reminding myself that I was seeing all this in the world of Islam.

It would have been so easy to get carried away and walk until we dropped here. Our time was limited and besides, the sweltering sun would soon be directly overhead. Deniz wanted to push on too, so we chose one part of this city to explore. The ruined Library of Celsius was a sight to see. It was built in nearly 2000 years ago and the architecture is fabulous. Now devoid of books and scrolls it still manages to speak volumes. One thing was for sure. This city placed a high value on learning.

There were bath complexes, temples, massive market places, an aqueduct, houses, official buildings and even a little private theatre. I liked the street called Harbour Street. An earthquake or something serious (Zeus throwing a tantrum?) had done away with any sign of a harbour. It was a lovely oddity.

What can I say in so few words about the biggest Roman archaeological site in the Eastern Mediterranean? (And that's saying something!) Thanks to Deniz the Meniz and Zeus I got to see it.

Soon we were off again and climbing up a small mountainside. Why? Deniz, who'd never struck me as religious said he wanted to show us an Islamic shrine. Okay. Before I had time to even consider what that might be, we pulled up at a very pretty, isolated spot in the shade of lovely trees. A lone man sat beside a stone structure that appeared to be an ornate tunnel entrance leading into and under a small forest beyond.

But no! It wasn't a tunnel entry. Believe it or not this Islamic shrine was the tiny House of the Virgin Mary. Who knew? Like all good stories it's disputed but the story goes that St. John brought her here to fulfil his promise he made to Jesus to 'care for her'.

Since I was a small kid I've known that everything's a story and history is a heap of them. My grandad told me. He also warned me not to get stuck in one.

For months we'd been seeing larger than life evidence of warring factions everywhere. Forts, castles and walls built by a million invaders and travellers convinced me my grandad was right. What I realised right now was that all of those marauders and tradesmen carried their favourite stories with them, and the stories that caused the most harm were the ones they'd got stuck in.

After years in the telling these stories and their tellers had lost the plot! History and Religion picked and chose the bits they liked; deleted bits and embellished bits in exactly the same way as the original tellers had done.

That's why I was only vaguely surprised that Islam and Christianity shared this shrine. I was genuinely surprised that such a place existed though. Being brought up a Catholic you'd think someone might have mentioned Mary ended up in Turkey! Not so. I learned that she gets more mentions in the Koran than in the Bible.

All this naturally took me back to Father Christmas. Deniz was telling us earlier that the 4th-century Bishop gave all his wealth away to help the poor, especially children. See what I mean? I can imagine the makers of modern Christmas in the west saying, "Oh. We like that bit. We'll have that bit and since Jesus came from the East too, we'll keep the stable, the manger, the donkeys and the wise men on camels. They can all stay."

The House of Mary was nonetheless beautiful in its simplicity and tranquillity.

Outside again in the sunshine and Deniz announced our next leg of the journey was at least three hours. "Were we happy with that?"

"Um? Let me think. Where else was it I had to be? Oh yeah. Nowhere."

We intrepid three were trundling and rolling along when we took a sudden corner. What?

There, right before my eyes, in among some trees and close to a very roughly-built snack shack someone had plonked a massive wooden horse. Oh! Gotcha! This has to be Troy. Get me! I was lunching at Troy.

Just like that, in a remarkably dusty, dried-dirt car park, I found myself in the pages of Heinrich Schliemann's favourite boyhood stories! Stories of the Trojan War and the Iliad. For one brief moment I caught that buzz and tingle Heini must have felt one hundred years before me, when those treasured boyhood stories sprang to life, right here. Food first though.

I had to laugh. Who wouldn't? We were tucking in to some delicious kebabs and lemonade when a small urchin (and that's exactly the right word!) sidled up to me and stared at me with his doleful, large eyes. He held out his hand and said a number in Turkish that I couldn't catch. In the palm of his hand was an ancient coin he had just this minute found. Did I want to buy it? Nice try my boy. Nice try.

What's a girl to do? There weren't exactly swarms of tourists and I admired his ingenuity. I closed his tiny fingers back around his treasure, pulled out a Turkish note and tucked it in his pocket. His grin widened. Deniz shooed him away. The loveable rascal ran, stopped, came back, placed the fake coin by my plate and ran away again. Sweet.

Pat and Deniz were determined to walk around the site. Not me. I took the lazy way. I climbed up the ladder between the horse's back legs (and that's not a sentence I get to use too often) to get an overview of the site. I knew Schliemann and his crew had found level upon level of settlement here right from the Bronze Age but even still the site was confusing. There was no wooden walkway around it as there is today and the humps and bumps of oddly-shaped hillocks and mounds shouted that there was still some digging to be done. I was thrilled though. This is where Odysseus set off on his epic journey back to Ithaca and Penelope. I could relate to that. I was on my own epic journey, wasn't I?

Back in the shack I ordered a coffee and spotted an English newspaper. It made me curious. Well, what do you know? The old country was experiencing its worst drought for decades and yawn, yawn something called The Cod Wars were going on. Inside I read about a new rock band called Queen. I guessed by the time I got home they'd be yesterday's news. The same went for some outfit called Abba from Sweden. Nothing to make me homesick then! Not missing anything.

We were off again. Deniz wanted to get to Assos where he had family to visit. Where we were going to stay the night? We couldn't care less.

Settled in with his family Deniz was beaming. Once again the family decided our fate. Late evening they drove us in an old jeep to the fantastical little fishing harbour of Sivrice. A quaint little restaurant was nestled alongside the sea. Only a small wall separated the few old wooden tables with their check cloths and small lanterns, from a tiny strip of sand just four feet below the veranda. Food was cooking and our spirits high.

In the dark of night the jeep climbed and climbed until we came to a small, wooden house not big enough to be a barn. This was our home for the night. With comfortable mattresses and oil lamps lit we were more than ready for sleep. Zeus blew out the lights.

We woke to the sound of the jeep's horn and gobsmacking views of the sea below.

After a lazy morning we famous three arrived in that magical house in Assos where I knew that Santa Claus spent his free time. The little house I mentioned quite some pages ago. Remember? We've come full circle.

Wham! Bam! Byzantium.

I never did get to grips with who the Byzantines were exactly. I wasn't losing any sleep over it. I was in the Orient!

I don't know about you but sometimes I play at seeing my life from above. You don't? Oh well, it takes all sorts. I don't do it often but occasionally the mood takes me. You know the old rumour that your whole life flashes in front of your eyes in a second as you're dying? Well, me? Sometimes I imagine a huge Maggie with a handheld camera filming the whole affair called my life. I can play parts of it back to myself from time to time. D'you know what I always say after I've watched a long bit? I always end up saying, "This is so badly edited. There's absolutely no continuity."

After an age of empty beaches, forests, the sea (and most recently, being driven through the Old Testament in an orange, soft-top Beamer), arriving slap in the centre of Istanbul struck me as one of those 'poor continuity' moments.

As soon as we hit this sprawling metropolis my senses were bombarded. They were bombarded by dazzling colours, mouth-wateringly new aromas, exotic sounds and the general buzz of that distinct energy given off by masses of people living together in one place. Hanging over it all was that wonderful and unmistakeable salty scent of the sea.

It was sad saying goodbye to Deniz. Relationships of any sort get a lot more intense a lot quicker on the road than in normal, everyday life. On the other hand I felt that high of being free again; of my life and whereabouts being back in my own hands; of that thrill of not knowing what comes next. When he wasn't looking, we stashed a small roll of Turkish Lire in the car glove compartment before hugging our goodbyes.

I half- expected to see Aladdin walking down the winding, back alleys where Deniz had dropped us off. At least I wasn't expecting a reindeer! The quirky, cobbled ways rose and dipped and rambled. I'd be bitterly disappointed later if I didn't hear the cry of "New lamps for old" from our cheap, seedy hotel window or at least catch a glimpse of a few magic carpets flying overhead. I know. I know it's cheesy and naive but give me a break! I was young and impressionable then (as opposed to now when I'm just impressionable.)

We couldn't wait to get out and about. Pat knew her history. Founded as Constantinople in 335 A.D, this place fell to the Ottomans in 1435. Some size! Some history or what? Old Constantine would have been rendered speechless to witness the mayhem and magnitude we found ourselves let loose in. For heaven's sake! We'd hit the Silk Road.

Our tall, narrow and very old hotel was tucked away down a side-street only a stone's throw from the Blue Mosque. We wasted no time on checking in, dumping our stuff to rush out of the room and back downstairs. We never actually made it through the front door, not at the first attempt anyway. Curiosity got the better of me. Just before the aged, wooden exit door was another one, off to the left. It wasn't actually a door, more of a doorway. Some incredibly worn stone steps led down to somewhere. It was impossible to see where exactly because the stairway curved to cut off our vision. It smelt all crumbly, dank and old. It felt old. We couldn't resist.

We were below pavement level from the very start but the steps kept going and going, down, down and down. So did we. Strangely, it never got so dark that we couldn't see. That kept us going. Daylight was coming in from somewhere below us. Intriguing. Even more intriguing was a faint sound of running water. We could tell it wasn't a tap flowing but couldn't work it out. Then, wow! Just wow!

We stepped out into what might have been a bath-house. Daylight was flooding in from a grating high overhead. I assumed this was what was meant by Turkish Baths but the faded mosaics on the walls and floors were a lot like the Roman stuff we'd seen. Spinning around, we saw this room was only a part of something once much bigger. To our right the ceiling was a massive half-dome that had been chopped off abruptly then plastered over. The patterns and figures on the gorgeous designs were only part-there at the edges. To our left was a large rectangular stone basin or bath. It was made up of a million tesserae too and had also been chopped. Its leaping fish collided with a solid flat wall.

No-one ever used this place now. That much was clear. At the far end an extraordinary stone wall-fountain had a carved sun face as its water spout. That was the source of the running water we'd heard. The water dripping from it was disappearing, draining away into the base of the bath. It must be finding its way out but heaven knows how. The echo in this chamber was fabulous. I played at being senator Carunculous Flatulence for a while, shouting my demands for shampoo and soap. I will never forget the feel of that strange cellar. Could it actually have been the remains of an original Roman bath-house? I'll never know. Maybe it's better that way.

We made our way back up to what passed as a lobby and stepped into the alleyway. There was only one place we could go, wasn't there? We headed for the Blue Mosque.

After those past months of boat rides and being in places on earth where the car was still a rarity, traffic seemed a ridiculous invention. A city seemed a strange concept too. I guess you have to live outside of them for some considerable time before you can see cities for the insanity they truly are. Even on that first afternoon I could feel the world shrinking; its new boundaries reduced and defined by the city limits. For the many souls hurrying about? This was their world. It had everything they needed to keep body and soul together and keep them entertained or at least preoccupied enough to avoid thinking about what they might be missing. For us? This was the East!

Around that first corner an enormous tree-lined square heralded the vast and majestic building. It stood about 140 feet high. On that day afternoon sun rays were targeting the enormous mosque and turning its blueness into glaring orange, piece by piece. The rays were gradually painting the vast, patterned dome with fire. We knew one thing. We'd have to wait to go inside. We needed some fabric to tie around ourselves as skirts and some larger headscarves. It could all wait.

For me our stay in Istanbul swirls into a kaleidoscope of startling images in my memory. I suppose the kaleidoscope analogy lingers because of the fragmentation cities tend to bring and because of the millions of intricate, Islamic patterns that greeted us wherever we looked. Islamic artwork is not only intricate but is composed of tiny contrasting bits and twirls like the specks in those childhood toys. All of this imagery was in the architecture, on fabrics, on the walls, on ceramics, in cafes, and reflected in the ever-present water running through the city; a vast waterway where enticing, lantern-lit and oddly-shaped boats played at being restaurants. They sent out their delicious smells and magical music as their unique contribution to the whole, heady carousel.

We walked as far as the massive bridge, the real gateway where East meets West. From there the city looked alive and full of coloured light; illuminated minarets and mosques, standing tall against the sky-line allowed us no doubt about it. This was a world far, far different to old Europe. It was exhilarating. It was awe-inspiring. I couldn't believe I was here.

In my mental kaleidoscope I can see me standing, twirling inside the Blue Mosque, its turquoise blue and white patterned interior bedazzling. I am staring up at the dome and quietly singing the word 'Alhemdoo.' (Praise Be). It can only be in places as wonderful as this that Arabic vowel sounds come into their own. The acoustics of this glorious place were designed and fashioned for maximum reverberation. Any utterance called out directly under the dome carries on and on and on. My own word echoed and echoed and echoed. The purpose, it is said, is that I might pray a thousand prayers at once.

I twist my memory toy as I write and, through the pinhole that time permits, see myself so clearly walking along avenue after avenue

in the cavernous, high-ceilinged and chaotic Grand Bazaar: Along
avenues where sack is piled upon sack, every one overflowing with
strange, brightly- coloured spices: Then more and more avenues where
men rest on their haunches, slowly rocking back and forth, waiting to
make a sale. Each shop front is no shop front at all. It's the entrance to
a cave jam-packed with crockery, ceramics, fruit, vegetables, carpets,
leather goods, rugs, tapestries, fabrics, metal-ware, wooden crafts,
jewellery, pots, pans, coats and jackets. Everything is everywhere. It's
all crammed in. It's hanging. It's propped up. It's precarious and it's
overpowering. The colours oh! The colours! Deep darks and lighter
terra cottas, rich greens and mellow vibrant blues, lush reds and dusky
yellows paint pots of all shapes and sizes or clothing even. What a
stroke of luck it was that I was travelling and travelling light. I wanted
to buy everything immediately and all at once.

Then I turn the wheel on my magic kaleidoscope for my mind's
eye to spy the endless, winding back streets where men with few teeth
sat at outdoor tables, smoked their hookahs and played weird-looking
games that made them shout suddenly and laugh raucously. I can
recall the street sounds, the children squealing, the cars beeping and
honking and that unmistakeably Eastern music blaring from overhead
verandas or from inside the murky depths of small cafes squeezed in
among the crowded housing.

At night in our little, sparse room we talked about the onset of
winter and the need to 'top up' the old money pot. It was great being
free again but it meant thinking about practicalities. There was no
way of knowing where our next jobs would come from or when. All
the world over city life is expensive. We couldn't afford to risk it. We
couldn't afford to stay here for long. We decided we'd keep going
east. Iran was our preferred destination. In the bottom of my pack I
had that letter of introduction. My Iranian friend had said there were
plenty of opportunities to teach English and to make good money in
Tehran. Tehran it was then. We'd spend three more days here. We had
a train journey to negotiate and arrange somehow.

For those next three days we walked and walked. I never once felt
threatened or at any risk in Istanbul. The people were friendly, kind
and generous. They couldn't do enough to help us. The man who
owned and ran our hotel took a liking to us, his 'Two English ladies.'

He took it upon himself to bring us breakfast every morning and left it outside our room each day with a 'tap, tap' on the door.

He also introduced us to his nephew George. They both reckoned that someone who spoke English would come in handy. They were right. George took us to a small railway station help us book tickets for Iran. He also took us into a fabulous tea shop inside the main Bazaar. We'd never have found it in a million years. I felt like Lauren Bacall as we sat in this café with walls and floors of brightly-coloured marble tiles. It was made more beautiful by a fountain at its centre and wrought iron trellises laden with vines that served as partitions for the clientele. Bring on the belly-dancers I say! No, sadly not.

When he went to place our breakfast order with the waiter, I stopped him. I was confident I could order it in Turkish. George was a bit taken aback. They whispered among themselves. It was my turn to be surprised. The guy turned and walked away. He did come back of course. He came back with a stout wooden stool that he placed right by the fountain. Then, panic, George told me "If you stand here on the stool and order in Turkish language, we eat and drink free." So I did. Everyone in the place applauded and howled with laughter. "What did I say? Oh-no! What did I say?"

George was chuckling along with the rest of the crowd. "No. Perfect. Perfect but you know? You sound so cute. You sound like a young child who has maybe 4 years old. Like you are only learning to speak! Wonderful." It dawned on me. I'd just sung for my supper!

I could go on and on about the tourist sights of Istanbul but you know what? In the end travel comes down to the people we meet and all the unexpected delights that present themselves if we let them. For instance George insisted that on our last evening in his city, we go on a boat trip up the Bosporus. I ask you. How could a girl (or two) say no to that?

That Train!

Play along with me for a moment. I'd like you to think of the words 'Train Journey' and what images they conjure up. I can imagine what they are. When you've considered carefully and have a clear picture in your mind's eye, I'd like you to wipe it out. Erase it. Press mental 'delete' and forget you ever had it. There is no way on earth that your imagination comes anywhere close to the train journey we had from Istanbul to Tehran. Think old films, think about a time when Great Britain held the Raj and imagine trains are a comparatively new and rather splendid invention. There were things called compartments on trains. These were immensely commodious and self-contained rooms to travel in. At most 6 people sat in these and had more than ample room to swing a cat. "Divine Daphne! Why not swing two? "

Eight compartments made a carriage and roughly ten carriages made a train. Carriages were linked to each other by couplings that were huge metal nuts and bolts to be basic. Every carriage had a long corridor running along beside its compartments. Windows were in abundance and sashed and passengers flung their heads out of them willy-nilly; when the spirit moved.

You can work it out! The average train was designed to carry about 500 people (give or take) including the railway staff. This was luxury. There was sometimes a bar and always a restaurant car that catered for a body's every need. Toilets weren't in short supply either. You might, if you were finicky, grumble about legroom but, on the whole, the service was par excellence.

This was the style of train that was standing waiting for us to carry us to Iran. I use the term 'style of train' because ours had seen far better days. The restaurant car was long gone as was the concept of luxury. Toilets were few and far between as it happens and so were staff. Apart from those minor differences the train brought back a few memories of the '50s. What altered the whole experience beyond recognition were the hordes of multi-coloured, multi-national, multi-luggaged and multi-lingual travellers currently amassing in the concourse of Istanbul Railway station that morning. Never in a million years was this mass going to fit into that one train. There must be some mistake, right? Wrong!

How naïve can a girl be?

To be honest, someone had been thoughtful enough to add on about 10 more carriages and 'okay, okay' that meant 80 more compartments. But that meant more people could pack themselves into the thing so no amount of added space was ever going to be enough.

By the time we were on the train there were ten of us squashed into our compartment made for six. Presumably this was the same in every compartment because the corridor was full. Like in some nightmare scene from a yet-to-be-written sci-fi thriller (presumably expounding the perils of Earth's over-population) noses, hand palms and flattened cheeks were pressed up against the compartment glass right next to me.

The bustle and noise was unlike anything the original Victorians could ever have imagined. I was having a hard time imagining it and I was in it!

Like grains of sand in a bizarre hourglass they must have shaken themselves into unseen corners because, as we set off, they had dispersed and settled enough for me to see out. Looking around our own little haven of a compartment, we were ten in all. Of course there was supposed to be enough room to seat people comfortably but hey! It's astonishing how insignificant comfort seems when you have more important things on your mind... like surviving.

Each of us looked around. The word I would use is stealthily. We each sneaked a crafty glance at the others and then put our heads down as if contemplating something incredibly important. I have no idea why we went through this ritual. We all knew that we all knew that we all knew we were here for the duration. Yep. We all knew this was it for two days or more. The timetables didn't bother about specifics.

If I had simply told you "I travelled from Istanbul to Tehran by train for two days many years ago," you might have gone all misty-eyed and become slightly envious. No need. Seriously. No need. If you would rather hold that notion, read no further.

I have to admit though. It was packed with the most hilarious little scenarios that are unforgettable. At times I laughed until it physically hurt.

Where was I? Oh yes, in our compartment. Directly opposite me (and also by the sliding door to the corridor) was a chubby, clean-shaven, Cheshire cat –grinning Afghani. Don't ask me how old he was. He just was. He wore one of those funny little astrakhan hats on top of a head that seemed perfectly spherical and was lit by two huge, almond eyes brim full of mischief. He sat with his flat palms on his knees, legs slightly opened and clothed in wonderful baggy trousers. I got to know him well even though we never spoke. I daresay he remembers me just as well and is to this day somewhere up in the Hindukush, telling anecdotes about me and that train ride. You see he and I were directly opposite one another for hour upon hour upon hour. He remained a bit of a mystery.

To my right was my companion Pat and on from her three Aussies, young guys heading to India and 'full of it'. That leaves the five on the far side. There were three men from Britain (the North to be precise). Two of them were young and the other was past retirement age. The second mystery man among us was a Pakistani who also kept remarkably quiet, only speaking when spoken to. I imagined him to be a business man of some sort but why? I'm not sure.

We'd brought a mountain of bread and cheese, fruit, quite a lot of cake, some sweets to suck and a dozen or more bottles of water and um…more cake. Most of this was crammed into our rucksacks on the creaking overhead luggage rack. We had water purification tablets too. The one thing we never wanted to do was to run out of water.

For the first few hours everyone did what most people do on crowded trains. Some of us were reading, some chatting quietly and some just idly watching the landscape fly by outside. Strangely, we were all acting as if we were on some brief jolly to the seaside for the day or some such. Perhaps the thought of more than 48 hours in each other's company was a bit too much for our human brains to contemplate.

With a little bit of manoeuvring and a lot of courage we could get out into the corridor to reach the bathroom. At first it was clean and the tap water was cold enough to wake us up a bit. You will have guessed from that the 'at first' slipping in there, that things were about to go pear-shaped.

The reserved 'I don't know you so I'll behave' attitude didn't last more than a morning. The Aussies had been dying to quiz the Afghani about any possibility of dope to get them through this ride. They were loud but they were hilarious. To every loud question they asked him, the little man rolled his wonderful big eyes and the edges of his mouth turned up a little more. "What's in there?" One of them pointed at the mysterious and very cumbersome cloth bundle over the man's head and asked. "Aw c'mon mate? Whatcha got in there, eh? Eh?" What possessed him at that precise moment to imagine an Afghani would come close to understanding English, let alone a bastardised version, remains one of life's unanswerable questions. The Afghani stared at him like a child might when a parent first refuses to buy a lollipop. His expression was friendliness personified with a hint of non-understanding mixed with charm. They wouldn't let it rest.

From where I sat he looked like a man who could play to a crowd. When he was ready and they were gagging, he put a finger to his lip and in conspiratorial mode beckoned them close to him as he fumbled in his pocket. They got off their seats and huddled around him to stare. He pulled out a small, gold trinket-type box and lifted the lid slowly. They stared some more. He took out a pinch of the substance in the box and theatrically sniffed it before breaking it into three and handing them each a tiny piece. Then he stuck his own piece up his nose and snorted it. They followed suit.

For the next twenty minutes they spluttered, choked, wheezed, bellowed and sneezed until their faces went crimson and their eyes watered. In a flash the little guy was gone, vanished, disappeared for now anyway. The rest of us cracked up laughing.

Back in those days it was cheaper to travel around with a student identity card. In some countries it made travel up to as much as 50% cheaper. By the time the ticket- collector arrived, we were a good day into our journey so we all knew a bit about each other. The Brits were from Newcastle in Northern Britain. They were miners who'd gone through the fights and squabbling around pit closures and taken early retirement. The oldest guy looked like Captain Birdseye. He was seventy, long white beard, curly shoulder-length white hair and a weathered old face. The Aussies were in their late twenties and did not show any signs of a formal education. They struck me more as what we used to call 'Jack-the-Lads.' As for the Pakistani and the mysterious Afghani? Who could tell? They were definitely not students though. Enter the ticket-collector.

The lamb to the slaughter stuck his head inside our compartment and sang,

"Tick- itz."

Everyone held theirs up. After he'd looked at them all he could see they were all reduced price, thought about it and asked "Eh-Stew Dents?" We all rummaged.

That was the moment folks. That was when I pulled out my virgin poker face. I had to. We all needed that face. I knew what was coming. Laughter was rising in me. My face began to melt and distort in anticipation. I dare not look at my travelling companions in case eye contact made me crack. My mind was scanning like crazy. I'd set it the exceedingly important task of finding something, anything, any memory of a funeral or an appalling film to help me get back my serious, innocent head and face. Great! What did it come up with as reference aid to my present predicament? A short film of the first time I ever peed myself laughing. Ain't the human mind a wonderful thing? I daren't lift my gaze. I had to.

It was like we'd all rehearsed the rules of a crazy card game we'd invented. We held up our trump cards. I was gonna die if I cracked. I saw the cards -Video Club Member, Provisional Driving License, Food Coupon, Miners Union, Miners' Union, Library Card, Library Card and Diners' Club. Ours were the only ones even related to education. When the poor man left, we slid the door to, gave it a while to make sure he was out of earshot and then exploded with raucous laughter.

When the inspector had gone our Afghani returned. The Aussies were now convinced he was a smuggler. They started in on him about that.

An hilarious game of charades ensued to establish his chosen career path. The whole lot of us laughed when he kidded them along only to ultimately say, 'Pro-fesh-in-al-toor-ist.'

I can't honestly remember all those hours spent in that carriage. I know the buffet disappeared somewhere on the first day. Not long after that, the water dried up. Without water the toilets were stinking. We ate bread and cheese and cheese and bread and shared when things got desperate for the less prepared. The Afghani came and went. The Pakistani said less than ever. Even the Aussies were growing weary. Walks in the corridor were impossible. Almost every inch was sleeping bag with bodies in there somewhere. I slept fitfully and on opening my eyes the instinctive thought was "Oh no! I'm still on this train!"

I woke like that in the middle of the night once. Only the Pakistani and I were awake.

He looked at me and smiled a lovely kind smile. Then he whispered,

"This is the crazi-ness. Is it not? All of your peoples is going East. There they are saying 'I want to see east. I must be in East. East is most fabulous'. All of my peoples is going west. There they are saying, "I want to be in West. West is best. West is fabulous.' East, West, West East, everybody are coming, going, going coming, here, there, there here and when my peoples is arriving West, they are not happy. 'Where is the chapatti like my mother making? Why is this so rainy here?' Then when your peoples is arriving east they are saying, 'It is so hot here and where are the chips and fish like in my home?'…….. East, West always coming and going. What will be becoming of us all?"

It was the funniest but thoughtful rant I'd ever heard. He spoke calmly and with such a wry smile. I knew I'd remember his words forever. To finish off he asked me,

"What is the meaning of this? What is the point to it all?" We both knew it was rhetorical and settled back down to sleep.

A new day dawned. We were all feeling we couldn't go on for another minute. Then! The train slowed and ground very noisily to a halt. We obviously had to disembark but the scenery was what you might call 'the middle of nowhere'. It took ages for all the nearly dead bodies in the corridors to shake themselves and grab their stuff. The train that wouldn't die chugged away again, ever-slowly forward until there was …….. silence. We got off. Some people fell over. They hadn't used their legs for a while I guessed. I gazed straight ahead. What? Who put that there? Why didn't anyone tell me?

There was the most enormous lake. Clunky passenger boats were waiting to take us across.

This was Lake Wan.

Mayhem, Miser & Madness

If you were to ask me at the end of that journey how long it took I would've guessed about a millennium, give or take a few days. On second thoughts I would've guessed more like 500 years. What with the wait for the original train, the boat ride and then the second train into Tehran it was definitely about that. You think I jest? My passport was stamped at some point along the way. When I figured out Farsi numbers, the year we arrived was 1354. Okay so we went backwards.

Like all half-baked student ideas, perhaps it wasn't the sanest. It certainly seemed insane now anyway. We were standing outside a complete stranger's front door, down a long alleyway some 2000 or more miles from home and clutching a scrap of paper scribbled on three years earlier by an Iranian friend at graduation ceremony. But, here we were. We chuckled at the realisation of what we were actually doing. Then we giggled at the thought of, 'it could have been worse.' We could have just turned up and said, "Ali sent us."

Whatever our circumstance, a young woman in full veil opened the door. Our intention was to give them greetings and news from their son in England then ask them for a few guidelines about cheap accommodation and agencies for work teaching English. We never imagined in thirteen hundred and fifty-four years that this would be our home for two weeks. But then we didn't know what hospitality means in this corner of the planet. A guest is an honour. The guest has to ask to leave; no-one else would so much as imply they should leave. We found that out in our first few days. It's a good job we did. I'd still be living there now some 664 years later.

We slowly got to know the Reza family. Their kindness and generosity knew no bounds. In fact, they were all so generous and so kind it was almost embarrassing. They wouldn't take any money towards anything or take 'no' for an answer. If we were friendly enough to compliment them on say, an ornament or an item of clothing, they immediately offered it to us. After a while we had a running joke that went, 'Never tell an Iranian you like his haircut.'

So we'd made a start. This was our crazed introduction to the metropolis called Tehran.

It's a bit of a blur now but thinking about it? It was a bit of a blur then. I have strong mental images of our two new friends, our allotted guides, Shahram and Amir. They were two cousins who had a car to take us here, there and everywhere. Their English wasn't brilliant but it passed. They were most definitely Anglophiles.

Every day they were proud to show us around their city. Strangely, among the many and more famous sights, I recall a tarmacked slope where we sat in the car and turned the engine off. Shahram lifted the handbrake off too. The car defied gravity. Instead of rolling back down the hill, it moved very, very slowly upwards. Don't ask me where it was or if it was an illusion. I don't know. I just know we rolled upwards. Strange the things that register in the old brainbox. Let me give you a whirlwind introduction to the Tehran we entered way back then.

This metropolis was long, freshly-baked, pitted flatbread hanging from random trees, the sign of a bakery. The jubes (long wide gullies lining every road) that carried fresh- flowing melt-water from the mountains (in the north) on and on and through the city. The totally insane traffic where traffic-lights were mere ornaments, where green British double-deckers swayed ominously on corners, overloaded with crowds top and bottom.

It was cars and trucks attempting to avoid the jams by driving up onto pavements, where there were ornate, massive, brass water-turns on metal legs. These were to provide drinking water when summer heat was at its height. Shall I mention a baby lamb or stray goat- or- two wrapped around the base of these water fixtures? The animals were seeking shade for sure but also drinking any drips and accidental puddles. What about the crazy mopeds? Whole families, mum, dad, three kids and a baby-or-two on the back, risking life and limb in all the chaos? And then the ever-present, devil-may-care orange and black taxis who picked up anyone who stuck a hand out and shouted a place name somewhere vaguely on their route. Not enough of a picture? Throw in the odd long, meandering camel train, bells jingling as it lolloped along the thoroughfares and determining the pace and flow the traffic. Such a train added a touch of colour. The camel drivers didn't give a hoot.

Turn up the volume! Somewhere in that soundtrack you'll be stopped short by the occasional, glorious 'call to prayer', the loud, haunting call of the unseen Muezzin in his minaret. His voice carried for miles. Yep. Welcome to Tehran.

Among all this, the Rezas provided a haven of calm and friendliness. Their house was far from affluent. There were no armchairs or sofas, no tables or upright chairs. Everything was carpeted and comfort was found in being seated, cross-legged on low, thin mattresses that also served as beds when the time came. We feasted on delicious home cooking of chickens, perfumed rice, incredible fruits, vegetables and a million homemade juices. Coming from a '70s Britain (where bananas were still the only exotic fruit available) I tasted fresh pomegranates for the first time and fell in love with all kinds of weird and wonderful fruits and nuts. Pistachio nuts were not 'ten a penny' but 'a ton a penny'. We ate them all the time. All of this food was piled on platters on a richly-patterned cloth stretched out over the living-room floor.

With Shahram and Amir's help we signed up with an agency and had teaching jobs at the Airport College within those first ten days. We also found a room to let with an American guy called Herman. Oh Herman! How could anyone ever forget Herman? The best that can be said of him was that he provided us with a LOT of laughs and introduced us to Joe. If he had known we had benefited from these, he would surely have sent us a bill. Get my drift?

Why do I include Herman? Herman has to feature. He epitomised the newly-found wealth of young Americans in Iran in that time period; far too much income and very little sense. He also struck me as a person I could use as a character if I ever achieved my dream of being a writer. That thought had never, ever struck me with respect to any one individual before. To explain the man is best done by verbal snapshots of what we three musketeers got up to under his roof. 'The Landlord's Manual' according to Herman roughly stated that 'tenants should know their place', be grateful for anything he may or may not receive 'and accept that a roof over their heads is enough. He genuinely believed that tenants should be neither seen nor heard.

Picture a reasonably modern kitchen with totally bare surfaces; the exception being a fruit bowl. Picture small post-it notes everywhere. The one on the fruit bowl says, "When I left for work this bowl contained 3 bananas, 2 apples, 19 pistachio nuts and 1 pomegranate." Now open any cupboard. The jars, packets and containers all have lines drawn on them and are dated so that Herman can tell at a glance if anyone else has used them. Joe Vasquez was to become one of my best mates. He was downright hilarious. His shock of thick, curly hair, full smile and Southern drawl all added to his charisma. We recognised each other as free spirits the instant we met.

He'd been living under the Herman regime for a month and was pretty fed up with it. When we arrived he was determined to find a better place to live for all three of us. Meanwhile we laughed our socks off at Herman's outrageous attitude to just about everyone and everything.

This may come as a shock but mid- September brought snow. I know, I know, it startled me too. I mention it because the house was freezing. We were freezing. Herman announced that he couldn't afford to put the heating on just yet. He followed up that gem with a request, "Are you guys around this afternoon? I'm looking for one of you to be here to accept delivery of my brand new Harley." Hilarious and unbelievable but the Harley got a room of its own with radiators on full. Yes! Subtlety wouldn't be a word you'd associate with old Herman.

Furniture in Iran was unusual. For some unknown reason the posh furniture available was all fashioned like something out of 17th-century France. Curly slender legs of chairs and sofas swept up to ornate upholstery backs and seats of a tapestry-type fabric that depicted courtly ladies in huge skirts and with head plumage worthy of Marie-Antoinette. It looked classy and expensive enough but it was all matchsticks. What it wasn't, was functional. Turned out the roofs and ceilings did a great impersonation of sturdiness too but that's another story. Why am I telling you all this?

To help you understand the straw that broke the camel's back and drove us to escape was a Halloween party. Herman had made an unusually friendly gesture. He called us together to talk about a Halloween party he was going to throw. My god! He was including us? After a long talk about how much food and booze he was getting and how many people were invited he threw us a curved ball (as Joe put it.) 'Would we mind giving him a hand decorating the place in Halloween style? 'Now the penny seemed to have dropped that we weren't Untermenschen after all, we gave him a rip-roaring 'Yes.'

We three got into it big time. We bought cardboard and huge sheets of paper to create a painted old grandfather clock complete with creepy crawlies on it. We bought spray cobwebs; black and gold balloons. We cut out a huge cardboard mantel piece and painted that too. We bought blue, red and yellow lightbulbs and made paper designs of so-say red bricks and stones to stick onto the walls as if the plaster was decaying. We bought rubber spiders and glitter to scatter around. Come 8 p.m. on the night the place looked a-mazing. When the first two guests turned up we three were more than ready to PARTY.

Classic Herman. He turned to us 'all eager for the treat' and said, "So where are you three off to tonight?" You guessed it! We weren't invited.

With anyone else we would have objected. There was no point. The guy was a brick wall. We went upstairs and laughed like drains.

If you could have seen us later when the place was filling up you would have had to laugh too. We stuck our heads round the corner of the room at the very back; getting a guilty peek at what kind of people would have a Herman for a friend. We literally were in classic formation. Me, the smallest had my head close to the ground, Pat's face was just above mine and Joe peeped over the top of us.

We would have stayed for only a minute or- two but then we were all gripped by something about to happen. There was no need to say a thing. We all knew what we were waiting for.

An enormously overweight friend of our Scrooge commented that she was feeling a bit giddy and another guest was dragging out one of Madame La Pompadour's chairs for her to sit on. All three of us stifled a gasp. She didn't sit on it immediately. She edged towards it, got distracted, edged closer to it and stopped and stood right by it. She could build suspense like a master horror writer. We knew what was gonna happen the instant her enormous butt hit the tapestry.

The suspense got too much. My chuckling and snorting started without my permission. Joe stuck his hand over my mouth. He whispered "Sh! Maggie Loo. We're getting to the good bit."

The elephantine beauty hovered. She lowered herself down in the belief she was going to sit. The chair didn't stand a chance. It splintered magnificently. We ducked back out sight and took a deep breath.

Everyone had run to her aid. Two or three people were trying to get her back on her feet. She was mortified. All she kept saying was 'Sorry. I'm so sorry.'

And what did Herman say to her apologies? What a Herman would say of course.

"It's okay. It's okay. Don't worry about breaking it. Don't worry about it now. We can settle the bill tomorrow."

We got upstairs to Joe's room as fast as we could run, shut the door and burst out laughing. Within two days Joe had found us all a better home, nearer to the centre. We decided to do a moonlight flit, to leave without paying our rent and with no warning whatever. On the night we were to escape Herman had gone away for the night.

I hope you can forgive us but we did a very bad thing. Armed with cotton-wool and superglue we hollowed out bananas, pomegranates and pistachios in the fruit bowl. We scoffed the lot and stuffed them all with the cotton wool, then glued all the skins and shells back together. We never saw him again.

The Shah and My Part in his Downfall

Take a hundred or more impoverished Western travellers bent on seeing the world but having to find work. Mix them up and spread them out into say, six or seven bedroomed mansions dotted about an alien city. Tell them you are going to pay them more money than they could ever imagine and watch as they all magically turn into English language teachers. We're not done yet.

Put them in the Middle East, let's say Tehran, Iran and let's (just for the fun of it) put them teaching on the Imperial Air Force Base and in charge of the language skills of hundreds and hundreds of air force cadets who have rarely seen Westerners let alone women! And those women are teaching them. Let's imagine these cadets come from poor, rural backgrounds and are gobsmacked at the situation they now find themselves in. But wait! There's much more to be stirred into this mix.

This is a country where alcohol is banned and dope is so abundant that it grows on trees. To be more precise, it's in trees along the four-lane dual carriageway that crosses through the city, a thoroughfare lined with trees that have large holes in them and where the local inhabitants stash their wares. It's where guys amble along and casually thrust a left hand out to dart inside the hollow and produce a lump of hashish the size of an average chocolate bar. But hey! It's legal and alcohol is not. 'When in Rome' as they say. You're beginning to get a handle on life in Tehran. Your mental image of it is building nicely, isn't it?

There are only one or two things you need to know to clue you in totally. None of us wanted to invest our ill-gotten gains in the type of clothing required to act the teacher. This resulted in jackets, ties, shoes and even trousers being passed from one bus to another as they crossed at the exit gate at change of shift. Oh and the English we were teaching was the American kind.

There are also British double-decker buses and a lot of Asians involved. The Asians were teaching English too and needed a considerable amount of help with linguistics. Muggins here got a reputation as being one of the very few qualified English teachers. How did this affect me? Remember the double-decker bus bit? Every morning I was captive on the upper deck. It was always carrying way too many people both downstairs and up. It swayed ominously, leaning over on corners. I use the word 'captive' because the Asians always had something, some point of grammar that needed explaining before they could even attempt to teach it. At 7 a.m. when I was still blurry- eyed and only barely in possession of my faculties, a typical tirade might be:

"What is the meaning of 'My watch is running slow'? I mean, I am understanding each and every word but this is not sense. How can a watch be running and then how can running be slow? It is not even helping if I am changing the slow to slowly, adverb, huh?"

Is there any explaining the vagaries of English let alone the American kind?

The Air Force base ultimately became known as The Home for Aspiring Parrots. The language teaching system we were expected to use involved a set of about 25 books working upward from simple to the more advanced. It was all American- English and involved an awful lot of repetition, an awful lot of repetition. No. I mean an awful lot of repetition. Follow it through! I dare you. What it meant was that set dialogues were repeated hour after hour after hour and day after day. First the individuals were asked to repeat something and then the group took over. The aim was to drill these guys until new vocabulary and phrases became the stuff of their dreams.

An unforeseen consequence was that it inevitably backfired. We all drilled ourselves in the process. Book 1 for example,

"Hi/Hi/ How are you? / How are you? / Fine thanks/ Fine thanks/ Where are you from? Where are you from?-"

See what I mean? Enough. Let's skip to book 3 or 4 where conversations got a bit juicier.

"Let's go for a picnic/ Let's go for a picnic/ Sure/Sure/ I can bring sandwiches/ I can bring sandwiches/ Peanut butter and jello would be good/ Peanut butter and jello would be good."

Okay cut to the more advanced, say Book 22.

Crossing the parade ground or navigating a corridor I often encountered one of the top brass. We both knew which book he was on. The first words out of his mouth were the dead giveaway. "It's a great morning." Completely by-passing any part of my brain my mouth wanted to utter the next line of that set dialogue. "Why yes it is. What are your plans for the day?" Since it was more than a bit inappropriate to ask such a thing of an officer, I'd bite my tongue, nod and then giggle later. Everyone on the base was suffering from ICTWBYO. (I can tell what book you're on.) We couldn't stop the recitations even when we were at home. Even a hint of one of those dialogues and the ensuing conversation was rattled off by whoever was within earshot.

The real insanity kicked in when American-English was impossible for even the Brits among us. It could get extremely annoying. The general set-up was that each class was three hours long. For one of those hours a massive, reel-to-reel tape machine was wheeled into the classroom. We teachers could give our vocal chords a bit of a rest. Things could go pear-shaped real fast. (I couldn't resist that Americanism even now).

Imagine spending two long and repetitive hours on the fascinating topic of the sound 'o' as in clock. Pretty straightforward, you think? Think again. Those tedious first two hours of drilling the relevant vocabulary and dialogues involving that specific vowel sound are wiped out in an instant. On the tape you hear, "Today's sound is the sound 'Aaaaaah' as in 'Cl-aaaaaaaah-k'. Best give up. Most of us did.

The ensuing mayhem was intensified by the thin wooden walls separating our classrooms. One day I could hear my boyfriend Michael next door. I heard him shouting 'Goalposts' then 'Score', and other football related words. Naturally I heard the group repetition too. That was odd. I knew which number book he was on and those words were conspicuous by their absence. At the end of the shift he had some explaining to do. His baby pilots had been asking about certain parts of the female anatomy. Now the football analogies made sense. My guess is that even today there are retired Iranian fighter pilots who snicker to think they know the English slang that makes for an interesting love life.

We only worked six hours a day. Six hours can be a very long time when it's spent repeating everything you say ad infinitum. I caught myself once and laughed. I started out the day by drilling, 'What am I doing?' First thing in the morning it rang out as a cheerful invocation to any language learner to engage in conversation. I don't need to say, do I? How the intonation and emphasis in that three word question can so radically change the underlying meaning?

Never mind. A six hour day with an early start meant we had more than enough time to get up to shenanigans. One particular afternoon Mike and I decided to teach ourselves the local lingo of Farsi. We began with the Arabic script. A couple of hours and we were sure we had this in the bag. To our completely stoned minds it seemed like a great idea to get a taxi into the city and test each other out. There must be simple things we could phonetically read.

Tehran being Tehran, obstacle one proved a challenge. We had to negotiate the rigmarole of hailing a taxi. Stick out a hand and shout where we were going. These were communal taxis so you took your chances. We hailed easily. Thank heavens. It was empty. Mike felt brave enough to sit upfront. I got the back seat.

This was a furry cave. Cabs were wallpapered with that shaggy, nylon, electrifying fabric so beloved of the 1970s. There should have been a law against it especially its eyeball- denting bright blues, reds and shocking purples. Hanging and swinging from everywhere in the cave were market-stall loads of beads and dangling bits and bobs. The soundtrack was eastern and most usually pop but always deafeningly loud. I wished I hadn't had that last joint. I was suddenly riding in a furry cave ducking and diving and swerving through the insanity of downtown Tehran's traffic. I gulped. I could handle this. I had this.

Then wouldn't you know it? We stopped. Two women, veiled from head to toe, jumped in on either side of me. All I could see were their eyes. Who wouldn't think of Cousin It in the Addams Family?' Mike looked around and turned away instantaneously. That glimpse was enough for me to see me in the back seat through his eyes. He was about to explode with laughing at the image. He was shaking, trying to fend it off. That didn't help my cause one iota. We survived. We got out in Tehran central.

He went first. "Okay then. Pick some writing, any writing and sound it out."

I looked up and I stared around. Ah ha! In huge electric, neon lights I saw...from right to left, the letter k. I pronounced 'kuh', feeling pretty damn smug. Then the next letter, 'Oh hello it's another 'kuh' and another 'kuh'? What the?' At this point, for those of you who don't know, anything about Arabic languages, they don't use vowels much. You supply the initial vowel sound and the rest follow suit. Let me give you the example of an Arabic word we use in English 'b.n.n.' If I supply an 'uh' sound after the first b then I create 'bununuh' which is ...you got it! Banana. Once you've put that first vowel sound all the others match. That's how easy it is to spot Arabic words that have come into English.

I persevered. The second word didn't end with anything I recognised but then I got it! Duh, duh! The last consonant was an L so 'luh'. I was pretty proud of working that out. I strung my scholarly findings together and said it out loud. "Kuh, kuh, kuh, luh."

We split a gut laughing. We were absolutely helpless. We fell about.

Right next to the neon letters I'd chosen. There in glorious technicolour but more importantly in flashing, moving neon lights and standing some 15 or 20 feet high was a bottle of Coca Cola being filled and poured by the magic of the dazzling light display.

"Okay smart ass." I said when we got ourselves together. "You find something trickier." We were gonna pick up some Farsi vocabulary by this method if we had to die in the attempt.

Mike decided the best place to look was down a side road. We wandered into a busy one and we found ourselves among colourful stalls with food sellers cooking all kinds of delicacies on large bright braziers. After a while Mike got cocky. "All right then. I'm gonna pick a hand-written sign. Here's one." We stood by the stall. He began.

"Huh" he sounded out an h with real glee. You could've been forgiven for thinking he'd found El Dorado. "Yeah! It's an h. It's an h. He sounded it out again .huh….no, no, don't tell me, and don't tell me mm for 'm'. I'm on a roll now. That's a b as in 'buh', oh my god that's an r. What the?" He struggled for a bit with the g that came next but he got it. Then at the end came rrrruh and sss.

"Okay. Here we go huh, um, buhrrrr, guh, rrrrs."

Yes. In his infinite scholasticism Michael had discovered that he was standing right next to a hum-bur-ger stall!

The smell filling the alleyway should have been a big enough clue all along really. We abandoned all hope of getting fluent in Farsi, for that day anyway. I couldn't stop laughing again all of a sudden. He asked me what was so funny now.

"You were right back there you know? When you said you were on a roll."

We aimed for the central bazaar and some telepathic backgammon with the mysterious and mystical old, toothless guys who adorned the chai shops and lured us in.

"What time have you got?" Mike asked

"I'm sorry. My watch is running slow."

"Shut up and pass me the hubble-bubble.

Ships that Pass

Funny but as I remember all this, my thoughts are wandering off at tangents. It's my book though so I'm allowed. I have absolutely no clue who coined the phrase 'memory lane'. It's glaringly obvious by now that I don't have one of those. I've got highways, byways and cul-de-sacs of memory that lead off all over the shop. Oh! I've just sussed where the idea of 'memory lane' came from – a narrow mind.

I'll take a diversion. This deserves to be said. I was talking about that dreadful electro-statically charged nylon that put in an appearance in the '70s. I have a vision of young bucks striding and strutting into discos in the transparent pretence of being god's gift to women. With hair reaching to their shoulders, handlebar moustaches and side-burns they convinced themselves they looked like Burt Reynolds, Ginger Baker or John Travolta.

Bri-nylon was the thing. Let's be brutally honest, the invention that should have stayed as the toothbrush it first was in the '30s got a bit out of hand in the '70s. Soon everything was made of it - socks, swimsuits, woollies, car upholstery, swimwear, jackets, the ubiquitous non-drip, non-wrinkle shirt and, most deadly of all, the carpets.

Those young bucks, dressed in bri-nylon from head to toe, would strut into a disco across the carpet and spark.

In the dark of the disco we could see the electrical discharges. Worse still, when you added those new, fandangled ultra-violet lights? The ones that made all things 'white' glow in the dark? Well you had sparking men dancing around with disembodied items of clothing from blouses and hairbands to shirts and trousers. The spectacle would give today's ghost hunters an orgasm. The staggering affects of ultra-violet lighting lost many a buck his chance of scoring. Dandruff is white.

Back in that earlier world of the '70s a train journey was a brilliant experience. Trains were the perfect place to meet a glorious and random selection of people. Amazing conversations were up for grabs. Sadly, the very layout of modern trains encourages isolation and escape into a personal bubble. The shell hardens with those dreaded little screens everyone holds. People thumb-dance their way to a destination and need never interact with the stranger.

In the '70s long corridors allowed a traveller to catch a glimpse of pockets of strangers' lives in different compartments. These were like little sitting-rooms where interaction could thrive.

Why do I even mention this? Because, the further east I travelled the more I realised I was armed with the wisdom of a high court judge. I would never have met him but for just such a compartment. I was on my way back to University once, on a very crowded Bristol Leeds train. On my long walk to the loo I saw that First Class was all but empty. I thought I'd try my luck.

I quite fancied a compartment with only one old guy in it. He looked a bit Dickensian. I moved in. Sure enough we started chatting. I'd never met a high court judge before. When the ticket-collector appeared, I knew my cover was about to be blown. My new friend reached in his pocket and pulled out his credentials. He flashed them at the inspector and said, "She's with me." I liked him.

Even at that age I'd noticed my life had a tendency to stray innocently into the pages of some novel or other. Right now I was momentarily caught up in John Buchan's 'The 39 Steps.'

Anyway, it was the time in Britain when the oil crisis struck. Ted Heath's three-day week was hitting hard. Driving was restricted to a maximum speed of 50m.p.h. even on motorways, and power cuts were pretty much par for the course. If memory serves me well, it was the time when the phrase Winter of Discontent was first commandeered to describe what we were all going through.

Of course the judge and I got round to politics and international relations. We talked about the Suss laws or stop-and-search, and a raft of other contemporary stuff.

I asked why marijuana was still illegal after the recent publication of Nixon's Shafer Report. Why was dope banned in some countries but booze banned in others? Who makes the rules round here? His answer made perfect sense to me. Not only did he tell me that the Shafer report had got the wrong answer and consequently been tossed in the bin, but he explained that countries generally tolerate two drugs as legal and acceptable. It scarcely matters which but any more than two and the fabric of society is threatened. The West legitimises alcohol and nicotine; the East chooses hashish and nicotine or hashish and opium or any combination but always two. He also added that after that it's simply a question of economics. It was arbitrary.

That man removed any prejudice or judgement I might hold towards the customs and habits of other, more alien cultures outside Europe.

Here now in Iran, I was witnessing his words as a reality. Opium was available over the counter and hashish was everywhere. To accommodate the thousands of westerners employed in his country (the judge's 'question of economics') the Shah permitted access to alcohol. The purchase of this drug was restricted to only a few select and very exclusive places. A place in point was

The Tehran Hilton which, when we fancied a drink, was our local pub. Remember William Kempe when I take you in there. I'm still Morris-dancing my way around this globe and, being a William Kempe groupie, I also tend to bump into things.

Picture now if you will those old, glamourous, black- and- white movies of the '30s and '40s where posh folk lollop around in luxurious lounges; small lamps on their tables as centre-pieces. Cocktails and caviar are brought around to them on silver trolleys by handsome young waiters in penguin suits and the ambiance is so laid- back even the soundtrack's dozing off.

That soundtrack is unquestionably provided by the white grand piano centre-stage. On this piano a black female goddess with a sultry voice lounges or is draped as she occasionally and lazily targets an unsuspecting guest to aim her love song at. Yes. Now you have it. You're with me in the Tehran Hilton.

There's always a 'but', isn't there? Why hasn't she chosen someone to croon to I wonder? Why? Would you?

Her audience in Tehran was mostly burly truck drivers from Britain just passing through and regularly popping in here to tuck into their fully- fried English breakfasts and mugs of tea. Their scintillating conversations usually entailed all matters oil and diesel and how cheap everything was here in Persia.

Then to add to her woes, members of our household were liable to turn up, always doing our best to look and act not stoned and to blend unnoticed.

The question on my mind was always 'Do un-stoned people smile? Should I look more miserable?' But that made me laugh the more.

One visit stands out. We were in high spirits. Don't get me wrong. We weren't unruly; it was rather that in our casual dress we represented, shall we say, that group of wealthy who don't give a rat's backside about what anybody thinks. Some might say we looked out of place but one thing I'd learned was that the filthy rich are expected to.

Six of us were around the table. We'd ordered two magnums of the best champagne. They'd just arrived and were in fancy ice- buckets on their trolleys. The banter kicked off. The laughter began.

I relaxed into the evening fun and gazed at my surroundings. The lounge was huge but I'd never been down the very far end. That was where our waiters went to fill trolleys and collect drinks. There was obviously a bar but no-one ever did anything quite so common as to walk down there. Certainly, since we'd been coming here, I never went there. This particular night I kept peering at it. I got mesmerised watching the bartenders working. All I could see over the bar was the neck and shoulders of the servers. It dawned on me that they were all extremely short. I didn't mention it but kept an eye on them just to see if any tall people were employed there. Not one.

As the champagne went down I couldn't stop wondering why the policy of the Hilton was to only employ dwarves as barmen. It didn't matter but it was curious. The lounge was full now and there was a hubbub about the place. The chattering glitterati had arrived and had definitely livened the place up a lot. Witty banter at the table drew me back into the group.

Scott was the only one among us who never smoked. Everyone knew it but in his drunken, playful state Michael offered him a cigarette.

"If you want, I'll teach you how to smoke it."

That caused a group giggle but it was when Joe snatched the ciggie and said,

"No. No. No. Let me show you how I learned." With that he stuck the cigarette behind his ear. He pushed back his long, thick and permed hair to make more room for it, then cocked his head out ridiculously and joked, "Spark me up."

As quick as a flash Michael said, "Yeah. You're right Joe. I'd forgotten" and leaned across the table with his lighter held out, sparked it into life and put it to Joe's ear.

The clientele of the Hilton lounge were instantly treated to the once in a lifetime spectacle of Joe's hair on fire. Sadly for them but luckily for Joe it was a sight that only flashed for a split second in a kind of whooshing way.

Babs exhibited an unconscious and amazing reflex when she grabbed a jug of water gliding by on a trolley and threw its full content over Joe. The hiss and sizzle heralded a large puff of smoke that rose majestically and lingered, hanging there mid-air.

Joe lifted his champagne without so much as a change of expression or even a raised eyebrow. 'Cheers'.

Have you ever done something like that in a public place when you were drunk? Ever fallen over most unceremoniously and stood up ever-so quickly then carried on regardless? You can convince yourself and genuinely believe that no-one noticed a thing.

That was us. We carried on as if nothing had happened even though, for a while, Joe's head was still steaming.

We should have seen it as an omen. We should have guessed there was more to come that night. Joe had that tell-tale look of mischief in his eyes. He directed those eyes at me. Hair steaming or no, he rose to announce he was going to the bathroom.

In a couple of seconds he was back, leaned over me and whispered "Get yer ass off that goddam chair Maggie Loo. You juss gotta come see this. Now!"

I was up for it. Whatever it was I was up for it. I went with him unquestioningly. As we made our way out of the lounge towards the huge, ornate foyer I got a revelation. He was dragging me on a short cut past that end bar! There were steps down into a whole new lounge area I'd never seen. Down there the bartenders were full size.

"Hey they're not dwarves!" I shouted at Joe.

"Who aren't? What?" His face was a picture. Maybe he'd never thought they were dwarves in the first place.

"The bar staff," I said, still amazed at the revelation.

"What in the..?" He spluttered

"What in the...?" I echoed his words but because Joe had tugged me right into a scramble and barrage of constant bright flashes and a lot of people calling out.

"It's Liz Taylor." He laughed like a drain, "Goddam it...Maggie Loo! It's Elizabeth Taylor!"

"Yeah right!" I muttered but I'd go along with his fantasy. Why not?

Okay. Take 1. Scene 2. We're back with those black-and-white movies. You're watching a scene where the Hollywood paparazzi are huddled in a pack, scrabbling and brandishing those huge, old, hand-held cameras with the massive silver flash bulb thingies? They're all jostling and shoving around some star or-other to get the best shot. They are all shouting at that glamorous star to get her to turn and face their way.

Yes! Here they were and there were we.

It still hadn't sunk in fully that this could actually be Elizabeth Taylor. I'd only come out for a quiet drink. Why would Liz be here? I caught a peek. Nah! I turned to Joe amid the chaos "That's not Elizabeth Taylor. She's too freckly and way too small. Elizabeth Taylor? My.........."

On that cue the crowd of extras catapulted me forward and I was jolted, mid-sentence and spinning round to steady myself. Then, face to face and virtually nose to nose with the said Elizabeth Taylor I finished my sentence... "arse!"

All I can say is she looked a tad surprised.

I often wonder if her mind ever went back to that evening and if she ever asked,

"Why did that strange young woman say 'arse' into my face'?"

A Knight to Remember

I had accumulated a lot (and I mean a lot) of money. Plans to go on to India were coming along nicely. There was a trap looming. The very mundane and routine lifestyle I'd shunned by going travelling in the first place was catching up with me. Perhaps I'd caught up with it?

I had the steady job, the big house albeit shared and the feeling of being settled with its comforts. They were tempting and threatened to take hold. £1000 a month tax-free in 1977 was an enormous amount of money. Some of it was just begging to be squandered. When a week's public holiday cropped up I got a fit in my head to follow my heart to the Greek Islands for a few days. I missed them. With a wad of cash in hand I went to the British Airways travel agency and got myself a first class return ticket to the island of Rhodes. I needed to see and breathe in the Aegean.

Travelling with no care to money makes things so easy. From Rhodes airport I caught a taxi and booked myself into modest rooms by the sea. It wasn't to save money (that was the last thing on my mind). No. It was the charm of the old place, the familiar blues and white, the wooden floors and shutters opening onto the beach. Here I spent a blissful five days walking, swimming, sketching and breathing in that atmosphere that is uniquely Greek. After months in dusty lands the island was spectacular.

Time came as it always does, to go home or at least back to Tehran. I figured it would be a leisurely trip; a taxi to the airport; a short flight to Iran and another taxi home. Hell! Work the next day would be no problem.

The check-in lady informed me there was a very slight change of plan. 'Hello.' I took a deep breath before she explained there was to be no direct flight but that all I had to do was go straight into the transit lounge in Amman in Jordan and wait for my connection. It was a holding lounge. I wouldn't even have to go through Customs or even leave the restricted area of the airport. A short wait and I'd be off again. She reckoned it would only be about an hour's wait. Okay. I could cope with that. It seemed straightforward enough.

Life has a very strange habit of being cussed when it wants to be. I didn't know it of course but this was one of those times.

Sure, the flight to Amman was cool. The man next to me was a riot. He was a self-made millionaire. How had he made his millions? Yes, folks I met the man who invented that little handheld gadget that punches out all those sticky little price tags on the stuff we all buy. He was a character and no mistake. We fell to talking about travel and flying in particular. I mentioned that the whole experience had changed even since I was a kid. That got him talking about really early air travel and one story in particular. It went like this,

"We were in this little aircraft and back in the day the toilets presented a problem. They worked on a suction basis. Difficulty was, space. They had a small foot-pedal that operated the suction. Lack of space demanded the damn thing was right by your feet. There were only fifteen or-so of us and we all got to know each other pretty well. When the woman across from me had been gone a bit too long we all got worried. We stopped to listen out carefully for the sound of that suction. It never came. What did come were muffled screams. Well! Cut a long story short? It took four grown men to pull her off that thing. I'd never seen a cone-shaped ass before!"

With stories like that the time flew as fast as our plane. I told him my story, how come I was on this flight, how come I was working in Iran and some of my better anecdotes. I explained that I'd wanted to go straight through but had to stop off in Amman but it wasn't a problem. When I got to the bit about simply having to go to the transit lounge and wait an hour, he went all serious. He suddenly looked a bit worried. That didn't actually inspire confidence. "Look." He said it with a listen carefully tone of voice. "This is the Middle East. Things happen. I'm gonna give you a little note for the guy who's meeting me off this plane. The company I'm working with have asked him to be there. I'm flying down to the Gulf but I have to hand him some documents to deliver in Amman. I'm leaving on a private plane so I'll be off in minutes. No time to hang around. I'm gonna ask him to make sure you're okay. It's just in case there's a hiccup." Sure enough he scribbled a note, handed it to me and made sure I put it somewhere safe.

When the plane landed it was evening but the air was hot. The light was fading as we crossed the tarmac to meet the go-between. The guy was standing at the steps of a small, private aircraft on the apron and ready to go. After brief introductions my only ally was gone. I was convinced I wouldn't need this other guy. Why would I? What could possibly go wrong?

Inside the tiny airport I headed straight for the transit lounge. I was stopped abruptly and taken to Customs. My helper was close by. Despite all protestations I was issued out through Customs and found myself outnumbered by Arab men, all of whom were in full Arab regalia and all of whom were staring at a young white woman, very tanned, in a long summer dress and sandals. She had the facial expression of the stereotypical rabbit in the headlights.

It was probably my overactive imagination but they looked like they were closing in for the kill.

My Jeeves picked up my bag and whisked me to his car. I never saw this coming. His English wasn't great. I gave him the note. After that he kept muttering 'Hotel, hotel'. My heart sank. I'd never thought about how much money I had on me. Why would I?

As the night drew on we went from hotel to hotel to hotel; most of them full. Amman was experiencing a massive influx of Palestinians fleeing Israeli hostilities. 'No room at the inn.'

One hotel had a single vacancy but when they saw me, they wanted £150 a night. I knew I didn't have that much on me and anyway 'how long was I going to be here?' And come to think of it, where exactly was 'here'? Suddenly we were back in the car heading for downtown Amman. God it was hot. The air was clammy. My brain was working overtime. I was tired, hot, hungry and very much alone.

Here we were then in a Travel Agent's in downtown Amman. This was a main shopping street but by now everything was shuttered. No-one was about. My man opened the door and led me through the shop area to some stairs out back. A single light-bulb lit our way up the old wooden steps and into some kind of storage area. I know, I know, by now I should be panicking, right? Strangely enough I wasn't. My senses were on full alert but whether it was shock, the innocence of youth or my brain being otherwise occupied in fathoming how to get through this – I can honestly say I was not feeling fear.

Jeeves opened up a small bathroom to show me. He pointed to a long leather couch and gestured 'sleep' by two hands clasped by his face, head to the side. He made an attempt at English. "Me. Tomorrow. Come." He rattled the shop's keys in front of my face. I was relieved when he left.

I rolled my sleeping bag out on the couch. Maybe the adrenalin was wearing off but I felt exhausted. I remembered a Sufi maxim, 'Trust in god but remember to tie your camel'. It prompted me to climb in fully clothed. He did have the keys after all.

I must have dozed off because a dream was suddenly entangled with a sensation of something moving right beside me. A hand was inside my sleeping bag. As I slowly gained consciousness a sinister voice whispered in my ear,

"You want to come disco?"

What the.......? Who knows how the survival instinct kicks in so quickly? I knew middle-eastern guys; knew their adoration for their mothers. Out of my mouth, barely awake, cool as a cucumber, my voice said clearly and in a stern teacher voice "Now. Think your mother? What she say?"

He crumpled like a small boy, repeated 'Sorry, sorry' about a million times and practically ran from the room. That was that then. No sleep for me. I waited until I heard the door to the street close, sneaked a peak and lay back down on the couch. I was in the dark and in the stifling air. I was staring at the ceiling. I tossed, turned and tossed again. I had a thought. The small bathroom had a tiny window. I noticed earlier that it had a little plastic fan fitted into the glass. I opened the door wide and felt the draught. I went back to my couch again. At least I had some air now. Maybe I could have some rest.

Eventually dawn broke. Very faint light was coming in through the little window. It was then I saw them. On the other side of this loft, in the dark until now, they lurked. It was an army of cardboard cut-out air hostesses on the march. Freaky! Their cheesy smiles and perfect grooming didn't fool me. I just knew that at any minute Dr. Who's Tardis was gonna materialise and come to my rescue....or not. I have never looked at those posh birds who are camouflaged as air hostesses in quite the same way ever since. I know where they are spawned! I saw the nest.

This had to stop. It was nearly day. Even if the guy did come back, what then? It was time to explore. I ventured into the Hostess nest and beyond. In the shadows I found another door. It opened into a tiny room that at least had a bigger window. More than that and unbelievably it had one of those old telephone exchange thingamabobs. You must have seen pictures if not the real thing. It was an old, upright wooden switchboard with lights and wired coils with jack-plugs that are pulled out and swapped around to connect with lots of phone lines. I had seen one a few times when I was a kid and my mum worked as a telephonist for the G.P.O. (General Post Office.) Surely to goodness this thing would not work! But hey! There was a light flashing on it.

Right next to this contraption sat the Jordanian Yellow Pages. I flicked through looking for an advert for some prestigious hotel. It was pretty likely that the staff in such a posh place would speak English. Not only that, but the advert would be in both Arabic and English, surely. Success. Now to the machine. I put the earphones on and pulled out and inserted any wire I could find hoping to hear a dialling signal.

I couldn't help it. I burst out laughing. I couldn't stop. Here was I, in Jordan, in a cupboard, in a half-light, trying to get a signal, trying to get a message out. I just knew the Nazis would barge in at any moment. I was in occupied somewhere-o-other. I was a secret agent. I was Odette. 'Get a grip.'

Success! I had a dialling tone and a number for a posh hotel. 'Wait a minute! What on earth am I going to say?' Hysteria set in. Deep breaths. Keep this simple.

"Oh. Hello. Do you speak English?"

"Of course. How may I help?"

"Um. Sorry about this but 'Do you really, really speak English?' What I mean by that is,' do you speak English or can you just say 'Hello', 'Can I have a beer please?'" Working at the Air Force made me sceptical!

The calm and friendly voice on the other end of the line said,

"I assure you my English is fluent. I studied for many years in London. Why?"

"Well. You are about to be told an interesting story. Are you ready because I need help."

"I am ready. What's your name? I am, call me, Mark."

"Hello Mark. My name's Maggie. I am a European working in Iran. I am a teacher. It is a long story but....wait for it...I am stuck upstairs and locked in a Travel Agents' shop somewhere in your wonderful city. I have no idea where exactly. I need to find my way back to Tehran."

Bless the man. He didn't as much as falter or laugh. The main blessing was that he didn't hang up. I think I would have done.

"Very well. Stay calm Maggie. We need to establish where this shop is exactly. Find a piece of paper and a pen, leave the telephone and go downstairs. Look out of the windows and get me a list of the types of shops directly opposite. See if you can see what they sell. I will wait."

"Whoever you are I love you and I want to have your baby. Please don't go anywhere. I'll run." I heard him laugh but tore down the stairs.

Five minutes later mission accomplished. I was thanking my lucky stars that Mike and I had spent that time learning Arabic letters. Mark was as good as his word. Admittedly he laughed a lot at my childish sounding out of phonetics of those shuttered shops but the one café helped. It had chairs still left outside and a shoe shop next door with its windows crammed. He assured me he knew precisely where I was.

"My shift finishes at 7.30. I can be with you by 7.45."

"How will I know you?"

"I am the extremely handsome man in a pin-striped suit with a white shirt and a blue tie. Anyway, you're bound to be the only girl in the Travel shop, right?" That made us both laugh.

"My life depends on you Mark. Oh. What time is it now?"

"6.30. I will see you in about an hour Maggie. Bye for now."

I gathered everything up and made a bee-line for the downstairs shop to wait it out. I plonked on a very bouncy, comfortable sofa facing the large shop front windows, my bags beside me ready to go. I was obviously a lot calmer because I nodded off. A general hubbub and hullabaloo woke me up.

Quite a crowd of swarthy, curious Arab men (complete with headdresses) were lined up about three-deep from one end of the glass to the other. I assumed they were chattering about a young white woman locked in a shop. I must have been the talk of the town.

Through them all, a very handsome young man in a pin-striped suit and blue tie managed to barge his way through. He smiled a warm smile and waved. At 8 o'clock the owner of the shop barged through too, totally bemused by the queue waiting for his services. Our eyes met as he opened the door but I was gone.

"Breakfast?" Mark asked. That was a no-brainer.

In the most beautiful of cafes within a quaint little bazaar we ate nan, eggs and goats' cheese washed down with gallons of sweet black tea. I felt human again. We chatted about everything. When I apologized for bothering him he laughed out loud.

"Life is a funny thing Maggie. Just before you rang me, my colleague and I had been talking about old stories that we were raised on and loved as children. We were just saying there was no chance to rescue a damsel in distress nowadays and....there you were."

Something registered right then and there. Of all the times I've met what some might call angels, who appear in the nick of time, I had never once considered my part in their narrative. It dawned on me that these encounters have to be mutually magical. They wouldn't work any other way.

"Now," he said. "We'll go to British Airways' main office. If things are going badly I'll put a thumb down by my side. Can you cry on demand?"

"How did you know that was one of my many talents?" I said it but I thought about the train journey from Istanbul when that talent had deserted me. Usually all I had to do was think about my granny's sudden death when I only four. No. I could do this.

"Okay, if you see a thumb down that is your signal to burst into tears."

At first British Airways insisted there was no flight available for a week. I saw the thumb go down and cried like a baby. Miraculously a seat was found for the following afternoon.

He offered me accommodation at his 5-star hotel but I couldn't accept. I opted for a Youth Hostel where I could afford to pay my way. After a lot of friendly arguing Mark insisted we go out for a meal that evening and that he take me to the airport for my flight. At 8 p.m. that night he turned up with a fabulous Arabic outfit for me to wear. What a night that was. What food. What great company.

"Can I call you Dr. Who whenever I tell this story?" I asked him at the airport. After all the ups and downs of my story, including the creepy air hostesses, he understood the reference and chuckled.

"Of course but you do know that no-one will believe you." He looked at his watch.

"The Tardis is parked in a no-parking zone. I've got to dash! I've got a universe to save, again!"

As he walked away he didn't look back. He knew I was watching because a hand was lifted and his fingers folded ever-so gently and only once in a warm farewell.

Let the Good Times Roll

It was great to be back to this house in Tehran that had strangely become home. Everything was quiet. I went to the kitchen for a drink of water and bumped into Babs.

"Any news?" I asked her, expecting none. She gave me a welcome back hug and then the bad news,

"Joe's moved." I was gutted.

Joe Vasquez was my best mate in Tehran. He was the crazy Texan whose hair caught fire in the Hilton, who introduced me to Liz Taylor and had laughed so much with us in Herman's house. In his long, slow drawl he called me Maggie-Loo. Funnily enough he was also the first bi-sexual I'd ever met, to my knowledge. When I first got to know him I asked him outright,

"What in heaven's name made you come here?" His answer was Joe in a nutshell,

"Well Maggie-Loo, when you go to a party and your girlfriend and boyfriend both propose to you in the same place in the same hour? It's time to get the hell outta that place."

We laughed so much, me and Joe, wherever we went. The news that he'd moved was devastating. I was gonna miss him like hell. Babs took one look at my reaction and burst out laughing. She beckoned me across the hall with her and into the living-room. There was Joe plonked on the low mattress that served as a couch. She handed me two small Polaroid snaps that were scarcely dry and said

"I took these just now as evidence." They were two photos of Joe. In one he was sitting to the left of the Esfahan cloth hanging on the wall. In the other he was slightly to the right of it. "See? He's moved."

That just about summed up our lazy weekends in that house. He opened his eyes and his smile lit up his face,

"Maggie-Loo! Where you been? I been worried."

"Having adventures. Miss me?"

"Sho' did."

If you take a group of twelve intelligent and lively young people, put them thousands of miles away from home and pay them each a totally absurd amount of money, weird and wonderful things are bound to happen. We never batted an eyelid when we opened the door to see Persian carpets being delivered, huge marvellous samovars, wall hangings, pottery or expensive jewellery coming in with trains of delivery folk. As for me? There was no point in accumulating stuff. I was heading for India.

I thought of different ways to spend some of my ill-gotten gains. One time I thought it would be nice to send my mum some money for her birthday. The procedure in the bank was pretty straightforward. At the Air Force school we could choose the currency we got paid in. Rials were the best bet. They kept decreasing against sterling. So, when I sent the £500 I took the chitty and went to walk away. The teller called me back,

"Your change!" What? The guy handed me the modern equivalent of £75 back in change. Mad, huh? I'd bought £500 and got 75 of it back but my mum still got the full £500.

Apparently when my mum got the bank draft she thought it was 500 somethings. After my sister convinced her it was pounds, she fainted. When she came round she uttered a priceless quote, "Oh. I can go and get that trouser-suit from the charity shop now then?" Yep. Weird and wonderful things happened.

Jack worked on the oil rigs in the Gulf. He came back for two weeks in every six. Goodness knows how much he was earning. After his first year he'd already bought a small ranch back in the U.S. Anyway, he and I had arrived back on the same day.

He came back with his own booty of three huge, silver, circular canisters of reel-to- reel film, the ones used in cinemas. He'd borrowed them from the cinema on the rig. His heart was set on a film party in honour of a dear friend Tom, on his way back from India and about to drop by. No-one knew when exactly. Travel and travellers don't work like that. We all got excited whenever visitors from outside came to stay. Over the next few days Tom became a mythical character exaggerated beyond all proportion. We couldn't wait.

That first night home Jack announced he had a surprise for us all, something else he wanted to share. Apparently we had to wait till dark and we had to be on the roof for it. We waited. The time came.

At about ten o'clock we joined him on the huge flat roof. The city of Tehran was laid out before us under clear, starlit skies. There were twelve of us, waiting in anticipation of something magical. I should mention the roof wasn't completely clear. Towards one edge was a concrete cube construction (some four feet by four) that housed the air-conditioning vent. We followed his instructions and stood still with eyes closed. There was an almighty, ear-splitting 'Whoosh'.

Like kids we gawped in shock with our necks strained and heads bent right back, our eyes boggling. A monstrous oil rig flare shot up like a N.A.S.A. rocket hundreds of feet into the air. Eventually an enormous pink parachute opened way, way above us and the whole of Tehran lit up in pink daylight. It was an amazing sight.

We were so completely captivated by the pink sky that it never occurred to us for a single second that the whole population of Tehran could see exactly what we were seeing. Then...'Uh Oh!' something else dawned. You know that maxim 'What goes up must come down?" Exactly.

Giggling like wayward adolescents, twelve adults ran for that little concrete cube to take cover, hide from the aftermath and duck. We were actually shoving each other like maniacs to get the best spot. It was insane and hopeless. We threw ourselves flat out on the roof and dare not move. The sound of sniggering must have carried for miles in the night silence. We peered up at the parachuted debris descending and drifting. Down, down and down the glorious and massive electric-pink parachute fluttered. Then an even more heartfelt "Uh oh" rose. The thing was on fire.

We watched helpless as it wafted while it made up its mind where exactly to wreak havoc. Which collection of electric wires or telephone cables should it aim for? It decided and the decision caused an almighty bang and fizzle before the lights of the city below began to go out in blocks, one after the other. At first it was nearby but then there was a domino effect. Block after block went out fast. Darkness kicked in across the city. That wasn't all though. The bottom of this flaming thing had only clipped the cables. It kept going. It was heading straight for a full washing-line in a garden not that far away. 'Yikes'.

As our neighbours' undies ceremoniously burned, we escaped one by one, like prisoners of war in some old grey and pink movie; crawling out of our tunnel just short of the woods! We wriggled across our roof to the loft steps then scrabbled indoors to hide.

"Damn that was good!" Jack laughed. "Sure as hell don't look that spectacular out across an ocean."

Two days later Tehran had its power back. They fixed it pretty quick. In retrospect they should have waited a few days but who was to know?

They should have waited (like we did) for Jack's amazing, lively, kickass mate Tom to turn up and until after we'd had this famous film party. Anyway, the legendary character eventually managed to telephone to give us a date.

When we were not at work we got into party mood. We made popcorn, cakes, plans, more popcorn, more cakes, invites, even more popcorn, cakes, decorations and did I mention cakes? The only snag we had (and it was a big one) was finding a projector big enough and powerful enough to show those enormous reels of film.

Jack almost gave up. At long last he got a lead on a guy who could rent us one but only on the strict proviso that he and his assistant come with it to operate the monster. 'Deal done.' All we had to do now was wait a few days for this Tom guy and then......party! Party! Party!

The day came but Tom didn't. The evening came but Tom didn't. Guests arrived but no Tom. The doorbell rang. It wasn't Tom. It was the projector and the crew of two. I don't know about you but I've never seen a massive projector bundled up in muslin and sackcloth and perched, (precariously balanced) on a small man's head before, but hey! That's how it came.

His boss stepped over the threshold first. The porter stood dutifully behind him. They both had a look of sheer terror at entering the lion's den alias a house full of aliens. On this occasion the tradition Iranians follow of taking their shoes off before entering a house proved very unfortunate for us. Usually it was cool. Tonight it was not so cool. The young assistant had a severe foot problem. He hadn't only brought the projector into the house but a dreadful stink too. It was bad. It was so bad it made us want to heave.

Joe, a consummate stoner, was on it like a flash. When all polite attempts at getting the guy to put his shoes on failed, Joe rushed for the can of air freshener. For air freshener read Zyclon B. That stuff could kill anything unwanted. He started spraying the stuff so liberally at the poor guy's feet that he got a bit carried away. We all nearly choked. In his stoned state he genuinely believed that the poor young guy hadn't noticed. I have flashbacks even now of Joe spraying that can at that lad's feet throughout the entire evening.

We got set up.

The bemused Iranians had absolutely no clue what the film was about. Even when it started they were none the wiser. You can't really blame them. Seeing a massive image of the crazed Little Richard thumping out his thing on a piano is quite baffling in anyone's book. Their eyes nearly popped out of their heads. Credit where credit's due they stood, arms folded, expressionless and glued to the one spot, without as much as a word. There was still no Tom.

And so, with a houseful of guests we settled to watch 'Let the Good Times Roll' a film packed with classic clips of good old rock'n'roll (at least I think it is). Until we read the end credits scrolling up after 45 minutes we'd never even noticed we were watching the last reel first. No-one cared.

Just as the second reel began to roll we assumed Britain had lent Concorde to the Shah for the night and that it had just broken the sound-barrier right over our house. The bang was out of this world. Oh. Wait a minute, the film's stopped. Then a kerplanging sound like a cosmic afterthought threw us into total blackness .... again.

Joe peeped out of a window. 'Uh oh!' the whole neighbourhood was out.

We lit a million candles and carried on. Michael played his acoustic guitar in the hallway.

"Wassup?" Jack shouted as he bounded up the wide spiral staircase, pushing his way through a big queue of people that had formed for some reason. Someone was in the upstairs bathroom but not responding to knocks or shouts. Jack took charge. He hammered on the door to no avail. Three guys broke the door down. Everyone stared at the semi-dead occupant.

Inside was what might be a human. It was an unnatural contortion, draped around the toilet bowl. We ascertained it wasn't dead but was hugging the porcelain with a dead man's grip. Jack grabbed a tuft of its thick permed hair. He lifted the head upright and turned the face to his own so as to get a good look at it. He was like a frenzied and demented head-hunter (Conan perhaps?) displaying his trophy. Then he rested it back down in the bowl and shouted "Tom's here!" With that he walked off back down the stairs. He was so delighted to see his old mate the circumstances didn't matter.

As for the long- awaited, much-anticipated live wire who could climb mountains by gripping to sheer rock with his teeth or drink yards of ale without so much as belching? He slept for the next thirty-six hours straight.

He'd crept in unannounced and, hungry from his long trip, tucked a little too enthusiastically into a whole tray of hash brownies in the kitchen. How was he to know they were the ones laced with hash?

Michael played the Little Feat lyrics 'There's a fat man in the bathtub with the blues.' Joe started changing it by substituting 'toilet' for 'bathtub' and a bit of a singsong got going. When they had gone a long way beyond needing musical accompaniment, Michael grabbed his guitar and he and I went back up to the roof.

The stars were incredible, on a glorious warm night. Very, very softly he played

"If I was a sculptor, but then again no, Or a man who makes potions in a travelling show Oh I know it's not much but it's the best I can do, my gift is my song and this one's for you."

I listened, spellbound and deeply in love.

"Could it get any better than this?" I whispered. He carried on singing.

When he reached the words, "I sat on the roof and kicked off the moss," there was the faint but unmistakable sound of popcorn cracking.

"Hear that?" I asked "Someone's making more popcorn."

He smiled a very strange smile, leaned over closer and whispered in my ear.

"Sorry darlin' but that's automatic gunfire. Sounds like the sound of things to come. But hey. Let the good times roll."

The Army of the Dead

This wouldn't be an odyssey if I hadn't diced with death at least once. And life was about to get dicey. Somewhere along the line I let my guard down and ate something that didn't like me. I mean it seriously didn't like me. In fact, it was out to kill me.

Endless, miserable and painful days were spent hugging a toilet or sitting on one. The days turned into weeks. Of course I went to doctors. At first (and who can blame them?) the Iranian doctors were convinced it was nothing more than 'something foreigners experience.' After weeks that didn't hack it any more.

They gave me unctions, potions and remedies. They gave me prescriptions for god- knows-what. I neither knew nor cared. Jahan's relatives gave me old wives' remedies. One even persuaded me to swallow heaped teaspoons of dried tea leaves. I'll leave it up to you to imagine what that was like, trying to swallow that advice when I was constantly dehydrated. After a while even boiled, warm water refused to stay in me.

Michael and Scott had rented a car to go down to Esfahan, Shiraz and on to see Persepolis. They said they weren't going without me. That made me feel worse (if that was possible). Michael and Pat insisted on taking me to a specialist before I could even think about going on the trip. After testing, probing and interrogation, the guy resorted to injecting me with a very large needle. I'd lost over 2 stone and weighed in at 5st.12lb. To be fair, over the next few days the injection seemed to work. I started to drink soup and keep it down. I began to eat bread and a little potato. I had colour in my cheeks. We all agreed the trip was on.

Esfahan stole my heart. I'm not at all sure about reincarnation but the feeling I got there of having been here in a previous lifetime was powerful. The city is an oasis in an arid land. Given life by the river Zayande roud (which means 'Life-Giving') and cooled by a constant breeze from the Zagros mountains not that far off, it must have seemed like heaven to those ancient travellers coming in from the deserts along the Silk Road. It certainly seemed like it to me.

Esfahan is some 2,500 years old. History oozes from its every pore. Yes. The buildings scream it but the history I'm talking about can only be sensed. I felt I was being embraced by a million people, people who'd passed through here from everywhere and every century since time began. In a mysterious way they've left their own residual and very tangible imprint. We realised how much we had been missing that feeling flowing water brings. We'd been living without it in Tehran for months on end.

Unless you have wandered leisurely under arabesque archways shimmering and brought to life by intricate tile-work that sparkles in glorious sunshine, paraded along the wide boulevards they shade, and inhaled the heady perfumes of the gardens they skirt, you cannot grasp where I was. This is the largest market square in the world. These are the arcades of the Myden (now a World Heritage site I believe.)

Here, men in long white robes and loosely-wound headgear sat cross-legged, drank tea, smoked and put the world to rights while their wives believed they were keeping shop.

Some of them were. Some sketched, others cooked appetising flatbread on their small stoves. Many sold glassware, silver filigree, fabrics, spices, beads, precious stones, sandals, framed paintings, metal-ware, mats, hats and the kitchen sink. What else would you expect? This was the Silk Road. Every single one of these traders looked happy, their skin weathered and wrinkled, their laughter warm and their broad grins genuine.

Esfahan's bazaar occupies one side of the vast square. Inside here are a million stalls selling a million items. Dozens and dozens of tiny shops are dedicated to, and packed with, the blue and white ceramics synonymous with the city's name. It's exquisite. Everything about Esfahan is exquisite. The Persian architecture of the mosques (inside and out) is beyond belief. All around the city are those gardens painted into childhood imaginations the world over by tales told from the Arabian nights.

In this very bazaar I sat then, the guys drawing on beautifully crafted hubble-bubble pipes and me feeling a lot brighter, taking in all the aromas, colours and chatter as I sipped black tea through sugar cubes held between my teeth.

On the outskirts of town we pulled over to visit the shaking minarets. Following an old man's advice we split into 2 by 2 and climbed our respective towers. Apparently one couple should stand still while the other rocks their ancient edifice to and fro for a while, before stopping. I kid you not! The swaying of our tower made the other rock in resonance. Is that magic or what?

One day later and we were in Shiraz. I wasn't feeling too good but I said nothing. I wasn't about to spoil everyone's adventure. Shiraz is the city of gardens and home to poetry and literature. It lingers in my mind as a city of open spaces. I can never forget walking up the long avenue lined with orange and lemon trees that led us to Qavam House, a late 19th century town house built for the rich folk. How can anyone forget that porch-way? The walls and ceilings were completely mirrored. To stand in it, look up and spin around; then to look back out at all the fruit trees, fountains and huge date palms was surreal. All of that stood against the backdrop of a huge, paint-box blue, cloudless sky. My mind must have taken a snapshot because I am right there now as I'm writing this, forty years after the fact.

Where was I? Oh yes. The unforgettable. Picture a pink mosque; bright pink, a kid's custard kind of pink. Yes, domes, minarets and the huge vaulted entrance, every bit bright pink from top to bottom. What would it be like inside? Gaudily painted? No. This, folks, is the Nasir-ol-Molk and nothing can prepare anyone for this. Wow is what it was like inside. Just wow.

Stained-glass windows of the most magnificent design and glaring colours work with sunlight to paint the cavernous, bare interior with kaleidoscope patterns in every hue of the rainbow. This magic lantern effect doesn't stop at patterning the many pillars, no! It spreads itself into dazzling mosaics over the vast polished-mirrored floor. Playfully, in turn, the floor mirror reflects to throw the magic back up. There it decorates concave miniature domes above; small domes formed by the pillars and the stone mason's love.

I was blown away. This is illumination. This is what enlightenment looks like.

How strange though, to feel so spiritually strong and yet so physically weak? I could tell the toxin inside me hadn't quite done with me yet.

A renovated ancient caravanserai of individual chambers framed an open quadrangle. We took shelter there for the night. Our rooms had archways front and back, each altered to hold flimsy wooden French Windows. We flung them open, flopped on the bed and watched a breeze playing with the muslin curtains, gently lifting them and letting them fall; lift and fall, lift and fall until they lifted us, then let us fall...asleep.

I felt okay the next morning. I even ate breakfast. I must have been worrying about nothing. Good job I hadn't spoilt anything. We were off to Persepolis today. 'The wealthiest city under the sun.'

We are off to Persepolis! We were all thinking it but not one of us could bring ourselves to say it! Alexander the Great and his men must have said exactly that at some point and look what happened next! They completely sacked it in the year 330 B.C, more than 2000 years before we ever dreamt of coming here.

Michael was tired of driving and I was too weak to help him out. We decided to get a shared taxi to make the 40 mile trip. We were excited.

Perhaps things have changed now. Perhaps better roads have been built but then the ruins of the great city were way, way out in the sticks, a wasteland that only the hardy or the history buffs would venture into. Our journey became more and more desert-like.

We had driven through some swathes of desert to get this far. We'd seen camel trains, carpets drying in vast numbers stretched out to create enormous mosaic tapestries on drifting dunes, wondered at the occasional mirage and even caught sight of a camel post- office. But this was different, this was the route into Persepolis.

I was dumbfounded when, in an area where sand stretched in all directions and as far as the eye could see, a guy among us shouted "Ham Inja" (Just here). What? I say 'what'? Am I missing something here? I spun my head round to double check. Nope. There was nothing. How on god's dusty earth did this guy know where his stop was? Hey Ho. He got out, paid and wandered off into the shimmering horizon.

As soon as we arrived at Persepolis I felt bilious. I pretended I didn't. For some reason I was asking myself if there was a famous quote, 'See Persepolis and die' or had I just imagined that? Or was that Rome? I shrugged it off. I have weird random thoughts like that. Doesn't everyone?

The ruined city of Persepolis is immense. The structures are gigantic, epic and comparable in size and strength to anything the Pharaohs conjured up. This dead city made Ephesus look small. Like Ephesus though, the view from ground-level was all a bit overwhelming. Scott had a bit of an old tourist guide booklet. We followed that. We walked. We walked a lot.

I don't know what it is with me. I've got a thing for standing inside huge, ancient and partially ruined buildings. They shrink me to where my worries and problems become laughably infinitesimal before they disappear completely. It's the timespan that does it I guess.

The other three weren't far away. I kept an eye on them. I wandered off to find somewhere to sit to view the whole site from a little higher up. When I got to the Tomb of the King it began.

I was bent double by a crippling pain that stabbed my gut. It brought tears to my eyes and took my breath away. I hobbled up to the lower steps of the tomb and managed to flop down. I wanted to fake it for as long as humanly possible so that the others got to see as much as they could. I willed myself not to need a toilet. If there even was one, it was miles away. I turned and looked up at Xerxes tomb behind me; an ominous opening carved out of the mountain side.

When I'm in a life-threatening situation (and I've been in a few) I get all philosophical. When that happens what comes out of my mouth can seem droll. At the moment I glanced at that King's tomb, I felt the blood drain out of me. I felt as light as a feather. I said to Xerxes, "Move over a bit, would you?" That was it. Those were to be my final words for a while. Pretty stylish, eh?

I have no idea what happened next.

I came to very briefly, being carried by quite a crowd shouting and chatting frantically. Want to know something extremely weird? They were fading in and out from living, breathing human beings to skeletons. My first thought 'Oh! I can see in X-ray.' Then, 'Nah! Don't be daft. Of course I can't.' Now I knew what they were. These were the Spartoi, the mythical skeleton army of the Greeks. Mythical, oh yeah? So why were they here then, eh, eh? Now this was making much more sense. What was it I had to do to get past them?' Delirium can do strange things.

I'm in a mini-bus coming and going between realms. Oh no! The people on the bus are still the army of the dead.

I'm in bed in our peaceful caravanserai. Michael is at my bedside and looks anxious. I wonder why. Oh.

"It's okay. It's okay" I said ever-so calmly. I reached out hand to touch his. "Stop worrying. I'm only dying. It's okay, honestly. I'm fine."

He got quite forceful and said, "Listen you. You are not dying. You are not going to die. I'm going to find a pharmacy that's got something I know about from the States. I'll come back with it and I'll come back quick."

"You think I'm dying too, don't you?" There was no energy in me or in my voice.

"No, I don't. Shut up and get some rest. No, I don't think you're dying. I'll be back soon."

He did come back. He woke me up with some water and the biggest pill I've ever seen in my life. I gagged but I swallowed it

I was 9 years old. I was in my primary school class. I was the pen-and-pencil monitor. My teacher, Sister Carmel had a very posh pencil-sharpener attached to the side of her front desk. I put a pencil in and heard that magic 'whiiirrr- ub' sound. It changed tone as I pushed the pencil in again. Hey presto! A perfect point! Wait a minute! That pencil someone's sharpening must be gigantic. The sound is deep, hollow and massive. In and out, in and out sharpening. Oh no! I'm in the land of the giants. I tentatively opened my eyes.

There was Michael standing smoking in the wide open doorway. His instincts were on high alert. He was on to it the instant my eyelids showed him signs of life. He turned and put a hand on my forehead.

"Liar!" I said, grinning.

"What?" I could see the relief all over his very tired face.

I'd spotted three ashtrays chock full of cigarette stubs. That said everything. "You did think I was dying!" My next thought was "How long have I been out? And "Why is a cyclops outside sharpening pencils?" He laughed like a drain.

"About 42 hours.........and we're right next to a timber yard."

"42 hours?"

He hadn't left my side for all that time.

I don't know what I won by facing the army of the dead and winning. I'm still expecting a delivery of a Golden Fleece...but then ...you know what delivery men are like.

Taking Flight

In much the same way as the first moon landing of '69 marked my own personal flight, the distant gunfire in Tehran heralded more than one revolution. It signalled a revolution inside me too. Michael had broken faith. I was shattered. I'd put on some weight. It was time to leave. The only way I could summon up the courage was to just do it, up and leave telling only Pat and Joe. I've always been useless at farewells.

By 5.30 a.m. I was at the central bus station, and in a right state! The emotional pain was beyond belief. I felt dreadful but I knew this was the right thing to do. Dammit! It was a national holiday that meant a long weekend. A bus ticket couldn't be had for love or money. Or could it? The depot was jam-packed and chaotic.

As I made to give up and leave, the desk clerk shouted after me. Someone had just that second returned a ticket they could no longer use. I went to pay but remarkably the guy wouldn't take my money. A man beside me at the counter explained the ticket was free. The guy who handed it in didn't want a refund. This was strange to say the least.

The only bus I could take was going all round the houses to catch up with a connection from some other city. I needed to change before the border and then go straight through to Izmir where I'd have a day's stopover before a transfer on to Istanbul. Anything was fine by me as long as I got away.

I slept a lot on those bus rides but I woke up at the Turkish border. Sleep is a great anaesthetic. When I woke up I was fine for the blink of an eye and then I felt that sinking feeling, that kick in the stomach, the pain I was trying to forget. We had twenty minutes here so I got off to stretch my legs.

I was about to turn away from the bus when a second one pulled up. That strange noise of air brakes was unmistakeable. Dust flew up. The door jerked open. Who stepped out? My heart fell to the floor. Michael! He'd decided to do a runner at exactly the same time as me.

For a split second that was an eternity our eyes met. We were like iron filings trying to fight magnetism. I tugged myself away, pulled my chador up over my head and headed away to put some distance between us.

On that chilly morning the sun was coming up and highlighting the snow on the mountain not far off. I stared at that beautiful, snow-capped mountain and broke down. I let it out. I sobbed and sobbed. I probably would have sobbed myself sick but a hand on my shoulder made me physically jump.

An old cigarette seller lit a ciggie, broke off the tip and handed it to me. I smiled and took it. His face was haggard and wrinkled but his smile was so kind. He pointed at the glorious mountain. My gaze followed his finger. "No...ah!" He croaked out. "No-ah."

I got the message. This was Mount Ararat where Noah's Ark came to rest or so the story goes. The lump in my throat dissolved into tears again. I fumbled in my small back pack for some tissues. I must have some somewhere for goodness sake. I felt so alone and friendless. I couldn't find any tissues but my fingers stumbled on what seemed to be an envelope scrunched up at the bottom. What on earth? With a nod to Noah my mind whispered, 'Floods of tears'. I pulled out the envelope and realised what it was.

It was Chris' card. I hadn't seen that since Amsterdam. I hadn't used this bag since then. I opened the envelope. On the cover of the card was a depiction of Noah's Ark! Despite all the odds, that made me smile. I turned the cover and read, "Go forth with a smile on your face and a cucumber up your bum. See you when you've come full circle. You and I know what a circle is worth."

The last bit made my smile wider. It was a lyric from a Loudon Wainwright lll song that goes,

'We've come a long way since we last shook hands- still got a long way to go. We couldn't see the flowers when we last shook hands. (Couldn't see the flowers on account of the snow.) What did you do with your burden and your cross? Did you carry it yourself or did you crack? You and I know that a burden and a cross can only be carried on one man's back. All my life I wanted to roam, to go to the ends of the earth. But the earth really ends where you started to roam. You and I know what a circle is worth."

The warmth of his words and the song reference warmed me to my very core. I knew where I was heading. Where else? I had a friend. Of course I had a friend.

The driver blew the horn for us to get back on the bus. Michael's bus was gone. I hugged the old cigarette hawker and thanked him. Every fibre of my being was telling me this journey was going to be extraordinary.

I disturbed the handsome middle-aged man in the seat next to mine. When he said, "You look a little better" I could tell he was extremely well-educated. His English was impeccable. I assumed he was taking pity on me. My eyes were bound to look red and swollen and I was still abnormally thin. Of course he'd noticed I was a mess. "Where are you heading?" His voice was kind and friendly.

"To my friend Chris in Sussex." I said it and started to giggle. "But I've only just told him." There was obviously no physical way I could have messaged Chris in the last twenty minutes on a desert border. I knew it sounded crazy but I didn't care. I was wide open and raw. I couldn't be bothered to pussy-foot around with anyone. He'd have to take me as I was, telling it like it is. I warmed to him even more when he didn't ask for an explanation but asked instead, "How will you know when your message is received?"

"Oh. He'll let me know. He'll let me know loud and clear." Suddenly we two otherwise strangers were both laughing. "Sorry, but I'm gonna sleep some more."

The next time I woke it was because the monotonous drone of the engine abruptly stopped. It cut dead. I'd twisted myself into some god-awful foetal position with the right side of my face squished up against the window glass. When I squinted awake I was pleasantly shocked. There, grinning wider than a Cheshire cat and peering directly at me was an unimaginably gaudily painted statue. The face of this thing was matt pink, not pink as in fluffy but pink as in blancmange. The turban on his head was in dazzling white emulsion and the donkey he sat on was matt chocolate brown. He was riding it ass backwards (quite literally) so that the animal's butt was 'in my face'.

"Who or what is that?" I looked at my new friend.

"That," he smiled, "is the Mullah Nasruddin." That was it.

"Message received then. Loud and clear." I quipped and he got it.

"Your friend is acquainted with the Mullah?"

"Absolutely. Chris was the one who introduced us. He led me to the Sufis."

"Breakfast?"

"Too right."

This lovely man and I indulged in a splendid feast of natural Turkish yoghurt, orange juice, flatbread straight from the oven, fresh cheeses and even fresher eggs. Then came the sweet black tea. I was on my way. 'Isn't everyone?' I asked myself.

For hour after hour we chatted. The subject of our conversations is another book in itself. I will say that he was from that part of the world once known as Sumeria and was an expert in cuneiform and clay tablets. When I found that out I was tempted to ask him if he'd just popped off his Ark to befriend me. I didn't. I chose to keep hold of it as a nice idea. We were in Izmir before we knew it.

My clearest memory of Izmir is a salty taste of the sea air, and bright sunshine. I was alive. I was on a wharf and daydreaming as usual. I didn't even notice at first that the light around me had changed from bright sunshine to an eerie grey. I snapped out of my reverie. A guy selling roasted nuts walked over and handed me a large piece of broken glass sooted by the smoke from his brazier. What on earth was this about? He pointed at a sun very gradually disappearing. Oh my god! We were about to witness a total eclipse.

There was a spell when the sun was hidden. I have no idea how long that lasted. It could have been a minute or an hour. All I know for sure is that when that sun disappeared my poetic Voice (as I call it) recited these words.

> 'In the mother's womb afloat, a pale pink something, a shapeless boat.
> From first arrival I would be the moulder of waters that moulded me.
> Christ turned water into wine, in doing so became divine.
> Who was he that he might form, calming waters from disturbing storm?
> Why must he maker and master be? Of all that makes and masters me?
> There I would go- no-one following me
> To form a foothold on a floorless sea.
> Like lonely sailors we seek land then become but footprints in the sand.
> If I am bound to be divine let no other footsteps follow mine.'

The lines of verse recited themselves over and over until I'd committed them to memory. I watched the sun's corona. It was an enormous golden finger-ring with a dazzling stone. Fool I might be but I'm not stupid. This journey was turning out to be magical.

I'd spent the day before with Hanuk and Zeki. I never told them I was coming. If they hadn't been at home I would have gone to a hostel. They were and they put me up for the night. It was brilliant to see them. Now I had to catch this next bus to Istanbul.

My friend was there again. He'd saved me a seat. It was comforting. I was going to miss him when we eventually got to

Istanbul. He was flying to Heathrow and I had to sort out how to get to Sussex. That was what I was chewing over when he asked if I was going to Gatwick. I told him that Chris lived near there, yes but I wasn't flying. I was going overland.

To cut a longer story short we didn't part when we got to Istanbul. He insisted we share a taxi, then paid and signed us both in at a hotel he'd booked for himself. Despite my insistence that I should find somewhere cheaper, he won the argument. It must have been when he took my passport for registration here, that he sneakily did some telephoning. How else could he have booked me a first class flight to Gatwick? Yes. That's what he did. He handed it to me in a restaurant in downtown Istanbul the following evening. I was wearing a dress he'd bought me too. To be honest I felt more than a bit embarrassed and told him so. His answer took me completely by surprise.

"The airline ticket was already paid for months ago. All I did was change the destination and the passenger details to yours. The hotel is owned by my cousin and I'm not paying either. The dress and the meal are a lesson for you to learn to receive graciously. They are also my thank you to you." Apparently I'd restored his faith in human nature. I had absolutely no idea how I'd done that but this was a very genuine man. To misquote George Bernard Shaw

'It's not only holier to give than to receive, it's a heck of a lot easier too.' I accepted as graciously as I could. I couldn't help thinking of all the people who'd helped me and given me so much on this whole adventure already. My mind went back to that Travel Agents' in Amman and my very own Dr. Who. I knew I'd learned something important from that 'angel in the nick of time' stuff. What was it? It took me a minute to recall. Ah! Their narrative and how I fitted in it. This all had to be mutual or it didn't work. I had to ask him.

"You're the one who made sure I got that bus ticket way back in Tehran, aren't you?" He went all bashful. Like a light coming on in my head I knew, I knew I was travelling in the place of someone close to him; someone he'd recently lost. His eyes were watering. I left it alone.

Being back in Istanbul felt good. A westerner going east for the first time via Istanbul, experiences the city as alien and typically eastern. Coming back after time spent in the Middle East it looks distinctly Western. But that's the magic of Istanbul. It's a bridge that spans two world views.

The flight to Gatwick was a bit quirky. I had never seen seats on a plane arranged quite like that. In sets of three some seats faced forward, some faced the wrong way rather like in a train. I flew to Britain backwards, facing where I had been.

The lady at the airport information desk was worried about me. I wasn't. She seemed overly concerned that I had just missed the main airport service bus that went through Crawley. Flustering and hurrying she explained I had a very long wait ahead of me now. I knew she was mistaken. I smiled then she piped up with "Unless?"

"Unless what?" I prompted her. I knew there was an easy way. My journey was bound to continue in the same vein it had since Mt. Ararat.

"Unless ..." She stepped back away from her desk and beckoned me over to a door with a sign saying 'Staff only.' Then she led me through and pointed in the direction of a building site. "Unless you cut through those building works. Then you might just catch the last local bus before it even starts its route. You'll have to hurry though."

I thanked her but didn't hurry. This bus was mine. It was waiting for me. Of course I'd catch the bus. I took my time across the rubble and gravel of the site, turned the corner and there it was. She was right. There was my empty bus.

It suddenly struck me. I had no English money. Come to think of it, hang on! I hadn't used money since I paid for the shared taxi to Tehran bus station. Now, there's a thing!

I hoisted my backpack up into the bus, stashed it on the luggage space and sat right at the front, by the door and the driver.

"Been anywhere nice?" He asked.

"Long story" I answered grinning. He and I sat and chatted for a while. I gave him a list of the countries I'd been in and the story of this particular trip home. When he shut himself into his small driving area, to set off, he laughed out, "Fair play. Fair play. This one's on me girl. This one's on me."

Something totally unexpected happened when I got back. I was seeing England for the first time. I was seeing it through the eyes of a foreigner. My mind was boggled on that ride. As the bus filled up, stop after stop, I could understand every conversation of every single passenger and hear them all at once. My impression was that England is quaint after all. It was Saturday night and people were out and about having a good time

I wondered at a landscape of greenery and villages that once seemed so familiar and also taken for granted. I got lost in it all. By the time it grew dark I was the only passenger again. We were pulling into Crawley. That was the end of the line. I grabbed my pack and stood by the automatic doors. "What next then?" The lovely man asked,

"I guess I need a taxi. Where can I find one?"

"Oh. You'll be lucky. No chance. This time of night, on a Saturday? No chance."

The doors swooshed open. He drove off. I sat on the seat in the bus shelter and laughed. 'Might as well have a ciggie while I wait for my cab then.'

I was smoking for no more than a minute or- two when my taxi pulled up. "Need a ride?" the cabby asked. "Just had a no-show."

With my rucksack safely in the boot he invited me upfront to sit beside him. I showed him Chris' card with the address on it. I explained where I'd been and where I was going. We had a good old chinwag.

It was getting close to the time to pay the fare. I thought I owed it to him to confess I didn't have any money. I asked if he'd mind waiting at my friend's while I popped inside and got the fare.

"But I thought you said you haven't been in touch with this bloke for years? How d'you know he'll be there?" Suspicion had crept into his voice.

"Oh. He's there alright."

We parked right up close to the small flats. I couldn't see a light on. I rang the bell.

Within seconds Chris opened his door and said casually, 'Hi. Come on in. Come on in." There wasn't a glimmer of surprise or hint of excitement in his voice or attitude. That's the sign of a true friend, isn't it? To carry on seamlessly, exactly where you left off. He was back in Amsterdam and taking me back there by repaying the prank I played on him at that breakfast.

The driver saw all this and shouted "You're pulling my leg, right?"

I played along with Chris and acted as if I'd just popped in from next door to borrow a cup of sugar. Instead of sugar I wanted to borrow the taxi fare.

The two storey house was divided into an upper and lower apartment. Chris's was obviously the top one because the front door led straight to stairs. On my right, inside the door was a small alcove and in that was a glass jar for loose change.

"Um. I haven't got any English money. The cabby wants his fare?"

He'd already climbed one or two stairs but turned and nodded at the jar. I took it outside to the taxi. I counted it all out. I paid the fare and there was just enough for a tip.

Reunited with my trusty rucksack, I climbed the stairs.

Now came our raucous "Waaaaaaaaaaaaaaa" and a hug.

Two mugs of tea in hand we went in and plonked in his living room.

"Come on then spill the beans, spill the beans. Where did you go? Who did you meet? What did you see? How did you get here? Come on, come on." His grin widened.

"How d'you think I got here? How would a Maggie travel?"

"Um.....magic carpet?"

"Give the man a coconut! Mind you. Transport's come a long way since those old days of Ali Baba's. It took me a while to recognise it."

I was about to have a stab at answering his other questions when the phone rang and he went to answer it. 'I wanna know' he slipped that in before he disappeared.

I thought about his questions. I ran it all through. What I was gonna say was,

"Well, since you're sitting comfortably? I'll begin. I met Pinocchio, the Pied Piper, the Snow Queen (in the form of a Russian train guard), Biggles (the pilot on that train) the Giant from Jack and the Beanstalk lurking everywhere in Russia, the Sirens in old Copenhagen, the Little Mermaid and most of Anderson's characters actually. I met a lot of Fagan's street kids, a knight in shining armour who might have been Dr. Who, Don Quixote now Deniz, Anna Karenina and Little Red Riding Hood who's morphed into a funicular railway car in Norway. I met Space Family Robinson lost in a hotel corridor in Stockholm, and they were a few doors along from Confucius now known as Confuse

Us. I've met Zeus, Hera, Chronos, the Army of the Dead, a cyclops who had a thing about sharpening pencils, and a fallen angel called Michael. Not to mention James Bond who skied over the top of my train and of course Elizabeth Taylor but does she count? She was real. I think.

I've sailed with Jason and the Argonauts and Capt. Haddock from 'Tin Tin', travelled through a lot of Monty Python sketches, a page or two of Rider Haggard's 'King Solomon's Mines', in trains from John Buchan's 'The 39 Steps', the pages of an Ian Fleming spy thriller, some of Tolstoy, Tolkien's 'Lord of the Rings', 'Alice in Wonderland', pages from the Bible, other assorted fairy tales, quite a few pop-up books and I ended up in some tragic love story worthy of Thomas Hardy.

I've starred in a lot of quirky sitcoms, had bit parts in several old black-and- white movies (especially in the bar of 'Casablanca' (renamed the Hilton Hotel) and oh was in dozens of road movies.

I walked in the footsteps of Vikings, Romans, Greeks, Ottomans, Phoenicians, Aristotle, Hippocrates, Byzantines, Pythagoras and the guy who taught him all he knew, Alexander the Great, Xerxes, Odysseus, Catherine the Great, Lenin, Stalin and Hans Christian Anderson. I mustn't forget the footsteps of the Evangelists at Ephesus, the Virgin Mary and everyone who was ever anyone who walked the Silk Road. Last but never least, Noah and the Mullah Nasruddin. Oops how could I forget? To make totally sure, I checked out Paradise and went to Hell and back again.'

That's what I thought I'd say. I didn't say any of it. Why? It dawned on me right there and then that book learning was okay but it was like studying theory. I was done with all that.

When he came back I was as pleasantly surprised as he was when this popped out of my mouth, "Ah well you know how it is. 'I've looked under chairs. I've looked under tables. I've tried to find the key to fifty million fables. They call me The Seeker....'"

With that, and with Chris on air-guitar, we sprang to our feet and bellowed

"I've been searching low and hi...igh......I won't get to get what I'm af...ter- Till the day....... I die."

Where there's a will there's ....

It was my birthday, February 13th 1979. The decade was sliding towards its end. Truth be told? Even after these last long months I was still having trouble settling back into what most people call normality. After my years of going where the spirit took me, the humdrum and the routine were totally alien and claustrophobic.

That wasn't the only reason I felt miffed and out of sorts. Those years of travel were supposed to have led me to India.

I've always had a strong intuition. I knew I had to be there. Well, I thought I did. Perhaps that was just wishful thinking. I never did have any clear idea of why I should be there. Perhaps I was wrong. It had taken heartbreak, chemical poisoning and a revolution to stop me. Now it seemed a highly unlikely dream. The trail from Europe to India overland was well- and-truly blocked by very real and fundamental changes in Iran.

I opened my birthday cards and then the only letter. I could see it was from the Youth Service. They'd told me they would write to confirm that my temporary contract had been converted to a permanent one. I read the letter lackadaisically. It was only a formality after all. What the…?

I was shocked. The council had run out of funding. Apparently I was now unemployed. I felt exasperated, flung the letter aside and threw up the sash window of my top floor flat. I yelled out, "Give me a break!"

That outburst made me feel a tiny bit better. I put coffee on to percolate. Hugging the mug of steaming coffee to warm my fingers, I went back into the living room. No sooner had my bum hit the sofa than I heard gravel hit the window pane. I peered down at the path and saw my old friend Pete. I threw the keys down for him.

While he was navigating the three flights of stairs I poured him a cuppa. I was cheering up a bit. It was great to see him.

We hugged. The first words out of his mouth were, "Hey. D'you wanna come to India?"

Seemed he'd inherited some money and wanted to go to India. He was in need of a chaperone because he'd never even been abroad before. I was the only person he could think of who'd travelled a lot.

"And so it came to pass," as they say, that a few weeks later, I was standing first in line to disembark from the British Airways jumbo jet just landed at Bombay airport. I was unemployed. I was skint but I was here. Perhaps I did have unfinished business from the journey I'd begun back in '75.

Charming Chaos

To be fair, Bombay is mind-blowing. I'd taken the precaution of booking three nights for us in a budget hotel and it was one of my better ideas. No sooner had we reached the arrivals hall at the airport than Pete went blank. I'd never seen anyone go into complete culture shock before. Up to this point it was just a term without meaning. We weren't even out of the airport.

To this day I doubt if he even remembers the ride to our hotel. I was now travelling with a shop-window manikin and I had my work cut out. But for now we were on a crazy fairground ride. We were in a dodgem car the Indians call a motorised rickshaw.

The little black and yellow tuk-tuk swayed impossibly on its three wheels, sped, stopped, jerked and dodged 'em all. 'All' included cars, bicycles, buses, cycle-rickshaws, taxis, stalls, street vendors, kids, a million other humans and of course dozens of strolling cows. Ah! Those cows. As if that wasn't enough to have to skilfully avoid, we narrowly escaped death by crossing a railway track. Our heads were thrown up to the fabric roof as what I think was a cumbersome old passenger train cut through the busy street. My doubt comes from never actually having seen those parts of a train that make it recognisable. All I saw was a topsy-turvy mountain of humanity sitting on, in and clinging to a moving something. It was only the repeated clanging of a loud bell that made me suspect we'd flown over a level-crossing. There were no gates or any other distinguishing factors.

The heat was intense, the noise and smells overpowering. To be honest I checked to see if our chariot was guided by a monorail, working on a pre-set course automatically. I couldn't see how else the driver was managing to avoid the sheer onslaught of obstacles. He must have done this before, I guess.

My eyes were working ten-to-the-dozen to take this all in. My ears and nose were more than a bit busy too. Pete still said nothing. He was frozen. He sat gripping his seat so hard that blood couldn't reach his fingers and with his mouth half-open. So that's what a white-knuckle ride means. His face was a picture but I wasn't quite sure of what. I was wondering how long culture-shock lasted. Then I had an even more sobering thought. "Did culture-shock ever wear off?"

Everything I've just mentioned formed my first impression of India. That said, there was more. The architecture was remarkable, not only because of the odd mixture of grandiose and decrepit but also because of all the signage hanging from it. Huge old buildings displayed billboards that were all hand -painted. They were selling everything. Cinemas advertised the current film with enormous metal pictures bolted together in segments and painted with gloss, piece by piece. From these the huge faces of unknown film stars glared down at us in garish and gaudy colours, each lip about the size of a London bus. Shopfronts displayed signs proclaiming "Suitings and Shirtings very cheaply" or "Freshly Fruits Today" and so much more in almost-English. Until now I'd believed that Oxford Street in London on Christmas Eve was crowded. I changed my mind.

We made it to the hotel. I paid the taxi-man and led Pete inside. We didn't know it but our room and this hotel reception were the perfect introduction to India. The furniture was a little too grandiose in that 'what epoch are we in exactly?' kind of way and made me want to ask 'By the way Sir, what room is Disraeli in?"

Our host was wonderful though. Perhaps he had seen other westerners as traumatised as Pete. I don't know. I do know that he helped me and our small bags get up to our room, brought up tea and sandwiches and some fresh orange juice. Pete collapsed on the bed. So far he hadn't said a single word since we left the airport. This was fun.

When he fell into a sleep-coma I took the opportunity to go out and get my bearings. I was in India! I scribbled the time on a piece of a paper and a note saying I'd be back in about half an hour. I grabbed some bottled water from reception and ventured forth. Not too far at all from the main stretch and its side roads, the utter turmoil subsided. I stumbled into a pretty square that was busy enough but only around its edges. In the middle? Nothing much was happening. I sipped my water and sat on a bench to pull myself together.

Before too long a guy started setting something up in the centre of the quadrangle. He appeared to be a street entertainer of some kind because he spread out a heavily patterned rug and began to open up bundles and packages. They struck me as stage props. I wasn't exactly concentrating. I was staring into space, over his head. I couldn't believe this! Out came an Ali-baba basket. Out came a long, wooden flute or pipe. He sat cross-legged on his rug next to the basket. 'No! Surely not! Oh yes!' This man was a snake-charmer.

My first instinct was to race back to the hotel and get Pete. There was no point. I had travelled enough to know that, from time to time, life presents you with a precious gift. This one was for me. I fumbled for my small sketch book and pencils in my cloth shoulder bag. I moved closer, sat in the same posture as the magician and started sketching. Funnily enough it was my sketching that pulled a crowd. Before I knew it I'd attracted quite a lot of people. The charmer gave me eye contact. His grin was so mischievous. I knew him, if you get my drift. Suddenly he had his audience, didn't he?

He didn't open his act with the snake bit. He knew how to work an audience. He pointed at me with an open hand. Goodness knows what he was saying. I kept my eyes on my page and my right hand clasping the pencil as it sketched frantically. The people around me parted suddenly. He said something directly at me. My onlookers explained, "He's asking what is your favourite flower?" I answered,

"Roses."

"He's saying, 'Smell the palm of your right hand'."

'What?' but I obliged. My right palm, clenched holding my pencil all this time, reeked of roses. Everyone near me leaned over to sniff it. They gasped and applauded in turn.

Then something remarkable. Every one of them turned to me, put their own two hands together, palm to palm and bowed to me respectfully.

That brought tears to my eyes. I welled up.

It would be wrong to say I had no idea what was going on. I had my suspicions, my own interpretation of all this but that didn't mean I was right, did it?

We all watched as the magician played his flute and a large snake wound its way upwards from out of the basket. It danced, mesmerised by the haunting melody.

As soon as they were otherwise occupied I packed up silently and crept away. "What on earth had just happened? How long had I been away from the hotel?" I found my way back there, sat in the lounge and sipped tea.

The owner and I sat and chatted about Bombay and our trip. I left the lounge with a fistful of pamphlets stuffed in my bag, a railway schedule for Poona and two cups of tea.

God only knows

The whole world knows the '60s and '70s brought a revolution in youth culture. What I didn't realise (or didn't pay attention to more like) was that most places in the same world weren't experiencing it.

It wasn't only music and fashion that exploded. Changes seeped into every part of everyday life. There was an excitement about. Something was in the air. Jumbled up in all of it came new ideas and all things eastern too, including the spiritual. The spirit of youth went seeking fulfilment and enlightenment. After Sgt Pepper, the place to be was India.

Strangely mysticism wasn't what attracted me there. I had no idea why the draw to be there was so strong. I figured I'd see it like buying shoes. Some have 'mine' written all over them. When I saw it, I'd know it.

Lots of crazy stuff was getting through to us back then. Some musicians who were our heroes (like The Beatles and Pete Townsend) were introducing us to a new word 'guru' and what that entailed. The world divided into seekers and followers. That's a bit simplistic but sounds right. The latter had no appeal for me whatsoever.

It turns out that India was littered with gurus. Very few of those had famous Westerners among their followers. What all this boiled down to in my world was that, by the time Pete and I arrived in Poona, the idea of following a spiritual leader wasn't strange to us at all.

Was I afraid of cults? No. A cult? A religion? Strikes me as only a question of scale. History records that even Christianity was once a weird little cult. Did I want a guru? No. It was only a few months ago I'd realised that in-tuition is exactly what it says on the tin.

I trusted mine.

Although we'd popped in here to fulfil a promise and deliver mail, this was a safe environment to hang out for a while. Full of westerners to meet and clean food and water guaranteed, Pete could take a few days here to calm down and get over his shock. We could cobble together a few loose travel plans too.

Poona was the location of the Rajneesh ashram. His full title was Bhagwan Shree Rajneesh. To some he was god incarnate. (Aren't we all?) His disciples or students were called Sanyassins and wore orange.

It was a beautiful setting. Only a short walk off the beaten track a huge area had been lovingly converted into superb gardens. It was an Eden where exotic trees, plants and flowers flourished and delighted our senses after the rush, chaos and pollution of Bombay. Residents had lovingly constructed pleasant buildings for shelter too. All of the outdoor spaces were alive with never-ending birdsong, delicious colours, wonderful perfumes and a heart-warming sense of tranquillity.

Bhagwan and his Sannyasins were a spiritual community made up of folk who were, by and large, pretty laid back and easy-going. We were just two more strangers who'd turned up unannounced.

Buddha Hall was the focal point. It was a massive, marble-topped plinth under a fascinatingly-shaped grass roof supported by hand-carved tree trunks all around the perimeter. Every morning back then, the Master held audience and took questions. The first time I saw him I got it! This man was as bright as a button, cool as a cucumber and downright funny. Why? Well, if you are going to help sort out the mental issues of a crowd of young western kids how better than to appear as an old man with long white hair and a flowing beard. All that was needed was a throne. He had one. It was perfect. 'Hit us where it all started, why don't you?'

I couldn't work out if this image that Bhagwan and other gurus present to the world is traditional or great marketing. It certainly works as a reflection to the western audience who expect nothing less. I'd already started giggling. Unfortunately my sense of humour didn't go down too well with some disciples. I got a lot of stern glares. With respect to our hosts we lay back on that marble floor some mornings to listen to what god had to say. Bhagwan didn't exactly help me in my attempt to cut back on my laughing. One morning, in a truly wonderful and slow, tuneful voice, (that floated on his breath to whistle slightly at the end of his s soundsssssssssss) he said,

"Sit up. Sit up now." So I did. I looked around the hall. Unbelievably, of all the dozens and dozens of people, not one other person sat up. He carried on. His voice sang

"You do not need a guru. You do not need me. Leave, why do you not leave?"

I looked around at the heaps of meditating bodies, semi-conscious on the floor and started to laugh again. I had to keep twisting my body to get first one foot and then the other over and in between each and every sannyasin in my way. Just as I made it to the very edge I heard "Many people are asking me, 'Where can I find God? And I answer 'Why are you asking me? You must have left him somewhere. Where did you leave him'?"

That set me off again. I sat in the empty gardens and laughed until my ribs ached. I really did like this man. We wandered around checking the place out and making friends. There was a ton of information on a thousand noticeboards. One of the courses attracted me. I was itching to have a go at three days of Sufi dancing and learn to spin. I can't remember what Pete fancied doing but there was a lot on offer. A few days here could be fun. News travel fast in any small town and this community was no exception. Pretty soon it was obvious I'd gained a reputation of being a sceptic through and through. I thought it was a bit harsh. After all the worst I could be accused of was laughing. They were convinced I hadn't taken the great master seriously; not treated him with enough respect. Now that was very strange. From my point of view I was the only one who had actually heard what he'd said and acted on it. When I asked Pete why he hadn't sat up and left? He'd simply never heard those words. Like most happenings in Poona (we would learn) 'you make of it what you will'. At least Sufi Dancing was physical. It would have nothing to do with all this mental supposition and acrobatics, would it?

To give him his due god started his day quite late. This meant that nothing much happened until about 11 when he'd finished talking and answering questions. This particular morning he answered a question that appealed to me, a lot. Someone had popped a question into god's box that went like this, "Is there any truth in the Bible?"

Now, whereas most would hear that question as loose, off-the cuff and non-committal, me and the Master took it at face value and literally. So he and I agreed on the answer. He put it so much better than I could have done though. It was that voice of his that did the trick; his soft, breathy and enticing tone; his sibilants that were drawn out gently into an oh-so soft whistle, and his wickedly mischievous giggle. Bearing those in mind, his answer came after a belly-laugh of some considerable length. He said, 'That's the only miracle in it' before launching into the helplessness of that belly-laugh again.

Yep! This guy was cool (or should I sssssay 'cool'?)

Thing was, I was having my reservations about this dervish dancing thing. Why? Well, over my light breakfast of herbal tea (the only kind available) and flat-bread, it occurred to me that the only time I had ever spun and spun for the sheer joy of it, was when I was a kid. Okay, so what? So what? Follow it through. What did that inevitably lead to? Right! Giddiness! Why on earth would I want to spend an hour making myself giddy? Of course, that question set me off laughing again. Perhaps giddy was my normal state of being anyway.

A pink man in a turban on a donkey somewhere in Turkey (and many moons away) goaded me on. I went back to Buddha Hall to dance myself into the dizziness that my inner child could handle and definitely loved. Why not? In for a penny, in for Ezra Pound! I also ought to say that by now I was dressed in a loose, dark red, cool cotton dress, both sleeveless and full length. I bought it from the Ashram shop. I couldn't face more orange so I went for dark red.

The other members of this group were already in the hall. I slipped off my sandals and joined them. The shade from the grass roof was more than welcome. Early morning didn't mean cool In India. At this time of morning the sun was still hot. The cold marble felt gorgeous to my bare feet, calming and soothing. It fact it cooled my entire body.

When we were calm and collected our instructor asked us to close our eyes, shake the stress out of ourselves for a moment and then stand stock still. Minutes later we were to stand, feet apart with arms outstretched to either side. Next we were to imagine a golden cord running down through the centre of our heads and down further through our whole body and extending outward to all four limbs.

Poised like- so, we waited. Prejudgement being what prejudgement is, I was expecting sudden, intermittent 'tings' of a Buddhist bell perhaps? No. This was Bhagwan's gaff! In that meditative and serene state we heard ....Pinocchio.

What was he singing? Of course he was. "I've got no strings to hold me down, to make me fret, or make me frown. I had strings but now I'm free. There are no strings on me.

Hi-ho the me-rri-o. That's the only way to be, I want the world to know nothing ever worries me" ....and do you know what? I'd heard that song a million times but that was the first time I'd ever heard the lyrics.

Pinocchio stopped. We waited. I was processing the words.

I knew I came to earth with no strings attached. On that particular day in that particular moment in time, I was privileged to be among a dance group of about 20 people re-realising it at one and the same time. Then it started.

I heard the insanely enchanting and head-bending rhythms of the Eastern music I love. It announced itself softly. Slowly, slowly it was winding itself up and up, faster and faster and faster we spun.

Fears of giddiness, speed and of falling over came and went in the blink of an eye. The music paid no heed to my mind. It went straight for my heart. Then it reached my soul. Fear was something to do with a mind my body didn't need right now. It didn't need it at all. With my feet on one spot my body spun. What use words when feelings take over?

In retrospect I was the eye of the storm. At that centre everything was calm and still. The world outside looked crazy; a speeding blur of giddiness spinning and running around me; madness with a strange hum to it. And here I was absolutely still, watching it all go on around me. At the outer edges of the blur, the colours of the gardens swept in and out. My body was a spinning top. Very gradually the music slowed.

At a moment of my choosing I stepped out into the melee. Cool, calm and collected, I stepped out through that fuzziness of activity I'd seen. Now it was gone.

There wasn't a hint of giddiness. We stood still and with eyes closed we listened. Did we need prayers? Advice? Meditation bells? No. We needed those deeply philosophical words "I've got no strings, so I have fun. I'm not tied up to anyone. They've got strings But you can see, there are no strings on me."

For goodness knows how long, I was a whirling dervish.

No Strings on Us

Okay, okay so it was cool and easy being in an ashramful of western seekers with easy access to all the amenities we were accustomed to but it felt wrong. Perhaps wrong's too strong a word but definitely not right. It isn't fair to generalise but on the whole the majority of people here didn't venture outside the confines of their comfort zone, physically speaking that is. We were in India for goodness sake!

I took my care-taking job of Pete seriously but he was acclimatised now. When we weren't involved in dancing or listening we took every opportunity to get out and about in the nearby town and explore our surroundings.

In brochures and glossy magazines the everyday things in India seem so enticing and exotic. Take bicycle rickshaws for one example. Fancy yourself being pedalled around to see and experience the very essence of India? It sounds great, huh? Now...do it. Anyone with a heart will soon experience the dilemmas Pete and I kept feeling. Frail men, young and often very old; worn out by the exertion of cycling and pulling a couple of overfed tourists in sweltering heat fought for that privilege.

On the one hand we just couldn't do it; on the other hand their livelihoods depended on us overcoming our concerns for their well-being. Crazy though it may seem we compromised. Whenever we came to any kind of upward climb we made an excuse to get down and walk and pretended to be looking at shops and stalls we had absolutely no interest in. This, of course, got us into deeper water. We had to buy trinkets and all sorts of nonsense at those stalls so as not to appear aloof or haughty. Needless to say we gave these away to the next ones who looked in need. Added to all this was the incredible poverty.

Initially a visitor to India feels obliged to give to a beggar. It is the right thing to do, or is it? We soon learned that one attracted two, attracted three until we were being followed by dozens and often mobbed. It was all too much. Even stranger was the fact that I had absolutely no money. I was poor but the word scarcely fitted me, did it? Try explaining that to those all around us who were living in abject poverty. It made me sad. It made me even sadder to go back to the ashram each day and witness the contrast. That's one way I learned about the absolute folly of the western mind, a mind which seems bent on creating problems that needn't exist only to spend hundreds of pounds to solve them. As a westerner I had mental issues too but now I could see they weren't life threatening by any means. In fact, I wondered if my main mental issue was that I had mental issues about mental issues.

It is impossible to explain but living in western culture certainly messes up the mind. All around me that fact was displayed in bright orange. Anyhow, somewhere along the way I stopped laughing and took a long hard look at my surroundings and the state the world was in. The friends I'd made in the ashram were still pressing me to take the whole Bhagwan thing more seriously, more to heart. They still accused me of not giving the experience my all. My all was invested in the India I was glimpsing outside of the compounds.

Those glimpses were affecting me deeply. "Who's running this world?" came up again as an unanswerable question. I remembered my friend the judge in the Leeds train. This was all arbitrary. If that didn't explain something, look to economics.

On one rickshaw ride I noticed huge fields spread out to my right and on into the long distance. They were just unworked fields, gone to seed and derelict. It was wasteland that stretched for miles. I stared and stared and realised they were overgrown with marijuana plants. In astonishment I pointed them out to Pete and asked, "Is that really dope?"

Quite calmly he said, "Well yes. It's not called weed for nothing, you know?" That did it. That started me thinking. Here were acres of weeds. Who on earth decided these weeds were illegal? I gave myself an answer. "The people who realised they could sell them."

Over the coming days we sketched out a travel plan as best we could. Going south was a no-no. It was already scorching hot here. Further south would be unbearable. There were times in the day here in Poona when the tarmac in the town began to melt. Besides, no trip to India would be complete without a visit to the Taj Mahal and I was determined to get as close to Tibet as I could. India being as vast as it is, the distances we had to travel were huge. We had to make a choice. North it was.

From people we met we learned that Varanasi, also known as Benares, was a sight to see. I got hold of a pamphlet that said the city was one of the oldest inhabited cities on earth, one of the seven most sacred sites in India. The pictures of it were mind-blowing. Apart from those rough ideas we had no plans. I couldn't wait to get moving.

When rumour spread that Pete and I were in fact leaving we came under a kind of spiritual bombardment. My guess was that people who have found a place where they feel they belong take great comfort in believing that anyone in their right mind would want to be like them. The fact that we didn't was proving a bit unnerving for them.

On the day before we were due to leave I was begged to think again and just give it one more shot. I had to put my whole heart into the experience. Today a very special guest was holding audience in Buddha Hall; a guest who was a great healer. If I took it seriously I would surely stay. In the end I promised I'd attend.

At about midday we made our way to the Hall. Lines of people were queueing for something. When we got to the front we were asked to consider deeply if we had anything wrong with us or a disease of some sort. We had to write it down on a fragment of paper and pop that into a huge box. Those friends who'd persuaded me to come sat close to keep an eye on my attitude. I was determined to enter into this wholeheartedly, so help me god.

I sat in anticipation. I watched respectfully. I'd scribbled my disease. I'd put it dutifully in the box. The great man was announced.

His name was 'He Who Has Been and Come Back.' Deep breath needed. 'O........k. He appeared.

Oh no! Please no. Please don't do this now. Not now.

Remember the Adamm's Family? (The original T.V. version?) Remember Jackie Coogan as Uncle Fester? He was here but in an orange robe.

I was so proud of myself. I didn't allow even a smirk. I gulped and gripped my dress. It couldn't last, could it? Believe me it didn't. He faced us. He rolled his huge eyes. His pupils flipped up under his eyelids and disappeared. Muggins here exploded. No, seriously, the laughter I'd been choking down genuinely burst out. Now of course I couldn't stop, could I? You must have been there, in that most serious of places, a funeral maybe? Where you must not laugh. I was there.

I was nearly wetting myself as I hopped, skipped and jumped over all the annoyed people just to get out. I was shaking, crying and snorting. I was trying to say something. I was trying to say "No. No. He's brilliant. Honestly he's brilliant. It worked. It worked. I'm cured. He's cured me, honestly, honestly, he's cured me. I'm cured. I'm cured. Let me out."

If looks could kill, eh? They didn't get it. On my little piece of paper I'd scribbled, "In danger of losing my sense of humour."

Outside in the garden my stomach and ribs ached but I calmed down. I was thinking about the experience in this whole strange Orange scene. What could possibly sum up the whole Rajneesh thing? I suddenly remembered something about George Bernard Shaw. The opening night of a play had flopped. Afterwards, backstage, someone asked him how he felt.

"The play, sir, was an outstanding success. The audience, however, was an abysmal failure."

Pop-Ups

Cast your mind right back to when you were a kid. Can you recall being sucked in and absorbed by pop-up books? The pages were huge, weren't they?

I always went inside mine.

Well, sometimes one of this world's most famous sights does that to me. It pops up in front of me wham! And I'm drawn right in. One in particular did it now.

Pete and I arrived at our cheap, little hotel in Agra very late at night after a very long journey. We should've been ready for bed but we were overtired. We weren't up for sightseeing but felt like going for a stroll. It was a hot night under a huge full moon when we stepped outside.

Across the narrow road was an old high wall. We crossed over and ambled along. It was great to be off the train we'd been on for hours and great to smell strange aromas from strange trees and unfamiliar blossoms. We hadn't been walking long when we noticed an arched doorway coming up. It was embedded in the stones of the wall. We had to take a peek, didn't we? Sharp, sudden intake of breath! Before our very eyes popped up.... the Taj Mahal.

The pages around and behind it were illustrations of a dark-blue velvet sky. The marble of the Taj was made silver by the moon. Leading up to it, the artist had painted a stretch of water with moonlight to turn it into a silver carpet. Fountains danced and tinkled. We froze, speechless. We were holding onto this moment to treasure. Neither of us spoke as we stepped in to those magical gardens. Ravishing might come close. We were dumbstruck I guess. What could we have said anyway?

The whole place was ours, not a soul in sight. Calm and amazed Pete and I plonked ourselves on the lush grass. The monument to love stood alone in the Indian summer night. It was big.

Stark shadows began to blur at their edges under passing clouds. Our surroundings grew dark. I blinked then blinked again. Tiredness was taking its toll on my eyesight. I rubbed them and looked again. Tiny, luminous-green lights were floating and dancing in the warm air. I looked away to rest my eyes by concentrating on the grass. It didn't help. Lights were crawling and wriggling along the grass. I closed my eyes to rest them.

Out of the black Pete said, "Is it my eyes or can you see little bright lights everywhere?"

Fireflies filled the air around us. Glow worms had come out to play on the lawns. How magical was this? Pete and little ol' me had our own private and enchanting light show in front of the Taj Mahal. We weren't sentimental by any means but we spontaneously held hands and squeezed. Words wouldn't have been enough. How long we sat there I don't remember. A tired but elated pair of travellers ambled back to their room to dream like the kids they truly were.

"Shall we do the tourist thing tomorrow and visit the Taj Mahal?" Pete laughed quietly as he fell into his bed.

"Why not?" I giggled. "Goodnight Jim Bob."

That was it. We giggled ourselves to sleep.

Save. Our. Soles.

Yes. Pop-up books were my favourites when I was a kid. The wonder used to engulf me. Best was to put them on the table and peer across at their pages while ducking down to be at eye level. From that position I could get in. That was a great feeling especially when the pages led me into the real world of a story I thought I already knew. Writing these memoires has shown me how I've stored these distant memories in that attic I call my mind.

Some are photographs; snapshots that come with feelings felt when I captured them. Others are more like short films that I can project on mind's wall to relive.

Some are exactly like those childhood pop-up pages because that's how I experienced them. Among these types of memories are stored a lot of the world's most renowned tourist sites. They always took me by surprise. A prime example is the Colosseum in Rome. When I first visited that illustrious city I had no clue where the Colosseum was. Come to think of it I have no idea where I imagined it would be. It was 1972 and I was in a V.W camper van packed with young American stoners who'd offered me lift miles ago. The van skidded, screeched and wove through traffic only Italians can create just on the outskirts of the capital. In the back we were being slung and flung all over the place. Nippy little motor scooters kept parping and cars honking. We swerved and I was thrown against the far window. Bam! Pop-up moment! "My God. It's the Colosseum. It's in the middle of all this traffic."

After breakfast the very next morning we took the camera, sunglasses, hats and all the stuff that tourists take to visit the famous Taj Mahal by daylight.

It was only 10.30 but the much-loved mausoleum was glaring under a sizzling sun. Hot doesn't even begin to describe it. The scene from our previous night had changed dramatically. It was 1979 and international tourism was still not readily or cheaply available to most. Visitors to India were either the rich or the adventurous on a tight budget. The crowds weren't there. Sure there were visitors but most were Indian couples or families on holiday. There were enough milling about to sharpen the contrast of our magical night.

The walk up the main avenue is longer than it looks in all those familiar photographs. There was no rush. We weren't restricted by a 'tour' agenda. I pity those who are.

Where grass and fountained waterway meet the huge building, a line is drawn.

Beyond that line shoes are not allowed. This being India, some twenty yards or so before the end of the lawns, a middle-aged man had set up shop to rent 'foot-coverings' for those (we assumed) unaccustomed to walking barefoot. I can't remember how much he wanted exactly but he thrust these covers at us and said, "Only 50. 50, 50 rupees."

Don't get me wrong. We did our best to support the ever-ingenious entrepreneurial spirit of the Indian people whenever we could but that seemed a bit much. Despite his protestations and his grabbing us by the sleeve (to make a sale) we shook our heads and walked on. We felt quite proud of ourselves that we'd actually managed to say no to an Indian selling us something. It's a nation of great salesmen.

We slipped off our sandals at the edge of the grass where a large area of marble paving began. A few large strides and we got it. We yelped, hopped and danced an insane dance like the idiots we were. "Ooh. Aah. Ooh. Oo. Aah." Duh! White marble, sizzling sun? 2 and 2 together? Equals scorch.

Earlier visitors watched us and laughed. I like to think they'd done this mad dance and were caught out like us. Maybe not though. I imagine it's left to those of us who don't come from such hot climates who show themselves up and dance like hillbillies around the Taj. The soles of our feet were singed. We Morris-danced off the marble at long last and made a bee line back to the guy, tails between our legs. (Bees don't have tails I know). He handed us the now much-coveted sock things.

"Only 150. 150. 150 rupees!"

Bargain!

Impressionable

After hours travelling propped up on this train's luggage rack, we were glad to get to Varanasi. The world and his brother were on here with us. To say it was full to overflowing is no exaggeration and at the station overflow it did. People dripped and poured off the roof where they'd been sitting and clinging for hours. People were being posted through windows by others who wanted to exit the same way. Groups were wedged tight in doorways in their rush to be out there in this city. This was a pilgrimage.

We waited for the human stream to run into a trickle before even considering leaving the comparative safety of the carriages. Left with us was an old, old lady. She was bent double; her spine locked at a right angle from the heavy burdens she had carried working in the fields, day in and day out from a very early age. Members of her extended family were roping a big bundle onto her back, deeply concerned that it was secure. Whatever was inside the sackcloth was big and extremely heavy. It took three grown men to lift it. They eventually got off the train and we followed.

The platform was heaving. The granny kept to the back of it all, toothlessly smiling. Then! Horror of horrors, she stumbled and fell. We rushed to help her. We weren't alone of course. The family ran back too. The only difference between us and them? They all ran straight to the prized package! They didn't so much as ask her if she was okay. Not a word. Not a glance. We helped her up. Aunties, uncles, brothers and sons proceeded to unwrap the hessian sacking. Inside was a 3 ft. high, solid stone statue of Krishna. It was imperative that God reach the Ganges safe and sound.

Welcome to Varanasi!

This place is so old. Difficult to grasp that the Buddha delivered his first sermon near here in the 6th century B.C. And here I was.

With a waterfront that sprawls for 8 miles along the sacred Ganges, this is the oldest, continuously-occupied city on earth. Indians strive to visit this holy place at least once before they die. The belief is that if you are fortunate enough to die here you will be freed from the wheel of Karma (of having to be reborn ever again), guaranteed salvation. To be cremated here is the next best thing.

Most people think that learning from life is hard. Personally, I find the unlearning more challenging. Varanasi was about to give me a masterclass.

Over its thousands and thousands of years of development the town has spilled over the sides of the steep embankments it sits on. It has crept down to the water's edge and then crawled slowly back up again. All of the stages in between are clearly discernible on the multi-tiered slopes. A peculiar mish-mash of buildings clings to the steep climb. Dilapidated homes and temples clutch each other at the edges of dirt platformed steps that make a thoroughfare. The way these narrow walkways twisted and tightly turned convinced me they were originally goat paths very gradually widened by the millions of footsteps I was now following.

On our first afternoon we went for a walk. The earthen main street was so narrow no motorized vehicle could use it. The surface had been compacted by centuries of passers-by. We did not know it was the holy path that every pilgrim longs to walk along. There were lots of things we did not know. But even we could feel the path pulling us downward, downward towards the great river.

A turn to our right and we were descending more steeply. To either side of us tall, decaying structures hemmed us in. We had to watch out. We kept our eyes on where we were stepping. We were concentrating so hard on negotiating the sudden bends and twists that we had no idea or view of where we were heading.

Before long, even that slow progress was halted. We were in a queue, a line, a people-jam. This was the norm apparently. Day and night, day in day out, lines of people squash and jostle down this hill, shouting out advice to each other on how best to manoeuvre and manipulate the homemade stretchers they carry over their heads. The things are lifted and held by means of long, wooden poles at either side. On those stretchers? The corpse of their deceased loved one, fortunate enough to be buried here.

My first thought? 'Well. This is a first! I've never been in a procession where I'm queueing up behind the dead.' In the blink of an eye I answered myself with 'You have. You've always been in one. You've just never realised it.'

There were plenty of other people here who hadn't come for the funeral rites. They were here to fulfil a lifelong dream. Those pilgrims on the slope didn't stand on ceremony (excuse the pun). Not for them the oh-so Western attitude of 'let's wait calmly then and show respect for the dead'. Not at all. They pushed and shoved their way past as if they were at the opening of the Christmas Sales in their favourite department store, all smiles and excitement. I started to laugh. For some inexplicable reason my mind whispered "As you were chaps. As you were!" I looked at the dead bodies then back at us all. 'Yep. As you were' is right.

We gingerly wound our way around that corpse and then the next and the next. The procession of dead bodies seemed endless. The compartments in my western mind that separated life from death were breaking down.

By twisting, turning, squeezing through and constantly watching our footing, our first glimpse of the open Ganges took us by surprise. Her waters filled the entire horizon. There was no opposite bank. This looked like a sea. The river was vast at this point. The steep, awkward passageway had opened up into an enormous auditorium of epic proportions. How do I even attempt to describe all this for you? Take a deep breath.

We spilled out into a chaos and mayhem that worked just fine.

The auditorium was like an amphitheatre. It was a series of long, very long, stone steps sagging under the weight of centuries of use. They could be climbed quite easily but served as benches too. They provided seating for the weary, the waiting, the day-trippers and the curious, every one like a spectator taking their seat for The Greatest Show on Earth. What that show was? We had no idea. For the moment we were blissfully ignorant, again.

We sat to have a ciggie. We stared out at water as far as the eye could see in all directions.

After a while my mind flipped my perspective. What if this wasn't the auditorium? What if we weren't the audience? What if this was a stage set and we the actors? What if The Goddess Ganges watched our play as she passed? How did this all look from the river's point of view? If ever there was a time when I wanted to stand up, step forward and speak an immortal line or two, this was it. There was only one line it could be, "To be or not to be."

The stage set of the burning Ghats is best appreciated from a boat on the river. (Enter Wossyorz.)

Wossyorz was a street kid who adopted us as soon as he spotted us. He never got the hang of "My name's Maggie. My name's Pete" or the purpose of us pointing at him and asking "What's yours?" He called himself just that. So be it. He was happy. He took to sleeping on the hard floor outside our hotel room door in case he missed anything. The proprietor informed us that Wossyorz desperately wanted to wake us early one morning in time to see the sunrise. Seemed a little odd but we played along.

At an ungodly hour we three set off and down the hill. We thought the place would be a bit emptier. As we reached the bottom of the hill it sounded as if we might be right. Seemed like most sensible people were still in bed.

I have never seen so many people crammed into one outside space in absolute silence and semi-darkness. Row after row after row, (fifty to a hundred people deep) stood, motionless staring out across the dark waters. It may be clichéd but every one of us would have heard that wayward pin drop. It didn't dare. Every eye was glued to the watery horizon. At first I just thought. 'Okay, so the sun's gonna come up,' and I diligently waited. I waited. I stared. We waited. We stared. We waited and waited. We stared and stared. Believe me or not the suspense was building to a point where I started to be more than a bit concerned. 'What if it didn't come? What if the sun didn't rise? Just because it had always risen didn't mean it would rise for ever, did it?' Still no sign. Now we were as one. 'Would it? Or wouldn't it?' This was real. Why on earth had I taken this for granted?

Then the upper rim of a gigantic, dazzling orb peeped over the line that separates the earth and heavens. The magical sphere slid upwards ever-so gradually, its glare shooting out across the water directly at us. As an audience we erupted into rapturous applause, chanting, singing and dancing. Many among us leapt into the water in sheer joy and thanksgiving. Flowers were thrown from everywhere. The waters were strewn with brightly coloured petals.

From the river's point of view the cast sprang into action as soon as the spotlight was on them. "Action!"

Our beloved little friend wasted no time. He led us to a rowing boat and we climbed in. From a short way out we looked back at the scene we had just left. Here I'll ask you to imagine. Imagine you're in the greatest art gallery on earth. You enter a huge room and sit in front of an enormous painting that covers an entire wall. You are so close to it that there is nothing else in your line of vision. What kind of place is this? You can't quite make out what's going on and why these swarms of people are gathered together. The backdrop is otherworldly. What is that? You focus. As you focus you are being drawn in.

The backdrop is a peculiar collection of buildings of different height and different places in time. Set after set of stone steps lead up to these towering shapes and back down to the water's edge. Flat stones. Stone platforms. Tree trunks. Stacks and stacks of cut tree-trunks piled high everywhere, in every available space. So many surfaces stacked high with them, to your left, right, above the people and beneath them.

There are temples, domes, turrets, spires and castellated remnants of a bygone age standing in line...oh! Look higher! Resting at the left edge of the painting and sitting at the top of the grandest steps are some magnificent decaying palaces. Maharajas once gave parties here. But now who are the guests? Enormous vultures sitting along their flat, ornate roofs show themselves by their unmistakable silhouettes, painted stark against the wide Indian sky. They lurk.

I jump. A vulture I was eyeing takes off from the old palace and swoops down so close to us, only yards away. Yikes! Wossyorz tugs at my shawl. He points at something in the river. I think I'm gonna throw up. The body of a small infant has surfaced, has slipped free of the stone that held it under. The vulture starts pecking at the dead eyes. I turn away and face the shore.

The mass of brightly clad people are eating, buying food, souvenirs, relics and posies of flowers from tatty umbrella'd stalls slung up at random. Boats and boatmen are scurrying, loading and unloading wood. People are bathing fully-clothed, holy men are chanting and making strange gestures towards the horizon.

You have been caught up. There's an unbelievable cacophony of all the sounds of this veritable hive. Oh! The smells. What is that smell?

The funeral pyres are ablaze by the shoreline now. The temperature needed to cremate a human body is immense. Amid all the living crowds the dead burn in full view.

This is where I am. This is all around me. There's the crackling of wood and flesh, the sparks and embers swirling upward and the Untouchables heaving more and more wood onto those pyres to feed the flames. The smoke thickens then wafts where it will, transforming the canvas into an Impressionist masterpiece after all. It's unmistakeable, isn't it? That gift impressionism brings. That ability and freedom it allows you, to make of it all what you will.

Rajbah

"Raaaj....baaaah!" He absolutely hollered. The 'he' in question was a mild-mannered, smiley Indian man standing not more than a foot in front of us. The yell nearly split our eardrums and made us jump. Until that point we'd been calmly negotiating the rental of a houseboat on the lake to our left. Without as much as a turn of the head he did it again, "Raaaaj...baaaah!"

"What the?" was written all over our faces. There weren't that many people milling about but those there were seemed oblivious to the random outbursts. We had no idea what the word meant. Was it some kind of religious outcry? (A bit like crossing yourself in Ireland when the Angelus rings from the church bell?) Nah. Unless he was the only member of the religion (which by the way is quite possible in India) it was unlikely. We settled for Tourette's syndrome. At least after the first two bellowings we were braced against any more.

I'll admit we were stoned. Of all people it was the bus driver that got us stoned. If you could see the roads (loose definition) we'd just travelled along for the best part of a day and a half, you would think it very unwise for any driver to be out of it. We did. That was until we experienced the rubble tracks only ever-so slightly wider than the bus, twisting around bends and corners designed by those guys who build the scariest ever rollercoasters. Corners and bends almost in cloud kept coming at us. I was a bit scared to look. There were sheer drops down to my left side, drops of about a thousand feet! Overhangs that didn't look like they were going to hang over anything for much longer scraped the top of the mountain of luggage piled on the roof. I'll spare you the occasional rockslide and the crumbling edges of the road. Let's just say the line between our life and our death got excruciatingly thin at times. Once you get to see it and be there, getting stoned seems like the best idea in the world. If going over a cliff is likely to take you out of yourself, why not do it yourself first?

Pete was already suffering from his previous and very recent brush with his own mortality. In the depot where we'd boarded this bus, we were watching it being loaded up. The bus was metal. Okay we could cope with that. The ladder the packers propped up against the bus was metal. Not too much strange there. The big problem for Pete came when the metal trunks were being piled and piled and piled onto the metal roof rack. It seemed like a 'Guinness Book of Records' attempt to rebuild the Tower of Babel.

My eyes couldn't help but follow the mesmerising antics of these wallahs. They worked as a team, tossing huge piles of stuff from hand to hand, catching them as if they were as light as feathers and building up teetering stacks. Then! Pete grasped my hand. What? Why? He was squeezing it till the blood was draining from it. His eyes were popping out of his head. He was rigid.

Ignorance is bliss. Unfortunately he didn't have that luxury. He was a qualified electrician.

Drooping ominously and precariously within inches of the latest highest trunk was an extremely thick electricity mains cable. It was already badly patched together with tape in more places than one. Bless him. Pete didn't freak. He whispered very calmly,

"Get ready to run."

As if on cue there was an almighty bang and blinding flash. The cable whiplashed loose and crackled, sparked and thrashed around like a crazed boa constrictor. It took on a mind of its own. Trust me! When Pete said "Run!"....we ran.

From the safety of the far side of the road we looked back, as the Indians chased the offending cable. "They're out of their minds!" Pete was mumbling over and over. "Insane!"

When the bus was eventually ready to leave and chaos overcome (for now) we got on it.

There wasn't a single landscape, form of transport, street, river or roadway in India that was ever devoid of people. Transport was always crammed. Imagine our surprise to be the last people boarding and find an empty free seat for two right up front by the driver. I did tell you there were lots of things we didn't know, didn't I? Naïvely we felt lucky. With a huge glass windscreen right down to my feet and wrapped slightly round to my left I could enjoy a panoramic view of the hill station scenery we were about to witness.

And that, dear friends, is exactly why the locals on this bus didn't want to sit there. The same locals who were all too aware of the death-defying ride ahead.

Srinagar, Kashmir, we'd arrived. We two were slightly the worse for wear but deliriously happy and somewhat surprised to still be alive. Back in those days Srinagar was a small, typically dishevelled Indian town. It oozed charm, other-worldliness and some magic. The foothills of the Himalayas were a nearby backdrop and the air was deliciously chilled after the sweltering heat further south. This was stunning.

Everything here happened on the Lake. We'd been told a great, cheap way to stay was to rent a houseboat on this- Lake Dal. Naturally, being from Europe we knew what houseboat meant, right? Wrong.

"Raaaj Baaaah." This time we burst out laughing. For my part I was by now imagining George Harrison, cross-legged, suitably garbed with sitar in lap singing the word over and over, musical trills 'n' all. I can't imagine what Pete's imagination was doing with it. I didn't even want to go there!

The said famous lake was to our left. Across the wide expanse of water houseboats were moored, packed together tightly enough for a person to step over from one to the next. They were actually house boats, that is they had something the size of a bungalow on their decks, complete with verandas and narrow gardens. There were dozens upon dozens.

We were separated from them by the calm, mirrored surface of Lake Dal some feet below us, and a rough stone wall along the water's edge. The wall was within touching distance so the pop-up moment was impossible to miss. No. It wasn't a building or tourist attraction. It was a Rajbah physically popping up.

A chubby little chap no more than ten years old popped his head up over the wall. When I say head, it wasn't his head exactly, it was the top of it. Two huge eyes and a little nose followed. They were under an astrakhan hat. To either side of this impish apparition, were two small hands, fingers splayed to grip the wall. The big, bright eyes rolled from side to side and back again and then again. Maybe he was scouting for any of his mates who might be about here on land. No joy there, those mischievous eyes fixed on us.

The mild-mannered man clipped him across the top of the hat and the vision disappeared for a second. Then we spotted and tracked his hat bobbing up and down as it moved away from us slightly, right up against the far side of the wall. It went up and in and out of sight until it revealed what was under it, sort of piece by piece.

The man (his dad we presumed) smiled serenely and in that head-nodding, neck bobbing way that Indians have, he said 'Rajbah' in a tone that carried oh-so many nuances but also forgave the kid from being who he was. The obvious nuance was one of introduction. The undercurrent said "Watch out!"

The Rajbah in question led us down the previously unseen steps and into a rowing boat. All the way across he asked questions. His English was excellent. This kid was as bright as a button. On that boat ride we heard our new titles for the first time. "Sa'ab and Mem Sa'ab."

I do not tell a lie. We were instantly transported back into The Raj. It wouldn't have surprised me one iota if Queen Victoria had sailed by on one of the gondolas being punted around us. (You should be getting the hang of this by now but just in case- 'No!' You don't know what Gondola means!') So successful was the Time Travel that we couldn't help ourselves. For a while there we were possessed. "Oh

Marmaduke dwah' ling ! Isn't it simply divine to be in the real India and ect-u-elly in the cumpenny of a native?"

"Now. Now dearest Christabel. Simmer down old girl. A bad case of your vapours will land us both up shit creek..... And without young Rajbah's paddle."

(I mention this because Marmy and Christabel accompanied us throughout the rest of our stay in India. They would just sneak up on us from time to time and dismiss us as one might a servant.)

For now all four of us laughed our way ashore, five if you include Rajbah (whose English couldn't quite keep up). He giggled like a good'un too. We liked Rajbah. We didn't know it then but he was to cause and share a lot of our hilarity.

At this minute though his job was to show us the houseboat! 'Oh my goodness that houseboat!'

Up on the Roof

Freeze frame! Hold the image. Three characters are drifting across the blue, mirrored-surface of a huge lake set against the dazzling white backdrop of the highest mountain range in the world. Hold that in your mind's eye a moment while I take you way, way back to 1957.

It was the '50s and television had arrived at our house. On weekday afternoons the fledgling B.B.C broadcast a series called 'Watch with Mother.' The series was a set of very different programmes for kids. There was one for each day of the week. I take you there to talk about my favourite -'Picture Book.'

A lady with that very distinctive, stuck-up British voice held a huge album on her lap. She turned the pages slowly. The camera angle showed us pictures page by page. At long last she would stop, the camera would zoom in and the chosen image magically come to life. It turned to film.

That, my friends, is how my mind works with my memories. Nowadays of course, we have computers to store our photos (a poor substitute for our own memory) but they count for nothing compared to the feelings and ability to relive that our own faculties allow.

Now press Play. (Unfreeze film.)

After a very, very short time it was obvious to anyone with a brain and heart that the people here were open, trusting and humble. It was also obvious why. The sheer size of the ever-present Himalayas on their doorstep and horizon whittles down a person's sense of self-importance pretty sharpish. The vastness of the sky and breadth of water invites openness. The rushing, hurrying and rat race back home was a million miles away. Here there was time to enjoy and relish human company.

Saab and Memsa'ab shrank the second they arrived. I'd shrunk so much that the houseboat to be our home for a week was a doll's house; a doll's house I could go inside instead of straining to imagine.

Quaint? Quirky? Ornate? Retro? Victorian? A poor man's grandiose? Do any of those help you conjure up this big wooden house on a big wooden base called a boat? Probably not. I'll have to draw on lots of comparisons as clues to bring you on board. Think wood. Think lots of dark wood. Think wooden safety railings, exterior decks and walkways. But when you think wood? See it all ornately hand-carved with very fine scroll and fretwork on every available surface. Step over the threshold into the lounge. This lounge is about 15 ft. by 12 ft. You are in the doll's house.

I'm guessing everyone alive knows the effects the British Raj had on India and its people. I do. What I never knew was the effect it had on interior design and home-furnishing. Who would? By the late 1970s the décor hadn't changed since those glory days of the empire.

Our sofas and armchairs were solid. The upholstery was thick, embossed, furry and heavily patterned. A large Indian rug covered most of the floor space. On this, at the centre, sat an oak coffee table with scrolled legs and daintily placed doyleys. I can't use the word curtains. These weren't curtains. They were antique velvet drapes from ceiling to floor, tied back with gold tasselled fixtures. The walls were of course wooden and allowed sliding panels to act as doors between the many rooms. The two large bedrooms had chandeliers (did you doubt it?) and four-poster beds with predictable drapes.

Suffice to say we two, Lord and Lady Oddsocks, had well-and-truly fallen down the rabbit hole. Wherever we were and whatever year it was, we were grinning like Cheshire cats. We grabbed a cushion or three each and headed out onto our front veranda. Unfortunately Fanny the maid had taken the day awf.

There in the late afternoon sun, Pete was reading about old British motorbikes and me? I was messing about with my sketch pad and acrylics; letting the water create its own marbling effect to capture the textures of the nearby mountains, white with snow but interrupted farther down the slopes by greyish splashes where bare rock came through.

The people here have lived on this lake for hundreds of years. It took some getting used to (I can tell you) to see shops of all denomination and size drifting past. Everything was bought and sold by boat. Further out on the lake were strange, brightly coloured gondolas. Lake Dal it seemed was the Honeymoon Capital of India. Young love brought newly-weds here to be rowed up and down for photographs to stick in treasured albums.

Dozens of these passed by day after day. I know what you imagined when I first said the word 'gondola'. Erase it. This isn't your open-air Venetian doodah. This gondola, my friends, is more like Cleopatra's barge only modified for the slightly less affluent. It's painted in reds and golds. At one end there is a cubicle of sorts draped in red velvet with more of those obligatory gold tassels. In all his finery the gondolier stands and punts behind it. The couple sit and laze in privacy (saving the eyes of hundreds of people they wave out to of course, oh! and the boating photographers beside them that they've hired to get some good shots.) It was fun watching all the commotion.

On our first night we decided to hire a rowing boat the following day. We wanted to have some fun of our own.

This is India so I probably don't need to tell you that the fun started long before we ever got into a boat. In fact it started when we casually mentioned the idea.

Still, for now, after hours and hours and hours on that bus, we relaxed and stared at the mountains. I don't think either of us could believe we were that close to the Himalayas.

Rajbah, bless his cotton socks, couldn't keep a lid on his burning curiosity for all things foreign and the antics of his esteemed guests. After less than an hour there was a tap-tap on the sliding exterior door beside us.

We called 'Come in' and that little cheeky face peered around the edge of the narrow slit he allowed himself. "Chai?" he asked, hopefully. When we declined he said, "Ride in boat?" Well now, that caught our interest.

Before we knew it we were in a long, narrow boat being manipulated by the kid's uncle. Rajbah couldn't sit still. He wanted to show us everything and all at once.

Um. How did we miss this? Why hadn't we thought to look out back?

We were in town. Hardly anyone here goes over to dry land. They have everything they need on the water. The waterways are narrow with shops either side. If it wasn't for the fact that I was in a boat, I could easily have mistaken this for a day out in a typical high street back home. We were boating along and through shopping centres. Shops packed side by side as far as the eye could see. Okay, okay so the shop fronts looked Indian and were on stilts…but hey.…..shopping is shopping, right?

Needless to say we were fair game. There was no pressure to stop and buy but there was so much excitement from the tradesmen. They were all so keen to be 'the one' that Sa'ab and Memsa'ab chose. We didn't want to buy anything. In the end we felt bad about that. We stopped at the most extraordinary papier machee factory (No! not factory as in machinery! Get real.) 'Factory' as in large space where dozens of smiling people sit, chatter, create and hand-paint incredibly delicate trinket boxes of all shapes and sizes out of grey, gooey mulch.

The traders fed us, gave us fresh juice drinks, fruit and nuts. We were torn. On the one hand it was clear the hospitality cost more than their profit, on the other it would be insulting to refuse.

When we eventually got back to our floating palace, we threw open the door and gasped.

I had never seen stars like this. No matter how stunning the stars of the Aegean and Nordic skies were, these weren't the same entities. They couldn't be.

In the heavens above us some unseen goddess had sprinkled her most precious jewels. Emeralds, amethysts, diamonds, lapis lazuli, turquoise, amber and multi-faceted crystals hung there.….in the sky, right above us, over our heads.

We sat in a stunned silence. I was honestly tempted to stretch my arm up and pluck them. A bedazzling heaven only knows how long we sat there in the very truest sense of the word awe. When our necks ached from jewel-gazing, we dangled our bare legs and feet over the side of our boat and stared into different space out over the lake surface. Something else quite extraordinary was unfolding for us.

We expected dark. While our minds were away the string of houseboats had lit paraffin lamps. Their glow stretched to right and left of us in twinkling chains. Further off, on the distant mountains, more stars began to come out to play one by one, moving down the slopes. Glowing yellow, these newcomers grew and grew in numbers until they reached as low as the lake horizon and by their reflection joined the lights around us. They completed a lantern show right to our feet. These random stars were butter lamps lit by small settlements way up in the foothills.

"Hey Pete!" He looked at me.

"We're sitting on the roof of the world."

Jesus was Here

I opened my eyes and saw planks. Oh! It's a ceiling! For a split-second I thought I was shrunk to a Borrower but then I got it. We were in this doll's- house of a boat in Srinagar. I remember!

Rajbah woke us at some ungodly hour. When I ducked to go out onto the deck, I realised my waking impression was spot on. I was a Borrower. The Himalayas just across the lake shrunk me again and instantaneously at one glance.

Good old Rajbah had spread breakfast out for us on the deck table. When Pete appeared just after me, we sat and sipped chai in speechless wonder at our beautiful surroundings.

For the British and the Irish predictable weather is, and always will be, one of the delights of travelling. To wake up and know it's going to be sunny (just like yesterday and the day before that) is something we never quite get over. It was early but it was sunny again! Our plan for the day was simple: hire a rowing boat, row leisurely around for an hour- or-so and then moor the boat up at the far side to walk a bit and take in some sights. What could be easier? Nothing could go wrong.

The idea was to make an early start before all the boat traffic started and before the midday sun could melt us. Besides, we wanted to be as discreet as possible. We were already conspicuous by our whiter skins and general alien appearance. We were ready. We'd had so many hours sitting in busses that we were up for a spot of physical exercise. It would do us a power of good.

I don't know what it is about us humans but, when we get a fit in our heads to do something we haven't done for a while (like rowing a boat) we completely and utterly forget any problems we may have encountered the last time we tried it and why we don't do whatever it is more often. That was exactly where our heads were at that morning. We were gung-ho about the whole thing.

Before I go any further you ought to know some more things that we didn't.

Tradesmen row on Lake Dal. Nobody but nobody else ever rows their own boat. For the honeymooners to row is unimaginable. For tourists to row is unthinkable. For the wealthy it's beneath them. (Excuse the pun). For a Sa'ab and Memsa'ab to row? (Bear in mind they obviously fit in those last two categories!) Well, that is best answered by the faces of all the Rajbah family when we simply asked for a boat.

Their eyes popped out of their heads. Their jaws dropped, and then they stared at each other and back at us completely lost for words. Then it dawned on them we were joking. They had a great laugh.

It took us a good half hour to convince them it wasn't a joke. We actually did want to get in a wooden boat, on our own, and use our own fair arms to row the thing. Their reluctance to allow us to partake in such a demeaning task knew no bounds. Neighbours were dragged in in great numbers to persuade us of our folly. What had we started?

We prevailed.

By the time the craft eventually arrived any notion of being discreet had become a fantasy. Rajbah and three others steadied the thing for us to step in. That's where the bit about inconvenient forgetfulness came into play. Ever taken it into your head to hire a boat in a park lake? Or on a quiet river? Yep. It suddenly occurs to you that starting off can be a tad embarrassing. It's something best done in private. Too late! We already had a large send-off party.

We were each handed a long oar with a heart-shaped paddle. That struck me as quite sweet. We just wanted to get this over with and cast off safely. As luck would have it I was facing forward. I had a great view of the family waving us goodbye, then an open lake, then the family waving us goodbye, then an open lake, then the family waving again. Got the picture?

After about fifteen complete circles and an awful lot of raucous laughter from onlookers (growing in numbers by the minute), Pete decided to try taking both oars and rowing as one might on a sunny Sunday afternoon back in Blighty. Up to a point it worked. It worked long enough to get us out of the sight and sounds of our audience. We were alone, almost. The shops had started floating by us by now. Much to their amazement and merriment they gawped at us and pointed us out to everyone else around. But for the most part they did not physically manhandle us in any attempt to help. To say progress was slow would be an understatement. The current further out was stronger than we had thought. That's a lie. We hadn't even thought about it. We lost control. Whenever we decided to go one way the water sent the other.

I need to tell you something. I blame all this on Jerome K. Jerome. For the last week I'd been dipping into his masterpiece 'Three Men in a Boat'. It was taking me much longer to read than a small book should but every time I read a bit I nearly wet myself laughing. I soon realised I had to go careful where I read it or run the risk of being carted off to an asylum.

If you haven't read it? May providence permit that it finds you in such a perfectly apt setting as India. If you have? No explanation necessary.

That wilful human forgetfulness I was talking about? Well until we were stuck out in the middle of Lake Dal (aiming one way and going the other) the setting for that book never even crossed my mind. It was after we had been trying the one oar each approach again for some time (and unsuccessfully) that muggins here made the suggestion "Perhaps if you try my oar and I'll take yours" that the hilarity of the whole thing hit me like a ton of the best jokes I'd ever heard. I mean it hit me 'big time'. The oars were identical! (Read the book!)

That was it for me. I crumpled. I crossed my legs. I laughed until I cried.

Who knows how long my spasm lasted? I was snapped out of it by what sounded like a lot of people shouting at us. We assumed they were offering us friendly and welcome advice. How wrong can you be?

We stared at the honeymooning gondolas now out in full force. The hollering was definitely coming from their general direction. The wedding photographers (local paparazzi) were yelling at us for sure. It wasn't to warn us of impending doom. It wasn't to offer advice either. They were shouting out for us to say the Indian equivalent of "Cheeeeeese." Now that we were facing them? Their cameras clicked and snapped, to use their local parlance, like billy-oh.

I'm pleased to tell you that somewhere in India today there are elderly couples flicking proudly and nostalgically through wedding albums and coming across those priceless snaps they have of a Sa'ab and Memsa'ab

"Ack chew ally row ing their own boat on the lake."

Then probably adding

"They were soooooo funneeeeee" with that wonderful tendency they have to draw out the vowel sounds. Oh! and doing that wiggle of the neck thing they do.

With a bit of a tow from a vegetable shop we got beyond the deep current problems and got the hang of steering. We reached the steps where we'd first met Rajbah, tied the boat and climbed up onto dry land. The crowd at the top were appreciative of the entertainment we'd provided and every one of them wanted to shake our hands.

The narrow streets of Srinagar town provided a degree of welcome anonymity. It was a relief. Back then there weren't many Europeans visiting the area so we were always going to stand out. We did spot one or two 'freaks' as the Hippy-Travellers were called, but even they seemed to be busy buying tickets to get somewhere else.

Strolling around aimlessly brought us into a deserted little back-alley. Not far along was a strange, old stone structure. Curiosity got the better of us. It was all a bit rough-and –ready, all a bit weather-worn. There was a waist-high railing around the square block of a building. We wandered around it to find that the railing only ran along three sides. A scratched and barely-legible metal sign on a small gate read: "Tomb of Yuz Asaf." We went in. I can't even attempt to recreate the feeling inside that shabby, forgotten little place. Peaceful, sad, old? At some time someone had built a wooden framework around a big, worn slab of stone. The framework had windows to view through. This being India this screen thing was painted in gaudy pinks and greens.

On the screen was an information plaque in English among other languages.

Well! What do you know? This out-of-the-way, deserted and practically forgotten tomb was purported to be the burial tomb of Jesus. Buddhist and Hindu alike hold that he did not die on the cross but came here to live out his days. They hold that his missing years were spent here studying ancient texts and beliefs.

I came to believe it, standing in that humble place that day. The similarities between the teaching of Jesus and the eastern Masters were pretty obvious as far as I was concerned. The so-called missing years always intrigued me too. And in this glorious landscape? Who wouldn't want to live out their days here? Why was I convinced? No-one was coming here. No crowds were flocking to be exploited for their money. This was no propaganda ploy to draw in tourists and foreign bucks. I was moved.

The main street was humble, some might say poor. I loved it. It was welcoming with its antiquated and hand-crafted wooden shopfronts, slightly the worse for wear. We found a bookseller. I sifted through some children's' books with bright illustrations to help them learn to read. I bought one on Guru Nanak (the Leader of the Sikhs). It was a learn-English book with Hindu and English under each picture. I was going to make a stab at learning Hindu phonetically. I still have that book somewhere.

We walked and walked and walked. Srinagar is full of vast, elaborate Mughal gardens and strange enchanting temples. It breaks my heart to think that nowadays it is being torn apart in sectarian and political strife. I believe that nowadays too, the peculiarity of the once lonely tomb has been exploited after all. How lucky I was to go where I went, see what I saw and feel what I felt in a world where all of that foolishness was never even imagined.

On the evening before we left for Dharamsala, the three Rajbahs did something wonderful. Mr. Rajbah had been building something outside for days. It turned out to be an outdoor, clay oven. He'd built it especially for us.

For our farewell Mrs. Rajbah cooked us an apple pie and made custard. How sweet. They understood this to be 'Typi-call-ee British, no?'

The Stuff that Dreams are made of.

They say "All good things must come to an end." I've never been quite sure who 'they' are but they'd do well to adjust their thinking. In my book "All good things pave the way for more." For now though, this particular good thing was drawing to a close. It was mid-May and we'd been wandering around India for nearly three months. The decade was coincidentally coming to a close too.

There was no direct route from Srinagar to Dharamsala but then nothing is ever straightforward in India and I most definitely should not be confused with someone who takes a direct route to anywhere. It was a good thing. Because of it my memory is awash with astonishing and unforgettable images of the mountainous region that ultimately stretches to Tibet.

Buses and trains came and went. Landslides, rock falls and erosion, all wrought by the winter's ravages, conspired to slow our progress. Jaw-dropping valleys passed by outside the bus window as we climbed ever higher. There beside me, mysterious temples and remote settlements clung precariously to the many hillsides and fuelled my imagination. Tiers of waterlogged paddy fields defied gravity and occasionally caught sunlight. In those moments, water turned to glass. Through my daydreaming eyes they looked like massive fragments of a broken mirror, tossed aside by the deity in whose honour they'd been gathered and worked into collages to make the layered landscape even more spectacular.

Unbelievable scenery swooped and soared just beyond the window as I watched. We were in Hill Station country. Why it was called that was abundantly clear now.

This roundabout route was a good thing in a more practical way too. En-route we met a fellow traveller. We met only briefly but it gave us enough time to take directions to a place we could stay in Dharamsala.

We got there.

I suppose a book about travel should finish with our two intrepid heroes getting home. But whose home? That's the million-dollar question in this story. I'll take you there but there's no direct route. Let's go via Bombay.

Only a deadline imposed by an airline could have knocked us into shape and got our heads together enough to make us sensible at this stage. We had to leave time to be in Bombay to catch a plane. We estimated a week should do it. That week had the makings of a zany road-movie. We caught this train here and that bus there and made a thousand stops to make the right connections. Through the windows of all those trains and buses we witnessed some interesting things.

Our concept of normality had obviously altered beyond all recognition. Why else would the sight of rats nibbling the cake for sale on a railway cafeteria's shelf seem perfectly normal? How else could we not bat an eyelid when the toilet blocks on platforms turned out to house two or three large families?

Despite our apparent integration into this country's cultural vagaries, Mother India still had plenty of delightful surprises up her sleeve for us. I never thought it possible to build high scaffolding from wooden poles and rope. I never imagined I'd ever see a funfair with a large Ferris Wheel cobbled together from crates and poles either.

Farmsteads scattered in the vast open plains were still using oxen to turn huge wooden wheels, circling for an eternity to grind corn. Through those windows we saw great festivities taking place: Processions alive with colour where happy people celebrated (we knew not what) and led elephants painted psychedelically to who knew where.

At changeovers Porter wallahs grabbed our bags and led us on a merry dance through this train, that standing carriage, and across live tracks to assure us seats, hours before anyone came to join us or our train was due to set off. We couldn't have dreamt up the wallahs' striking purple uniforms. Trousers were baggy at the crotch and short at the knee. Their headgear was a fantastical creation and display of starched net reaching skyward at an impossible angle.

Who would have thought it necessary (or possible) to order a breakfast omelette some 15 hours before you want it only for it to be tossed at you through the open window of a speeding train the next morning and bang on time? The food-wallah was outside, clinging on tight while juggling with his other deliveries. You can tell I could continue but, enough

By the time we got to Bombay we were hot, tired and irritable. Cities, airports and a deadline will do that to you. By hook or by crook we caught our flight.

Now let's go back a ways.

Dharamsala means 'Little Tibet'. I don't recall any details about lodgings or street names and the like. Feelings flood back. Space, freedom and peace of mind are best experienced, never described.

I hear tell there's a big difference drawn nowadays between two parts of Dharamsala, that it's classed as a city and quite crowded. That's not the Dharamsala I have in mind and forever hold in my heart. There it is (and will always remain) a remote and tranquil piece of heaven-on-earth where few venture. Even fewer were visiting when we were blessed to be there.

Imagine wide open skies punctuated only by strings of pretty, brightly- coloured prayer flags, small and triangular, flapping and cracking in the crisp, pure air set against the singular view of the highest mountain range on earth, snow-capped and resplendent.

My feelings take me back to hours spent rambling along tiny tracks and paths up hill and down dale. One way led to a pretty monastery. From the pathway, a wall that skirted it was low enough to sit and rest on. When I did sit on it I turned and looked over. The world dropped away from me into a chasm hundreds of feet below. I had to smile in the days that followed to see monks snuggled up on that wall, fidgeting and snoozing. A picture paints a thousand words.

They certainly had beatific and often cheeky grins, those monks. They had a fine sense of humour. Hand-carved signs all along the walk dished out generous helpings of wisdom such as 'In the beginning God made man in his own image. Man has been making gods in his own image ever since'.

On a morning walk I was approached by a monk. How he knew I was a teacher I can't imagine. He led me to a small wooden shack of a school. It was for the children, refugees from Tibet. I was invited to meet the kids and teach them something. All I could think of was "If you're happy and you know it clap your hands." I'm smiling and getting the shivers as I remember that episode. They were so young, so small and so full of wonder. Their big bright eyes watched my every move. I was honoured. What fun we had. Needless to say, they fought to keep me there. I fought back tears of farewells.

. Imagine a street made narrow by tall buildings topped with pagoda-shaped roofs in reds and golds. Imagine friendly souls walking along that street, dressed in saffron reds, deep turquoise and plain-coloured simple garments, long-sleeved and drawn across the body to tie at the side. As a person walks along, a hand goes out instinctively to turn the row of huge and ornate, patterned prayer wheels set to one side of the route. Now and then a monk or three in deep red (over bright orange) smiles as you pass. Contentment is in the air and the expression 'never mind' reveals its deeper connotations.

After all the complications of the indirect route to Dharamsala I relaxed and let myself go on that final bus-ride. I didn't notice but I must have let go of a lot more besides. This was a 'peak' experience in every meaning of the word. I was high geographically but high on clean air and in high spirits and blessed to be so. There was no need for stimulants here. This was a dream come true; a dream I never even knew I had but may, if I'm honest, have suspected.

Back in Srinagar when I commented to Pete that we were 'on the roof of the world,' we were. Now I realised we must have been merely eavesdropping. I'm not a person who needs to climb Everest, to climb right onto the very top of a roof. This was more than enough. I felt satisfied. If we could get up as far as Leh that would be wonderful but a cake is a cake, cherry or no cherry. I felt at home here. Any notion of me being on a mission faded away. It was most probably a fantasy all along.

Around day four Pete brought up the subject of the Dalai Lama. Call me William Kempe but it had never occurred to me that His Holiness was so close-by. In my defence I had been travelling for most of the decade and not in a position to keep tabs on many world events. Pete wanted to go over to meet the esteemed Tibetan leader and so we asked if and when it was possible. It wasn't. The very busy man was not in residence. Leh was out of the question too. Apparently the winter had been a harsh one and the road was not yet open.

None of this bothered me. I was here. I felt joyous and ready to go back to Bristol.

On our last day in this staggeringly beautiful place, I wandered blissfully along unaware of anything but how pretty this small street was. Instead of one monk or a few individuals coming towards me this afternoon quite a small crowd of young Tibetan monks was heading my way. The surprise made me pay attention. I caught eye contact with one individual and a light went on in a recess of my mind.

Here's the sudden curve in the road. Bear with me.

I was very young when I learned the truth of the words 'Sticks and stones may break my bones.' The other half of that old saying took me a painfully long time to grasp. For many years I kept quiet for fear of ridicule and of what others might say. Now I'm of an age where I can accept the wisdom in 'but words can never hurt me' and speak my truth.

Were you one of us kids who had an invisible friend? What happened to him or her? Mine stayed with me. To the mind of the child I once was, his features were 'Chinese'. That was the only stereotype I knew. He had a very long name I couldn't pronounce so I called him Fred.

Here in this pretty little street, in this corner of paradise, I knew. The instant I caught eye-contact with the Tibetans, I knew. I recognised the features. I knew Fred was a Tibetan. In the spilt second I realised, a single shiver ran through my body. Something lifted off me.

His silent voice whispered,

"I'm home."

Other work by this author:

The Once & Future Queen (a novel) www.lulu.com
In Other Words (Illustrated Book of Verse)
www.xlibris.com & www.amazon.com

Contact: www.maggiespages.com

Acknowledgements

My sincere thanks to:

Stephen Warrilow. Proof-reader.The Who: 'My Generation' & 'The Seeker' (lyrics)
Rod Stewart & The Faces: 'Maggie' (lyrics). Loudon Wainwright lll: 'We've Come a long Way' (lyrics). Bernie Taupin: 'Your Song' (lyrics). Elizabeth Taylor. Peter Bullen: back cover review.
& The Blog Snorklers whose support kept me going.

All of the people I met on my travels. Some of whose names have been changed.

1. Setting off

2. HUGE STATUES : MOSCOW

3. MOSCOW WORKERS

4. MOSCOW to PETERSBURG TRAIN

5. RUBBER PENGUINITIS

6. ACROPOLIS

7. PARADISE MYKONOS

8. GREEK ISLAND HOPPING

9, ISTANBUL

10. BOAT TRIP UP THE BOSPORUS

11. BODRUM   TURKEY

12. SHOWN AROUND TEHRAN

13. CRAZY TEHRAN TRAFFIC

14. DRINKING WATER -TEHRAN SUMMER

15. PERSEPOLIS - PERSIA

16 . IZMIR   COMING HOME

CPSIA information can be obtained
at www.ICGtesting.com
Printed in the USA
FSHW010605070119
54867FS